Praise for SOVEREIGN

"Sovereign *is one of the most influential books I have read in years. It's loaded with ideas that will recharge your life and change the way you think and act right away. By far the most highlighted book in my library!"*

— **Tom Rath**, #1 *New York Times* best-selling author of *How Full Is Your Bucket?* and *StrengthsFinder 2.0*

"It is no exaggeration to say this book is life-changing. I couldn't put it down. Emma Seppälä gives us wisdom and guidance in the form of unforgettable human stories of fallibility and courage, of astonishing scientific research (for any skeptics among us), of humor and vulnerability, and inspiration that is nothing short of poetry. This book is a gift."

— **Faith Salie**, Emmy-winning contributor to *CBS News Sunday Morning*, panelist on NPR's *Wait Wait . . . Don't Tell Me!*, and author of *Approval Junkie*

"Sovereign *is an insightful and entertaining guide to living life on your own terms—backed by science, spiced with humor, and laced with love."*

— **Dr. Jennifer Aaker**, General Atlantic Professor at the Stanford Graduate School of Business and best-selling author of *Humor, Seriously*

"With clear stories, science-backed skills, inspiring poetry, and gentle humor, Emma Seppälä invites us to explore the key experience of 'sovereignty,' a state of clarity and well-being beyond simply our capacity to be self-governing. In this illuminating exploration of the essential ingredients of a resilient mind, rewarding relationships, and a meaningful life, we are empowered to develop and strengthen this liberating way of being grounded in our lives. Reading this book will be a gift that keeps on giving for all those in your life, including you."

— **Daniel J. Siegel, M.D.**, *New York Times* best-selling author of *Mindsight*, *Aware*, and *IntraConnected*

"With a science-backed approach and stories from her own experience, Emma opens the door to greater freedom and happiness as she skillfully shows us how to reclaim our sovereignty from the variety of thoughts, habits, beliefs, and distractions that otherwise keep us bound."

— **Sharon Salzberg**, *New York Times* best-selling author of *Lovingkindness* and *Real Life*

"For many, modern society has separated us from ourselves. Sovereign *is a deeply personal narrative that offers us a path to recognize our own agency and empowers us to reach our greatest potential."*

— **James R. Doty, M.D.**, Director of CCARE and *New York Times* and international best-selling author of *Into the Magic Shop* and *Mind Magic*

"Sovereign *is a gift to your inner spirit, a salve for anyone yearning to unleash their best self, and a masterpiece of insight about how to show up for life. No matter your background or circumstances,* Sovereign *helps you tap into your greatest potential and fan your own inner flame—today and every day from here on out."*

— **April Rinne**, global futurist and author of *Flux: 8 Superpowers for Thriving in Constant Change*

"In a world where sensory overload is a daily occurrence, Emma Seppälä's Sovereign *provides a step-by-step guide to help you stay centered, grounded, and focused so that you can handle whatever curveballs the universe throws your way."*

— **Alison Levine**, *New York Times* best-selling author of *On the Edge*

SOVEREIGN

ALSO BY EMMA SEPPÄLÄ

The Happiness Track

SOVEREIGN

Reclaim Your Freedom, Energy, and Power in a Time of Distraction, Uncertainty, and Chaos

EMMA SEPPÄLÄ, Ph.D.

HAY HOUSE

HAY HOUSE INDIA
New Delhi • London • Sydney
Carlsbad, California • New York City

Published in India by: Hay House Publishers (India) Pvt Ltd: www.hayhouse.co.in
Published in the United States by: Hay House LLC: www.hayhouse.com®
Published in the United Kingdom by: Hay House UK Ltd: www.hayhouse.co.uk
Published in Australia by: Hay House Australia Publishing Pty Ltd: www.hayhouse.com.au

Cover design: Kara Klontz
Interior design: Karim J. Garcia
Indexer: Beverlee Day
Interior photo: Tony Rinaldo

First published by Hay House India, 2024

ISBN: 978-81-97222-89-4
10 9 8 7 6 5 4 3 2 1

Printed at Replika Press Pvt Ltd

MIX
Paper | Supporting responsible forestry
FSC www.fsc.org FSC™ C016779

Hay House is committed to a sustainable future for our business, our readers and our planet. This book is made from Forest Stewardship Council® certified paper.

To humanity.

A love letter.

May you be sovereign.

CONTENTS

CHAPTER 1

INVITATION

Sovereignty is internal freedom and a relationship with yourself so profoundly life-supportive and energizing that you access your fullest potential. The fullest potential you were *born* for.

Trust me, you've felt it. You've felt the sovereignty fire, kindled, in the pit of your stomach at different times in your life.

It's the inner flame that lifted you up from rock bottom and kept you walking through the darkest of nights. It's the roar of defiance that helped you back to your feet every time you were knocked down—a declaration of your fight and right to live as you, no matter what. It is what has kept you alive despite everything.

Regardless of race, nationality, religion, gender, or social status, at our core we're the same: sovereign. We all have the same desire to live in the fullest expression of ourselves.

Sovereignty allows us to reclaim the treasure trove of possibility that exists within all of us, if we allow it.

Sovereignty is your birthright.

And somewhere deep down, you know it.

Take the example of Maya, who was born into a working-class family riddled with addiction in rural Indiana. She grew up in a trailer and suffered abuse as a child. She felt pride in herself for the first time in her life when she joined the Indiana National Guard. She identified with the values of service, commitment, and camaraderie, and began to feel hope. That is, until she deployed to Iraq. She was in combat operations during the day—with all the hellishness that entails—and at night, her very own commander, a member of her community in Indiana, sexually assaulted her and prostituted her at gunpoint to her own colleagues. If she ever said anything, her commander threatened, she would not live to see the baby she had left back home in the U.S. A modern-day experience of enslavement at the tender age of 22.

Maya was a participant in one of the studies my colleagues and I ran, a woman I would never forget. She stunned me because—despite it all—she was sovereign. She said that our research intervention (a breathing protocol I'll discuss in Chapter 4) helped with her PTSD and that she would otherwise most likely have become an alcoholic, but she also had the powerful flame coursing through her veins that you could see in the gleam of her beautiful eyes: sovereignty. Despite everything she had been through, she was determined to show up as a great mother for her son—with all the extra care and love needed for a child on the autism spectrum—and a kind and compassionate leader in her community. She went on to beat all odds as a successful high-level leader at one of the country's top tech companies.

Another example is Nasreen Sheikh. Born into poverty and undocumented in India in the early '90s, she was forced to labor in sweatshops under abusive conditions in Kathmandu as of the age of 10. Yet at 16 Nasreen defied all odds by becoming a world-renowned human rights activist and successful social entrepreneur to help other women who had suffered the way she had.[1]

Extraordinary people like Maya and Nasreen, who lived through hell yet thrive, through their existence show us what we ourselves are capable of—despite anything we might have experienced.

There are many historical examples of sovereignty. It's Diogenes, the Greek philosopher who, after being captured by pirates, was being sold as a slave on a busy marketplace yet remained sovereign. He pointed to someone and cried out: "Sell me to this man; he needs a master."[2] It is the Buddhist monk who, despite being beaten down, repeatedly sat back up in perfect meditation until his abusers fell at his feet in astonishment and devotion. It's Dandamis, a famous yogi of Alexander the Great's time, who, when threatened with death if he didn't come meet Alexander, remained unperturbed and unmoving, stating he had no fear of death.[3] It's Joan of Arc, a 17-year-old illiterate peasant girl with neither status nor education who rekindled the deadened spirit of an army of downtrodden and unruly French men, turning them into victorious conquerors. It's the enslaved Africans of South Carolina who—after the 1739 Stono Rebellion—had their instruments taken away from them yet still kept singing, dancing, and celebrating using their feet and hands, originating step[4] and tap dancing.[5]

These examples and so many others awaken in us a distant memory: the knowledge that the human spirit is a force to be reckoned with.

Because you can shackle someone and take the instruments away from them, but you can never take the song out of their soul.

You can't restrain the human spirit. The human spirit is indomitable. It is sovereign.

Sovereignty is your song. To quote Gurudev Sri Sri Ravi Shankar:

> *There is a song deep inside you. You are born to sing a song and you are preparing. You are on stage holding a mic but you are forgetting to sing, you are keeping silent. 'Til that time you will be restless, until you can sing that song which you have come on the stage to sing. It doesn't matter if you feel a little out of tune for a minute or two. Go ahead! Sing!*

I dedicate this book to you, that you may sing your song.

And that, my friend, is my dangerously powerful invitation to you.

You were born for this. You were born to be sovereign.

THE BOUND STATE

Yet sovereignty often feels far from what we experience daily.

To the contrary, we tend to live in what I'll call a bound state: Through life experiences, fear, and trauma, we start to disconnect from ourselves. We're dealing with distraction, uncertainty, and chaos on a daily basis—thus the subtitle of this book. We are prone to fear and easily influenced by outside forces.

The crises the world has been facing—from pandemics to senseless wars and environmental catastrophes—have dramatically increased mental health problems[6] and sent us further into a state of languishing.[7] The constant barrage of all sorts of news, media, and messaging accelerated by technology and influenced by corporate greed and divisiveness only exacerbates matters.

Research tells us that over 50 percent of people across industries are burned out,[8] uninterested (engagement levels are very low at 34 percent, according to Gallup[9]), overwhelmed, and down. Something feels like it's missing. Something is lost. Something is not quite right. But we can't quite put our finger on what it is.

The COVID-19 pandemic lockdown was the first time many of us consciously experienced a sense of being bound: total lack of control, autonomy, and freedom.

Though that time is now behind us, we have experienced living in a bound state far longer than that. A type of invisible lockdown. So old, and so common, in fact, that we fail to see it. So normal, that we don't even know it's there.

We're bound to destructive beliefs, habits, patterns, concepts, relationships, addictions, and misconceptions. It is the reason so many of us feel there is more to life. That life feels empty. It is the reason so many suffer from anxiety, depression, addiction, fear, burnout, and unhappiness.[10]

It's easy not to be aware of something when you're in it, just like the proverbial story of the fish that doesn't know it's in water because it has never experienced anything else.

Almost everyone is bound to something. Because it is the norm. It's social conditioning. It is what we have learned, what we have integrated, and what we have carried with us for generations. It's deeply entrenched in our own minds. And it is keeping us from living our freest, boldest, and most authentic life. It is also keeping us in a place of suffering, whether we realize it or not.

Take the models of success that society gives as an example: people with bulging muscles or bulging wallets, fame or power, beauty or balls. When you look a little deeper, they are often accompanied by misery, superficiality, or self-destruction, as we'll discuss in the coming chapters.

If you don't relate to yourself in a way that is sovereign, as my own experience showed me, those acts of power will also be acts of defeat, because they often also involve a fundamental betrayal of yourself, and that causes a profound energy leak.

SOVEREIGNTY

Sovereignty doesn't have an underbelly. It is about a deeply life-affirming, respectful, energizing, and enlivening relationship with ourselves and other people in such a way that fully preserves us and allows us to live in the fullest expression of ourselves.

The path to regaining sovereignty begins with becoming aware of the shackles binding us and then learning to break free from them.

There's a way to stay centered and grounded despite the chaos. Despite the unpredictable nature of these times. Despite the constant noise. Despite it all. And that is sovereignty. If ever there was a time on the globe when we desperately need inner strength, poise, and the ability to maintain equilibrium and power no matter what—it's now. Thus this book.

I started writing it shortly after the COVID-19 pandemic began. Though it was a tragic time, one powerful phenomenon that came from the pandemic and its aftermath of war and chaos and division was that, by making us face the reality of death, it also woke us up to the value of life and how we want to live it: on our own terms.

While my last book, *The Happiness Track*, invited readers—using science—to emancipate themselves from outdated and destructive theories of success to find true happiness, *Sovereign* takes things further. Written in as practical a way as possible, using anecdotes from my own life (Husband may or may not have decided to change his name after reading the manuscript) as well as stories from friends, science, research, case studies, and even poetry that came to me in the creative process, the following chapters are an invitation to you. An invitation to claim your sovereignty.

When you are sovereign, you not only experience happiness and well-being but also maximize your gifts and strengths, bringing out the best in yourself.

Just like your thumbprints are unique, your whole being is a unique expression of life with completely individual gifts you bring to the planet—whether you realize it or not. Sovereignty allows you to express them completely. In that way, sovereignty is not just a gift to you, it is a gift for everyone who meets you.

And sovereignty is contagious. A U.S. Marine Corps veteran who was in one of my research studies shared with me that, during grueling challenges, it wasn't the youngest and most able-bodied Marines who succeeded; it was often the smallest, oldest, or even weakest. What they had that made them different was inner sovereignty. And they became the leaders—seeing them succeed helped everyone else stand taller. Reminding someone of their sovereignty makes their flame grow stronger and brighter. If you don't want to gain sovereignty for yourself, then do it for everybody else.

This book is a manual, a road map, a manifesto by which you can systematically become aware of all the areas in your life where you have abandoned your sovereignty and what to do to reclaim it. *Sovereign* is designed to emancipate you from the many ways in which you subjugate yourself (knowingly or unknowingly) *at every level of your existence:* your self (Chapter 2), your emotions (Chapter 3), your mind (Chapter 4), your relationships (Chapter 5), your intuition (Chapter 6), and your body (Chapter 7). Each chapter will first describe how we bind ourselves and then how we can reclaim our sovereignty.

Chapter by chapter, this book is designed to make you aware of the areas of your life in which you may be keeping yourself tied up in knots—bound—and depleting yourself, and showing you how to set yourself free. At the end of each chapter, I'll recap the "side effects" (i.e., benefits) of becoming sovereign in that area of your life; I'll offer a tool kit full of practices to put the ideas in the chapter into practice; and I'll share a poem that came to me as I wrote, which I hope may resonate with you as we explore sovereignty together.

As you read this book, three areas of your life, in particular, will strengthen to a whole new level:

- Your awareness and discernment in your everyday experiences, choices, and interactions
- Your energy as you start to live in a more life-supportive rather than depleting way
- Your courage, strength, and boldness

Reading *Sovereign* may be challenging at times because it will awaken you to the extent of the subjugation, limiting beliefs, and inertia you have unknowingly placed yourself in. But it will also open your perspective to the possibility of living life at your fullest: with your eyes wide open, spirit soaring. As you free yourself, you will notice a shift in your life force, and this power, in turn, will help you free others.

Early readers of this manuscript reported that *Sovereign* unlocked many things for them. The chapters are designed to lovingly and deprogram you from destructive conditioning so you may live a freer and happier life. True to yourself.

I want to invite you to a playground of freedom and authenticity, vision and innovation, personal potential and fulfillment. This book will help hone these qualities and bring them to your consciousness in a joyful, practical way that will also hopefully make you laugh out loud from time to time. It's an invitation to the beautiful landscape of possibilities wide open to you and within you when you start living in your sovereignty.

You Did Not Come Here

You did not come here
To play small,
To hide yourself,
To blend into the wall.
You did not come here
To dim your light,
To crouch in fright,
To lie in a ball.

You came here
To light a fire
Within your own heart,
That it might
Warm and light the fire
Within others' hearts,
That it may set ablaze old
rotting beliefs,
That it may light the way to
greater truths,
That it may burn to ashes
systems of old
Grown toxic with mold,
That you may make room
for new plants to bloom.

CHAPTER 2

SOVEREIGN SELF

One Saturday I was slated to give the opening keynote at an online conference. I don't usually work on Saturdays so, without thinking about it, I took the kids to a park 45 minutes away from our house.

The kids were throwing rocks in a lake when this text came in: "Having trouble logging in?" The keynote. I had forgotten about it. We had planned for over six months, and now I was letting them down. Devastated, I cringed. It felt like I was wearing a full-body shame suit.

Ever had an epic fail? A humiliating moment? A total flop? Take a quick moment to think back on your latest cringeworthy mistake or embarrassing moment.

Once you've done that, think of the words you said to yourself right after.

Judging from the thousands of students and executives to whom I've asked this same question, the words go something like this:

You're such an idiot.
You're so stupid.
You don't belong here.
What were you thinking?
You always do this!
You're such a mess.

Read those harsh words one more time, registering how they make you feel. These are the abusive words humans tear themselves apart with.

This chapter is about how we relate to ourselves. Our relationship with ourselves can either bind us, which is what we'll talk about first, or lead us to sovereignty, which we'll talk about second. While being bound puts you down, de-energizes and depletes you, sovereignty is invigorating, energizing, and life-giving. The first curbs your potential. The second sets it free. We'll end with ways to reclaim sovereignty.

BOUND SELF

As a faculty member of the executive education program at the Yale School of Management, I teach hundreds of talented executive leaders every year. What I've observed is that the greatest hurdle standing in their way is often their relationship with their own self. One day a highly talented middle-aged woman, a leader in a Fortune 500 company, came up to me after class and said: "Well, I get an A in leadership and a D in parenting" before she walked off. My heart broke for her broken heart.

"I am not good enough" is sadly a viral program running in most people's heads. Eighty percent of millennials endorse the statement "I am not good enough" with regards to almost every area of their life![1] Our brains focus more on the negative than the positive, the well-known negativity bias[2] explaining why, during performance reviews or any kind of feedback session, for example, instead of celebrating the nine compliments you got, you can't stop thinking about the one criticism, dragging your spirits to the ground.

Self-Loathing

We often hear about "toxic relationships," but something we don't realize is that many of us have a toxic relationship with ourselves—and that's how we get bound and tied up in knots.

A bound self is having an antagonistic relationship with yourself. It depletes you, wears you down, and stops you from attaining your fullest potential. It's self-loathing. You may think self-loathing doesn't apply to you, but consider this: Are you self-critical?

When I ask my students across age groups, professions, genders, and ethnicities to raise their hands if they are self-critical, almost every single hand goes up. Every time. Chances are, you are self-critical too.

Reread the list of things people say to themselves one more time. Most people wouldn't speak such words to their worst enemy—yet they do to themselves. Psychologists define self-criticism as a form of self-loathing.[3]

Here's where you may be thinking, *Stop right there. Isn't a good dose of self-criticism healthy? Isn't it the key to self-improvement? Isn't it important to be hard on yourself so you don't fall behind or fail to reach your potential?*

Here's where we need to differentiate between self-criticism and self-*awareness*.

- Self-criticism is beating yourself up for your mistakes and shortcomings. It condemns you for not being up to par and keeps you reeling in shame. It's mean.
- Self-*awareness* is knowing your weaknesses without judging or beating yourself up for it. It is honest and supportive of your growth and learning. But it's not destructive or condemning. You are simply conscious of where you need help. It doesn't elicit feelings of guilt or shame or insecurity.

For example, in my case, my statistics knowledge is not where it could be. Self-criticism would have me beat myself up about that. Self-awareness is acknowledging I need more expertise and inviting a statistician to be part of my research teams—which is what I do.

The Inner Terrorist

Back to the mass confessions of self-criticism in my class. Interesting, isn't it, that we can be so hard on ourselves alongside others who are just as hard on themselves? Everyone beating themselves up in their corner. Self-loathing is such a widespread viral program—I say viral because it's (a) common; (b) contagious, running in families and entire societies; and (c) so destructive. Toxic.

When I ask my students how self-criticism is working out for them, I am greeted by uneasy squirming and awkward smiles. They know the pain of it but don't see how it binds them.

How does self-loathing bind us? Research shows that self-criticism is akin to having a predatory relationship with yourself. It is highly destructive, leading to anxiety, depression, impaired decision making, fear of failure, and decreased levels of motivation, performance, and persistence.[4] It burns you out and drains your resources and energy.

Imagine a terrorist walked into the room right now, threatening you with a weapon. Your sympathetic nervous system—the fight, flight, or freeze mode—would get activated: fear, anxiety, elevated heart rate and blood pressure, panic.

Your inner critic is like that terrorist. Only this terrorist lives inside you, torturing you. By increasing your heart rate and other measures of sympathetic activity, it wears down your physical and mental health over time.[5] No surprise that research shows self-criticism is a maintenance factor in anxiety, depression, and eating disorders.[6]

Self-criticism is internalized perpetration. And the weapon at your temple is shame. Shame makes your self-worth plummet; it's de-energizing. It drains you and sucks you dry. There's nothing good about it.

Ironically, you play the role of both the persecutor—the terrorist—and the victim—your own poor self. See that? Trapped and bound by yourself. It's like we're programmed to self-destruct. It makes no sense.

Lift the Veil

As I mentioned earlier, self-criticism is a type of self-loathing. It's social conditioning that runs in families, communities, and cultures. And if everyone's doing it, it's what you're going to learn as well. It becomes so "normal" you forget to question it.

That said, self-loathing is not universal. In some cultures—like Hindu, Jain, and Buddhist cultures, to name a few—there's an understanding that having a human life is incredibly valuable because of the belief in reincarnation. You hit the jackpot if you were born a human. After all, you could've been born a worm! You're fortunate to have a human body, free will, and the opportunity to learn, grow, and contribute.

Now here's an example of how deeply rooted—or you could even say *married*—we are to the self-loathing program:

In one of my classes for executives, I ask participants to request feedback about themselves from colleagues, friends, and family. Not the usual kind, *only* the positive kind.

Get this: participants are so uncomfortable with these instructions they sometimes can't sleep before asking! I'm not in the business of promoting insomnia, but you have to wonder what is going on here. Why is requesting positive feedback so anxiety-provoking? When I ask them whether they'd be more comfortable asking for negative feedback, I hear a resounding *YES!*

Why is it acceptable to beat ourselves up with self-criticism and to solicit criticism from others but not okay to praise ourselves or have others praise us?

It doesn't make sense.

HOT TIP: You *cannot* unbind yourself without questioning things, especially when these things are destructive to you. Look deeper, lift the veil, ask yourself, *Why should I buy into this?* It's only by calling things into question that you start to dismantle the destructive habits and conditioning that are running your life.

Besides, if the self-loathing program is not worth dismantling for yourself, then do it for your children or anyone you mentor. The most heart-wrenching example I can give is hearing my son talking about himself in the self-critical way he heard me talking about myself when I was in a dark postpartum period after his baby brother was born. He had internalized the same feelings he heard me express—as children do. I became determined not to pass this on more than I already had. The buck had to stop here. If there's one thing I want to pass on to my children, it's a sovereign relationship with themselves, one that is life-affirming and self-honoring.

The Need to Belong

Another way we shackle ourselves up is that we believe approval, accolades, and admiration from others will make us feel loved.

And yet we often tie ourselves up in knots seeking them out.

Yale is an extremely competitive university with annual admittance rates between 3 percent and 5 percent. Millions of students from around the world dream of attending this elite institution. So, when a group of research scientists asked Yale undergrads what emotions they feel the most, you might imagine the undergraduates' answers would be "proud," or "happy." Right? They were living the dream, after all.

Nope.

These go-go-go high-performing students responded "stressed" and "tired."[7]

How deflating.

Next, the scientists asked the students, "What emotions do you most *want* to feel?"

Before reading on, take a moment to think what that might be.

Fulfilled? Joyful? Successful?

Nope.

"Loved."

Loved!

All that tireless striving, stress, and fatigue is a desperate search for *love*.

It's not just Yale students who are desperate for external forms of validation. It's the most common thing in the world. That's why most people have at one point or another sacrificed their own needs in order to belong.

Of course, the need to belong is deep-seated, instinctual, natural, and healthy.[8] Across history, humans have lived in social groups, tribes, and families. From birth through old age, our connection to others is essential for survival. We need each other for physical safety, psychological health, community, and connection.

From an evolutionary standpoint, to be an outcast, in many cases, meant death. Maybe that's why we evolved to experience rejection as so painful—it activates similar brain regions to those activated by physical pain.[9]

Researchers have found that after food and shelter, positive social connection is our greatest need, benefiting our physical and mental health.* People who feel more connected to others have lower rates of anxiety and depression,[10] a 50 percent increased chance of longevity,[11] a stronger immune system,[12] faster recovery from disease, and even a longer life.[13] Low social connection has been generally associated with declines in physical and psychological health.[14] Loneliness is linked to depression, anxiety, a host of negative emotions and behaviors, and poorer health outcomes.[15]

We're wired to seek social approval. Babies as young as four months prefer voices that have the sound of acceptance as opposed to rejection.[16] From childhood we have been taught the importance of fitting into our family, schools, friend groups, and communities. Throughout adulthood, we continue to shape our behavior for our romantic partners, friend circles, communities, and workplaces. Consciously or unconsciously, we adapt to norms for gender, country, religion, community, and culture.

Even rebels conform. Many motorcycle clubs, for example, stand by values of freedom and defiance, as exemplified by motorcycle slogans like "To prove them wrong, be a rider," and

* What's interesting is that these benefits have nothing to do with how many friends or connections you have and everything to do with how connected you feel to others on a subjective level. You could be an introvert or loner and feel connected to others, or you could be a socialite that feels connected to no one. You feel more connected to others when you are sovereign because your well-being is higher. Fascinating research I'll discuss in Chapter 5, "Sovereign Relationships," shows that the better your relationship with yourself, the better your relationship with others i.e., if you feel more connected to yourself in a positive way, you're more likely to feel connected to others in a positive way.

"Ride free or die." Yet these clubs also tend to have strict codes of conduct, strong established hierarchies, and expectations of obedience to club norms. Their motorcycle club gear and tattoos may be a show of rebelliousness, but they're actually a standardized uniform. All humans—no matter how badass and tough they appear—have the same tender vulnerability: the need to belong and the desire, like those Yale undergrads, to be *loved*.

Shape-Shifting

However, this desperation to fit in so as not to experience the pain of rejection can lead people to shape-shift, i.e., put their own needs, preferences, and beliefs aside to put on an appearance they think will be more acceptable.

When I moved to China right after college, I didn't speak the language and felt desperately lonely. I longed for even basic human contact, like phone calls from loved ones back home. One day the phone rang while I was in the shower, and I jumped out soaking wet to grab that precious phone. To hell with a towel, I wasn't going to miss the call (no FaceTime back then so no one would know!). Ten minutes into the conversation with Mom, standing there naked and shivering, I noticed something out of the window. (The buildings in Shanghai are very close for lack of space and overcrowding.) There, barely one foot from my window, were not one, not two, but three Shanghainese gentlemen, leaning over their balcony and having a good look.

You may or may not have been on public display in all your dripping, naked glory in China, but chances are you've experienced the burning shame of being seen at your most vulnerable and awkward, cheeks crimson with mortification at some point. Everyone has.

That's why we try to keep up appearances—to avoid shame. It's why so many people are deathly afraid of public speaking—the possibility of ridicule, because that equates to rejection. No wonder we shape-shift to garner approval.

But adapting yourself to fit in is still a form of rejection from arguably the most important person in your life: your own self.

Sarah, the sister of one of my colleagues, was diagnosed with a type of disease that health-care professionals suggested could be supported with a healthier and cleaner diet. She refused to even consider the lifestyle changes that involved cutting out certain foods. Why? Because that would mean she would stand out in some way through her dietary choices and stop looking "normal" to her community. See that? Belonging was more important to her than surviving. Is there a more tragic example of our universal desperation to fit in?

Putting on an appearance that contrasts with who you really are binds you because it drains you and makes you suffer. You feel:

- **Fearful.** After all, there is always the risk that appearances will come crashing down. If people find out who you really are—not the person they think you are—you might be rejected. Clara Dollar, a former Instagram influencer, wrote a disturbing essay for *The New York Times* describing how she remained aloof and cold in her romantic relationship to stay "on brand" for her partner, believing he had fallen in love with her for her Instagram persona. Unsurprisingly, she ended up losing his love, which was all she really cared about in the first place.[17] Her Instagram account no longer exists.
- **Depressed.** Norah Vincent disguised herself as a man as an experiment for a year and wrote a best-selling book about it (*Self-Made Man*). While she successfully passed for a man even in hypermasculine circles, the strain of faking her identity for so long led to a depressive breakdown so severe she admitted herself to a psychiatric ward.

- **Depleted**: Whenever you conform when you don't want to, give in when you would rather not, or say yes when your heart says no, you're going against your own needs and desires, and that's depleting. It's akin to how well-to-do women used to bind their feet to minuscule proportions in pre-Communist China. Instead of walking, they hobbled slowly and painfully, completely deprived of much of their own power—bound by their own selves.

It's normal to fall in line with expectations and conventions for behavior in order to belong. That's how social conventions are built (and total anarchy and lawlessness avoided). But it's not normal if it goes so far as to lead you to abandon yourself: your authenticity, your wishes, perspectives, and even basic needs.

I experienced my first romantic heartbreak at 16. I had lost many of my friends through being immersed in my first relationship and felt desperately lonely after the breakup. I concluded that, since I wasn't lovable enough as I was, I would simply have to become someone else. Someone "nice," which I interpreted to mean complacent and passive and (mostly) ready to go along with what others wanted. I grew my hair and stopped biting my nails to conform to gender norms of femininity. I also started starving myself—metaphorically erasing my perceived unlovability and sowing the seeds for an eating disorder. In trying to adapt to what I thought others wanted, I slowly lost touch with who I was. I became annoyingly agreeable—the type who, when asked, "What do you want to do?" would answer, "No, what do *you* want to do?" A friend said to me one time: "You're apologetic for even being in the room."

Although I certainly hope you made more life-affirming choices than I did as a teenager, in many ways, small or large, knowingly or unknowingly, most of us have conformed to our environment's expectations, often ignoring our needs in the process and abandoning ourselves. We have all said yes when we knew better, and mostly the impact is as meaningless as eating an unwanted hors d'oeuvre just to be polite. But sometimes the impact is life-changing: saying yes to a job, home, or marriage. Eventually, those mistakes become glaringly obvious. To others you can feign innocence. But in hindsight, if you are truly honest with yourself, you always knew better. You just didn't dare say no. Because you wanted to belong.

Vulnerability to Control

What's more, conforming to others' opinions or norms over your own keeps you disempowered and subject to manipulation and control, sucked into other people's agendas.

A lot of people stand to profit from you feeling that you are not good enough:

- Organizations you work for that want you to keep striving to prove yourself
- Friends and family who want you to conform to their views and desires
- Politicians and leaders who want you to feel powerless, afraid, or complacent
- Marketers who want you to feel like you need their product to feel better about yourself

You stand to profit from remembering that you *are* good enough. Not just good enough. You are more than enough. Exactly as you are.

Self-Neglect in the Guise of Perfection: A Toxic Cake

No amount of love or acceptance from others can make up for a lack of love from yourself.

There's only one person who can mend that hole in your heart: *you*.

Luke seemed to have it all. Very attractive (he is often mistaken for a famous Hollywood actor), he always had a half-smile on his face, ready to crack a joke. His life appeared to be close to perfect: a gorgeous wife, an extremely high-paying job, and a glamorous career that took him all over the world.

And then he went through a painful divorce.

I had noticed that he always shied away from conversations that weren't superficial, so when he called me for advice, I gently suggested he might benefit from learning to communicate before entering a new relationship. That's when he gave this self-aware and heartbreaking answer:

"I don't even know how to communicate with myself. How can I communicate with someone else?"

Self-neglect and self-loathing under the guise of perfection is like a gorgeous, perfectly multilayered creamy chocolate cake that's actually made of horse dung. It stinks. From the outside, Luke had reached the pinnacle of material success, but on the inside he was lost and poor and felt like a failure—like a little boy, not the man he appeared to be. You would never know he suffered from self-loathing, although he admitted it to me. The contrast between his outward achievements and inner torment were stark. The three to four bottles of wine he needed to sleep at night were a clue for those who cared to notice.

Here is the irony of it all: In an attempt to pursue innumerable external things—recognition, status, popularity, follows on social media, attention, power, money—to gain others' approval, you dig yourself into a hole because you've abandoned your own damn self. And if you don't like you—no matter how rich, powerful, or famous (or not) you get or even how much other people like you—you will never feel happy or whole.

In China, I thought I was lonely for the company of people. What I didn't realize until later was that the most profound form of loneliness is the one that comes from abject self-neglect and self-rejection. Loneliness for your own friendship. That is a loneliness no one else can help you with because you've bound yourself with it. That's a loneliness only you can quench.

Worthiness Is Intrinsic

It takes courage to allow yourself to be seen for who you are, with all your weaknesses and insecurities, quirks and preferences, desires, differences, and boundaries. But it beats the stress and strain of hiding behind a façade you know to be a lie. Because that is profoundly draining.

I spent many years in a relationship with a very kind person who was not the right fit. We were interested in different things, and I felt like I had to conceal parts of myself because I was still in shape-shifting mode. When we finally did break up, I noticed that I had a lot more energy. Not just 10 percent more energy, more like 500 percent more energy. I was supercharged for about a year after our split. *What was going on here?* I wondered. Then I figured it out: It's *energy-draining* to hide who you are and what you need. Living an inauthentic life creates an energy leak. Once I was alone again, all the energy I had spent pretending I was something I was not was freed up. I could reclaim it. The experience was extraordinary. As one of my students once summed up: be yourself, everything else is exhausting.

Besides, people connect with vulnerability and imperfection. Think about it. You're at a party. Who do you most want to hang out with? The perfect-looking person who is putting on airs or the person who just spilled something on themselves, who is acting slightly embarrassed or goofy but is also totally natural, vulnerable, and themselves? You'll probably take notice of the first and maybe be impressed for a minute. But you'll want to hang out with the second.

You are also more likable than you know. Studies have found that most people underestimate how much another person likes them and enjoys their company—*the liking gap.*[18]

Neglecting your own needs, hiding your identity, living according to other people's desires, and criticizing yourself for being you is like dying while you're still alive.

Knowing that self-loathing is just a program running you, you can reprogram it.

When a baby is born, you don't expect it to do anything to be worthy of love. Its existence is enough. Why should it be different for you? You were born good enough.

You don't have to do anything to be enough. You don't have to be anyone to be worthy.

Your existence is proof of your worth.

Once you've tied yourself into an unrecognizable knot to conform to other people's expectations and fulfill external markers of success, it's hard to get yourself untangled and to know who you are in the first place, let alone like or approve of your own self. It takes awareness and some work. But it is possible. And worth it.

Now that we've examined what your bound self looks, acts, and feels like, let's see how different it looks when you are sovereign.

SOVEREIGN SELF

Sovereignty is reclaiming your right to exist as you. Reclaiming it not just from others but also from yourself. Sovereignty involves courage, awareness, and self-honoring. When you are sovereign, you show up with all your gifts, and you become a gift.

Deprogramming Self-Loathing

Remember when I asked the students in my class to think about the last time they made a cringeworthy mistake? And they told me all the painfully mean things they say to themselves in those moments? Well after that, I invited them to do something else.

I told them, "Think of your best friend or a person dear to you."

I invite you to do the same right now.

Imagine that person calling you right now. They just made a cringeworthy mistake. They feel ashamed, devastated, and embarrassed. Take a minute to think what you would say to them. Judging from what my students tell me, inevitably the answer will go something like this:

"It's okay."

"Don't worry."

"Everybody makes mistakes."

"You've got this."

"This will all be forgotten soon."

"I am with you."

"It's not as bad as you think."

"You tried your best."

Go back and read that list one more time as if you were speaking to yourself. Notice what you feel. Relief, warmth, and solace. There is nurturing, there is love, there is respect, and there is perspective.

Here's another question to ponder: Why is there such a difference between the words that we use for ourselves versus those for someone we love? Why?

What is the only difference between you and your friend?

There is only one difference: you live in different bodies.

See that? It makes no sense to treat yourself differently. It's just a toxic viral program. I'm inviting you to deprogram that right now.

With #selfcare hashtags exploding on social media, you would think it has to do with bubble baths and chocolate. While that may feel good for a moment, it won't make much of a difference over the long run. Honoring yourself involves reprogramming yourself from the inside.

Consider what would happen if you loved and cared for yourself as much as you do for others. How would you treat you if you were your own child? With kindness and understanding and forgiveness? Consider how that would make you feel.

Safe, comforted, strong, resilient, confident, secure, centered, calm, energized, and at ease. Powerful! At face value, someone might dismiss self-love as weak. But it's not. It makes you powerful beyond measure.

You, more than anyone, are deserving of your own love. After all, it's the only relationship you're guaranteed to have 24/7 your whole life. How will you choose to treat yourself, not just in the good times but also when you fail, when you're tired, when you're ashamed, when you're lonely, when you're flawed, scared, or at a loss . . .

When you make your relationship with yourself the best one you've got, you automatically become sovereign, unhooked from others' wants and from depleting and destructive conditioning that takes away your power. And that's one reason sovereignty is so energizing.

After all, we all long to be seen, heard, valued, and appreciated. We have a strong need to feel safe and to trust. Once you create this kind of relationship with yourself, you stop seeking self-worth in others. You stop looking for validation and recognition from the outside when you provide that to yourself. Sovereign.

Self-Compassion

You've probably heard the term *self-compassion*, pioneered by psychologist Kristin Neff.[19] It involves:

- Treating yourself as you would a friend (like we just discussed)
- Being mindful and aware of your emotions without adding fuel to the fire: witnessing your feelings and thoughts without judgment or blame, hope, or aim—just a neutral observation
- Remembering that it's normal to make mistakes. If you are human, you live, love, and learn—often by making mistakes. They come with the territory.

Just as self-criticism is like a terrorist living in your head keeping you shamed, shackled up, and tortured, self-compassion is your best friend calling the cops on that terrorist, moving in, untying your chains, speaking words of kindness and support, and giving you a hug. It simply makes sense.

As you start to tune in and listen to yourself, you will awaken to yourself: your needs, your wants, the tendencies of your mind, your desires, your self-talk. Being aware of painful feelings (embarrassment, shame, disappointment, jealousy, envy) will help you witness them without going down the rabbit hole of self-destruction (*You're such an idiot*). You will begin to go easy on yourself (*It's okay, you're doing your best*). As you develop acceptance and even love for yourself, you'll feel relief and ease on a visceral level. We are all just human beings fumbling along, making mistakes, causing chaos, and doing our best. Hurting and healing. Everyone is a work of art in progress.

What Do I Need Right Now?

I like to add an embodied perspective to self-compassion. Notice that the three main tenets of self-compassion invoke changing your thoughts. Deprogramming the self-loathing also involves changing how you *behave* toward yourself at every level: physically, mentally, and emotionally.

In those moments where we have failed, stumbled, embarrassed ourselves, and cringed at the horrifying situation we have created for ourselves, what if we stopped tearing ourselves apart by asking, *Am I good enough?*

What if we stopped going down that well-worn path of self-loathing and asked something different instead?

What do I need right now?

This far healthier question suggested by Kristin Neff's colleague Chris Germer, clinical psychologist at Harvard Medical School, invites you to build yourself back up and heal rather than tearing yourself apart and suffering.[20]

Inquire into what you need physically in that moment to help you with your distraught mind and emotions:

A hug?

A walk?

A break?

A nap?

A cry?

A meal?

A friend?

You decide. You are the only one that truly knows what you need.

Learning to ask "What do I need right now?" will lead to you to engage in habits that

- Rebuild your strength
- Restore your peace of mind
- Revitalize your energy
- Rekindle your well-being
- Reawaken your willingness to get up and try again

In other words, habits that reawaken your resilience. Your ability to bounce back. Your hardiness. Your inner strength. And that's sovereignty.

From Bound to Sovereign: Stephanie's Story

Stephanie struggled with self-loathing from her early 20s onward, which led her to alcohol and drugs. Things seemed to have finally settled down somewhat in her late 20s. She kept herself in what seemed like a stable marriage and had two children. Soon after the second child was born, however, she found out her husband was having affairs with not just one of her girlfriends but *almost all of* them.

She lost her husband and her entire friend group and support structure all at once. This dramatic experience of hurt, shame, and betrayal confirmed her feeling that she was not good enough. She lost her trust in others but, above all, in herself. She lost all sense of self-worth. Being a single working mom of two on a tiny budget made her feel even worse about herself.

A few years later, she entered a new relationship and gave birth to a little boy who was diagnosed with autism, challenging her to a whole new level of stress. Her painful relationship with the boy's father only added to it. As in her first marriage, her new relationship mirrored her relationship with herself: one in which she felt put down. She even went against her maternal intuitions for how to best take care of their son, squelching every last bit of sovereignty to do what her husband thought was best.

Stephanie's son is now a handsome teenager. Loving, vulnerable, yet also strong and loud. Standing tall at 6 feet 7 inches and weighing 176 pounds, he loves to wrestle with Stephanie, who stands at a diminutive 5 feet 1 inch and weighs 110 pounds. She does her best to keep up with him and simultaneously admits she always lives "on the edge." The stress has led to nerve damage that makes her body jerk uncontrollably at times.

The only way she made it through all these harrowing events and relationships was by finally befriending herself. She began to attend to herself with care and dedication—making room to process the pain and anguish that she had tried for so many years to mask with alcohol, drugs, and other distractions. After 30 years of struggling in partnerships, she allowed herself to finally separate from her second partner and make space for herself.

Remember Luke, who said, "I don't even know how to communicate with myself. How can I communicate with someone else?" Stephanie broke that cycle: she started to listen to herself, and in so doing, attained sovereignty.

Self-compassion saved Stephanie's life. It helps her stay patient and energized and loving for her son. "I find I no longer desire alcohol or drugs. Despite everything, I'm happy, and I know it's because I'm finally there for myself." Though her life is tough, and she has very little time and few resources, Stephanie does the best she can with what she has to take care of herself. "I feel blessed and privileged every single day of my life," she shared with me.

Stephanie takes care of her son—a full-on 24/7 activity—on the weeks when he is with her. The rest of the time, when he is with his dad, she devotes to her work, but within healthy boundaries. She has gradually learned to stop pushing herself past the limits of self-respect and instead acutely listens for messages from her body and mind. She catches herself when she needs rest or downtime and commits to restorative activities daily.

"If the only time I get for myself is two minutes in the bathroom, I look at myself in the mirror and say: 'I love you; I've got you,'" she shared.

Awareness: Listening to Yourself

So how do you deprogram yourself from self-loathing? You systematically train yourself to do the opposite: befriend yourself. As simple and even cheesy as that may sound, it takes skill and dedication to rewire yourself. And it's worth it.

The first step is to become self-aware. Awareness is such a fundamental element of sovereignty that you will see the word *awareness* pop up again and again throughout this book.

What is self-awareness? It's observing your needs and actually attending to them. Sounds simple but notice what we usually do. We know we're hungry but still skip a meal. We know we need more exercise but still stay lazy, sitting on the couch. We know we need healthier habits, but we're stuck to our destructive ones.

One study gives us a clue as to why we're so out of touch with ourselves: When the study's participants were given a choice between sitting in a room doing nothing or sitting in it and giving themselves painful electric shocks, participants preferred to go the electric shock route.[21] Really. That's how averse we are to being with ourselves.

After all, we tend to go *all* day being distracted (by other people, news, media, entertainment, technology, etc.). In fact, you can go your whole life without ever encountering yourself. Think of Luke. Many do.

Back to Stephanie. She successfully deprogrammed self-loathing by paying attention to her body and mind even during the difficult moments and then honoring her needs.

In short, by paying attention to the clear cues your body and mind are giving you, you are building new neural pathways—ones that are no longer neglectful of yourself but attentive. With practice, this habit becomes second nature. It starts to be common sense. And, in meeting your own needs, you become sovereign and so much more available to others—as Stephanie is for her son.

Her cup is full, so next time she is with her beloved son, she can have the joy and stamina needed to accompany him on the adventurous journey that is his life and potential.

The journey home from the misconception that you are not good enough involves deconditioning yourself by proving yourself wrong. Instead of neglecting your needs, you put yourself first on the priority list to the best of your ability. Instead of being harsh with yourself, you nurture yourself. Instead of twisting yourself into a pretzel to fit into others' expectations, you remain aligned with yourself. The transformation you feel from this will keep you doing it.

I once told a wise friend about the heart palpitations I had developed since having my second child—a symptom of depletion and high stress, among other things. She said something I never forgot: "Your heart will heal when you turn your love toward yourself. Take care of yourself as you do your infant baby." And I did, and my heart did. What would it look like if you took care of yourself as you would an infant, attentive to its every need?

Know that as you start to pay attention and respond to your internal cues, you may risk disappointing others or causing some conflict. Especially if they are not used to you prioritizing yourself. As a fellow mom shared with me, "There are times when I just have to say to my husband: 'I realize it may be hard for you to watch the kids, but I really need 20 minutes to meditate.' And be willing to tolerate his reaction." After meditation, she's better able to deal with the kids and the dad. Everyone is happier.

What Do You Do with the Shame?

Remember that moment I failed to show up for my keynote? In that moment I had a choice: spiral downward with self-criticism and beat myself up, try to distract myself in unhealthy ways for temporary peace, or be mindful of my shame, remembering that errors happen to all of us. I chose what I knew was best: self-compassion.

I felt shame through and through from head to toe for several hours. Excruciating. My stomach was on the floor, but I didn't take it further. I didn't beat myself up. Isn't the emotion itself torture? Adding fuel to the fire makes no sense.

Dropping self-criticism doesn't mean you suddenly go soft on yourself and become overindulgent or irresponsible to the detriment of others. No, like a loving parent to your child, you are kind *and* you stay disciplined. You move through the difficult experience with courage and steadfastness, and you make amends if you've made mistakes. I went home, apologized profusely to the conference organizers, recorded a talk for them immediately, sent it over to them, and asked them to cancel my honorarium. And then, with a little time, life went on, and I moved on.

Research shows self-compassion has a significant positive association with happiness, optimism, positive mood, wisdom, well-being, and personal initiative.[22] You grow and learn from your mistakes and are resilient even in the face of setbacks.

Shame makes you forget how powerful you really are. In fact, it strips you of your power. Self-compassion is the antidote. It makes you sovereign again.

Remember how self-criticism activates your sympathetic nervous system—your fight, flight, or freeze response—by acting like an inner terrorist. A nurturing relationship with yourself does the opposite: because it makes you feel safe, it activates the parasympathetic nervous system, which is often called the rest-and-digest response. In that mode, the body can restore itself and recharge so you can get up and keep going with resilience, even in times of failure or hardship. You're able to recuperate much faster and bolster your body's well-being. Your mental health is steady as you stop judging yourself and putting yourself down but instead show up and support yourself. Self-compassion is smart.

Reprogramming Yourself

Being hard on ourselves and sacrificing our own needs causes us to believe there's something fundamentally wrong with us.

Wait. Stop right there. Did you let that sink in?

Being hard on *ourselves* and sacrificing *our own* needs teaches us to believe there's something fundamentally wrong with *us*.

Who is doing all the action in that sentence? Ourselves!

And that's good news . . . because again, there's not much you can do about others. But there's a *lot* you can do about yourself.

Room to Breathe

Once you recognize this, the mistakes don't seem quite so big anymore. You see things from a broader perspective. You have room to breathe—even laugh.

At the beginning of the COVID-19 pandemic, I volunteered to lead virtual meditation sessions to help people with the stress of lockdowns. Inexperienced with Zoom, I had my first session hacked within minutes by penis-drawing hooligans.

The second time, I was so much more prepared—hackers, kiss this Zoom pro's backside! I had welcomed everyone and successfully started the meditation when my space heater started banging loudly. Although I was in my home's unheated sunroom and it was the dead of winter, I decided that removing bomb-like background sound effects from the meditation was worth sacrificing warmth. I quickly muted myself to turn the heater off.

Then, to put everyone back into a serene space, I put on gentle flute music and proceeded to lead the group in meditation, trying to keep my voice gentle and steady despite the fact I was shivering. We seemed to be all set for communal peace of mind when things started to go awry again.

The others seemed as inexperienced with Zoom as I was, judging from the fact that they didn't mute themselves. There was so much noise and activity, my eyes kept flying open in alarm at the commotion: I saw kids launching themselves across screens to attack meditating mothers, heard dogs barking, and watched partners ask meditators for TV remotes. Someone kept crunching snacks . . .

I repeatedly asked participants to please mute themselves, but no one complied. I attributed their unresponsiveness to the fact they were either in deep meditation or had had it with pandemic mandates and weren't also going to take a meditation mandate from me.

Then someone accidentally shared their screen. Then they started to look up Hulu videos. I repeatedly requested they please stop, but again, to no avail.

Suddenly, everyone got kicked off (including me) because this "Zoom pro" had a free account with a 40-minute max usage limit.

After all this, I found out that after muting myself to turn off the heater at the beginning of the session, I had never unmuted myself, and no one heard a word I said!

That evening, I couldn't sleep. Not because I was devastated with embarrassment and shame, as might have happened in the past, but because I was hysterically laughing, first on my kitchen floor and then for a good part of the night in bed.

Once you deprogram yourself from self-loathing and cultivate a more sovereign relationship with yourself, you stop basing your life on trying to look perfect and on others' opinions of you. Life becomes noticeably lighter—and a lot more fun! You're energized and invigorated. You don't just learn from your mistakes; you bounce back from them. Perhaps, unexpectedly, you even gain from them. The day after my infamous meditation, I received compliments from participants for taking them on an "epic silent journey." Go figure.

The Courage to Live Your Magic

Remember how I asked executives in my class to collect positive feedback about themselves? Times when they were their best self? When they read the feedback they received, they were shocked by the positive impact they had made on others and were often moved to tears. Turns out most people are walking around with low self-worth and absolutely no idea what a difference they make to others. If your self-criticism and shame are strong, it's a good idea to pressure-test this self-view with others' perspective. You don't have the faintest idea what a difference you're making in others' lives.

When you no longer walk around with high self-criticism, no one has power over you anymore. You become sovereign. We've seen that many "rebels"—like the motorcycle gangs I mentioned earlier—tend to be quite conformist. If you want to be a true rebel, love yourself. (And we'll talk about how to do that later on.)

Each one of us has qualities that are a gift to those around us. It's your magic, whether it's that you're great with children, music, cooking, building, crafting, teaching, writing, inspiring, mentoring, healing, or making things beautiful. Perhaps you make people feel safe, or loved, or inspired, or uplifted. You touch people through your humor, sensitivity, wit, grace, or compassion. Even if you really are irritating, you're teaching others something valuable: patience! Everyone has magic—the song we talked about in the first chapter.

Way-showers are leaders who have changed societies through their art, spirit, or ideas and brought in new ways of being. They are sovereign. They know their song and its magic, and they're willing to sing it, even if it goes against the grain or makes people uncomfortable. Even if they're criticized. Even if it's hard as hell. Way-showers aren't here to stay in their comfort zone or keep you in yours. They're here to pull the blinders from your eyes and to show you that you, too, have magic to share. They change the world for the better.

Eric Michael Hernandez was 14 years old when his teacher asked for student volunteers for a school cultural festival. Eric is a member of the Lumbee Tribe of North Carolina, and his uncle had recently taught him a traditional healing ceremony called the Hoop Dance. "The misconceptions and stereotypes about Native Americans made it hard to be proud of who I was," he explained.[23] He felt embarrassed and ashamed. "I was afraid of what my classmates would think of me claiming my native heritage . . . I mean, what do you think about when you hear the term

Native American? Do you picture a half-naked teepee-living bow-and-arrow-shooting feather-and-fringe-wearing savage? I knew that's what my friends saw. I mean, how could they not? Our history books and Hollywood were telling us that's what's real." Eric did not raise his hand to volunteer that day.

On the day of the cultural festival, however, Eric showed up wearing oversized clothes covering up a full set of handmade Hoop Dance regalia. He gave his teacher music to play, took off his cover-up clothes, and performed a Hoop Dance in front of all his awestruck classmates. The next day, his best friend ran up to him and showed him the school newspaper with a front-and-center picture of Eric dancing with his hoops and the headline "Lord of the Rings."

The next year, when the school hosted the cultural festival again, they had to extend it from a one-day to a three-day event because Eric had inspired so many more students to volunteer and share their heritage. Eric went on to perform over 2,500 shows all over the world as the lead Hoop Dancer with Cirque du Soleil's *Totem* show. "I challenge you to think about the times that you may have held back who you are," he said in a TEDx Talk he gave at UC Irvine while I was writing this book. "Embrace your identity, embrace your heritage, and embrace your passions because you can educate and you can inspire and you can make the world a better place because we all have something to share."

Please don't cancel yourself. Don't clip your wings, dim your light, or hide your magic; the world needs you as you are—real, uncensored, and free.

So what if they call you crazy for being you? They don't realize the craziest thing you could ever do is live life pretending you are someone other than you.

Have the courage to be seen. As you set yourself free, like Eric, you'll set others free too. And they'll breathe easy. Perhaps for the first time.

Sovereign Self: A Dangerously Powerful Proposition

"Caring for myself is not self-indulgence, it is . . . an act of political warfare,"[24] writes Audre Lorde, activist, writer, and self-described "Black gay woman in a white straight man's world." In a world that was antagonistic to her, she understood that the only way she could do her work with energy, inspiration, and strength was to make sure her own needs were well taken care of.

Because how do you want to show up on the battlefield of your life? Limping because you kicked yourself on your way there or overflowing with energy and health and in spanking-new shining armor because you freakin' loved yourself on the way there?

As Maya Angelou writes: "I learned a long time ago the wisest thing I can do is be on my own side."[25] Self-compassion is common sense.

I have seen Stephanie, whose story I mentioned earlier, struggle; I have seen her fall. I knew she was strong, but I was also worried. When she finally started engaging with self-compassion, everything changed. While earlier in our lives I was concerned about her, I now witness her as one of the wisest and most powerful women I know. A source of solace, compassion, and sage advice.

When you are a friend to yourself, you stop seeking comfort outside yourself. Instead of looking for comfort, you become a source of comfort.

That is why only those who have truly learned to love and honor themselves can ever help really truly love and honor another.

And that is why, by healing yourself, you heal humanity.

Few and wise are those who value, honor, and care for themselves. For they are sovereign. May you be one of them.

SIDE EFFECTS OF A SOVEREIGN SELF ⚠

- **Awareness:** You are in tune with your needs and take care of them.
- **Energy:** You save a lot of energy when you're not constantly trying to keep up appearances, make an impression, and look for approval.
- **Boldness:** You no longer fear being yourself and speaking your truth.
- **Serenity:** You're less stressed because you no longer worry about other people's opinions.
- **Leadership:** By dancing to your own drum, you inspire others to do the same. You become a *way-shower.*

SOVEREIGN SELF TOOL KIT

So what should you do the next time you fail or are hard on yourself? Or the next time you feel shame or the need to pretend to be something you are not? Or the compulsion to conform instead of following your heart?

Create the conditions for a sovereign self.

- **Make time for yourself:** To get in touch with yourself, you need time. Perhaps the most important meetings to schedule on your calendar are meetings with yourself. Meditate, take periods offline when you can, or spend time alone, whether it's going for a walk, taking a drive, or doing chores around the house. See if you can do these things without external entertainment shutting out your internal world. Start to relish time alone with yourself and getting to know yourself. Even if all you have is five minutes once everyone is in bed or all your work is done, make the most of that time. It will pay back in huge dividends.

Remember how people would rather give themselves electric shocks than be alone? It's not easy being alone, but it's key. And by the way, you're not alone, you're with yourself.

- **Listen:** What is the state of your mind? Anxious, frazzled, down, or jittery? What is the state of your body? Are you tired, hungry, worn out, energized? At first, it might feel awkward and even anxiety-provoking to tune in to yourself because you're not used to it. It might even feel overwhelming.

  But you will see that it is deeply healing. And as you practice, you transform your relationship with yourself. Think about how Stephanie became sovereign, replacing a life of destructive and impulsive habits with deep listening: to her own needs, wants, pain. As she got used to being with herself, she learned to relish it. With time, you too will begin to deeply enjoy these moments and understand them as time to honor yourself. It's in these self-loving moments with yourself that you understand how to best take care of yourself and fill your tank. They will become critical sovereignty builders. They give you that armor and protection to help you go through life sovereign. You will become your own best friend.

- **Meditate:** To learn to listen and to build your self-awareness, I strongly recommend a daily practice of meditation. As a scientist, I like to see if things work for myself. I encourage you to do the same. Set a goal to meditate every day for 40 days and notice the results for yourself. I personally use the Sattva meditation app because most of the meditations on it are by my meditation teacher, Gurudev Sri Sri Ravi Shankar.

Practice loving-kindness meditation, which my colleague Cendri Hutcherson and I found increases feelings of connection and well-being. In this meditation you practice directing feelings of benevolence to different people, including yourself. You can think of it as deprogramming self-loathing imprints by training yourself for self-compassion and self-kindness,[26] which may explain its broad beneficial impact on anxiety and depression.[27] You can find this meditation on the Sattva app, my Youtube channel, and my website www.iamsov.com. I'll also share a brief version of the instructions here.

Loving-kindness meditation: Close your eyes and imagine someone who loves you dearly standing on your right—either a real person, a person from the past, or perhaps even a person from your religious tradition—someone who loves you very much. Feel the love coming from them as you imagine them standing by your side. After a few minutes, imagine either another person or the same person standing on your left, sending you their love. Then imagine yourself surrounded by people who love you, sending you their love and their wishes for your well-being. As you feel yourself filled and overflowing with love, you begin to return those benevolent feelings outward. First, you can send wishes of well-being to the person who was initially standing on your right. If it helps, you can repeat a phrase like "May you be happy, may you be healthy, may you live with ease." Then do the same for the person standing on your left. Finally, start to bring in acquaintances, even people you don't know very well, and send wishes for their well-being, for their health, for their happiness. You may want to end the meditation by imagining the globe in front of you and sending wishes for well-being to the entire planet.

- **Give yourself what you need:** Maybe you're tired and run down, but it's hard to take care of yourself because you have kids and responsibilities. Do the best that you can with what you have. Maybe make sure to have a healthy meal instead of what you might have had otherwise, go to bed early instead of watching TV, or park farther away from the grocery store so you can take in some extra steps and daylight. Day by day, these little acts can have a significantly positive impact.

People often ask: "Well, what exactly did Stephanie *do* to heal?" Here's what Stephanie did: she took workshops that helped her become more aware and attentive to her body and mind, to soothe her emotions and meet her own needs. Trauma and self-loathing can sometimes go hand-in-hand with disconnecting from the body—as we'll discuss in the next chapter. Now she commits to reconnecting with her body through free dancing, breathing, bodywork, meditation, cold plunges in icy lakes or rivers—or, when bodies of water are too frozen to access, like when she came to visit me, birthday suit snow rolls! She also spends time with creative endeavors that bring her joy: drawing, building, painting, and crafting.

Deprogram self-loathing.

- **Learn to handle the inner terrorist:** Of course, you may notice some unpleasant things as you make time to listen to yourself. For example, you could become even more aware of the inner terrorist program. Remember that whatever you become aware of loses its power over you: it no longer owns you. This is true of your inner terrorist or any self-destructive internal program that we'll discuss in this book. What you see can't hurt you.

Some people give the inner terrorist a name to help create the distance from it: "Hey, Boo, there you are again. I don't deserve to be treated this way by anyone, including you. Come back when you have something nice to say. Toodles." Then, congratulate yourself on noticing it and not letting it drag you down.

- **Self-compassion:**
  - Treat yourself as you would a dear friend.
  - Be mindful of your emotions (like the shame I experienced when I didn't show up for the keynote) without amplifying them with self-criticism. Feel them but don't feed them.
  - Go easy on yourself, remembering that we all make mistakes. Take responsibility for righting any wrong, but don't beat yourself up about it.
- **Your secret weapon: *What do I need right now*?** If you feel yourself going down a rabbit hole of self-criticism or self-loathing or are in a difficult situation, ask yourself: *What do I need right now?* Maybe you're at work and things are stressful and people want you to do more, better, faster. And you let the inner terrorist sit at the head of the table and be the first to agree. Your stress response is in full gear and your usual MO might be to get more coffee and double down, burning yourself out quickly, feeling awful about yourself, and probably doing less quality work.

  In those moments, pull out your secret weapon. *What do I need right now?* What you might actually need is to get out of the building for five minutes and take some deep breaths in the open air. Even if it goes against what you would usually do. Even if it goes against what others think you should do. Every time you do this, you are rewiring your brain to nurture rather than confront yourself. It's guaranteed you will show up better, not just for those around you but also for yourself. There's science behind this (discussed in Chapter 3).

Get real about your magic.

- **Do the Reflected Best Self exercise:** Remember the exercise I have my students do, where they are asked to collect feedback on when they were their best selves? This exercise is deeply beneficial for improving well-being, reducing anxiety, and building stress and psychological resilience. It can help prevent burnout and even improve creativity. In brief, you collect positive feedback about you (moments when you showed up as your best self) from a broad group of people around you (friends, colleagues, family). It's an extremely moving exercise but also enlightening. You can find a link to the exercise and its details on my website at www.iamsov.com.
- **Do the same with yourself:** Praise yourself, acknowledge your strengths. Speak or write them out—if only to yourself. At night when we put our children to bed, we have a custom of sharing what we're grateful for. Our youngest, who was four at the time, would rattle off the list and always end with: "And I'm grateful for *me*, Christopher." Practice being grateful for *you*.
- **Have the courage to set boundaries:** Sometimes you're faced with situations in which you'd rather say no, and perhaps your usual program would have you override your own wants for the sake of fitting in, belonging, or being loved. In these moments, take a break and some time to walk away and really consult your heart. Saying no can be challenging, and people may not respond positively. It takes

courage, but practice saying no. The more you do it, the more it becomes second nature and the braver you will be.

Setting boundaries used to be so difficult for me, I would get anxious at the very thought of doing so. But practice is key: I would rehearse a sentence in my head (or spend hours crafting an e-mail just so) and then force myself to spit it out (or press Send). After doing this for a while, it stopped being a problem. I now hold my boundaries up firm—without anxiety. After all, am I not as deserving as anyone else to express my needs?

- **The magic list:** You have so long ignored your needs; it's going to require retraining your attention to prioritize them. Some people will need alone time; others will need company. Some will need nature; others music. Some will need spirituality; others comedy. Sometimes you'll need a run; other times you'll need a nap. It might be a letter you write to an old friend or some warm tea or a trip to the trampoline park. It doesn't matter. You know best what fills your cup—what brings you rest, rejuvenation, energy, vitality, upliftment, inspiration, and joy. Make a list of these things and keep it handy. Do those things. Prioritize them.

  The result? You'll keep your cup full. And when it's not, you'll know to consult the list.

For additional tools and ideas, visit my website at www.iamsov.com.

*Should Is Sh*t*

Wise words spoken by a friend.
In what areas of your life do
you live only by shoulds?
Do you squeeze yourself into
something you are not?
Do you permit yourself
to be bullied for who
you are?

Do you apologize for being
you?
Do you push yourself past the
limits of self-respect and
self-care to perform?
Do you bend and twist
yourself into something
you are most decidedly
not—just to fit in?

What areas of your life do you
feel free in?
Can you breathe in?
Do you feel like you can be
you in?
Authentic, carefree, and
natural?
Like a child that is secure
in her mother's love.

Where can you cry and laugh
and speak the truth?
Your truth?
In those places you are home.
At home within yourself.

What will it take to bridge the
gap between the two?
Where do you expand and
where do you contract?
What's keeping you stuck?
What's making you free?

Where and how can you relax
more and more into who
you are?
Finally let the shackles drop?
When will you feel safe?
Abandon fear?
Who decides?
You do.

Sovereign.

CHAPTER 3

SOVEREIGN EMOTIONS

In my adolescence and college years, I struggled with emotional eating. Not the occasional cozy-up with a pint of Ben & Jerry's. More like a compulsion to gorge every time I was feeling down, a desperate attempt to subdue my emotions with anything edible. When I was done, feeling overly full and still upset, I would end with crying. It was a hellish cycle. And I was stuck in it. An addictive self-soothing mechanism, an escape, a false promise, a destructive habit that kept me captive and bound.

It was during that period that I first tried meditation. At the time (1996), meditation was considered weird in some quarters, but I couldn't pass up the opportunity to hang out with my crush—a freshman I heard attended weekly meditations at the campus chapel.

I dragged my fellow introverted roommate to a social situation we could feel comfortable with: the peaceful, calm kind. I also felt less anxious with a wingwoman—even one who was shyer than I was. Little did we know the type of meditation we had walked into was far from the relaxing mental hot stone massage and spa music we had envisioned. The silent hour we spent there was more unpleasant than the boisterous frat parties we avoided, even though I was sitting on a meditation cushion that was right next to my crush.

The teacher's stern instructions were not to move. My legs felt like they had been anesthetized, and after a while, everything was aching. While others were drifting into their Zen zone, I was silently swearing to myself never to come back. Never mind my meditating neighbor—no one was worth this literal pain in the butt.

When the meditation finally ended with a loud gong, I attributed my relief to escape from the torture session. And yet as we exited, I shared with my roommate that I felt noticeably different. My mind had fallen stiller, like leaves that had gently settled onto the ground after a windy autumn day.

I had never felt so good in my life, *and* I was never doing that again. Ever.

The meditation's impact didn't seem to last. The very next day I was feeling down again—as was often the case in those days. When I spotted a cold leftover pizza, I had my usual reaction: *Perfect, a chance to binge.*

That's when I had an epiphany. A realization that had never occurred to me before: *Emma, you always cry after you binge. This time, why don't you cry first and binge afterward?*

So I did. I lay on my bed and sobbed.

When I was all wept out, I noticed the impulse to binge had disappeared. Completely. I was shocked.

By giving full expression to the unpleasant emotion, the impulse to bury it with food had disappeared. The awareness that dawned thanks to one 60-minute session of meditation ended my eating disorder. I'm not surprised that several research reviews have since shown that meditation can help curb binge eating and emotional eating.[1]

I never binged again. Nor did I ever date my crush. But who cared? It was the beginning of a lifelong committed romance with meditation—and therefore with myself.

What happens when you are triggered or angry? Do you know what to do with those feelings?

No matter how educated you may be—how many Ph.D.'s, M.D.'s, or any other letters you do or do not have behind your name; how many skills you've mastered; weights you can lift; dishes you can cook; employees you can manage; crossword puzzles you can solve; and languages you can speak—chances are you have as much formal education about what to do with your big, bad negative emotions as a five-year-old.

That's why most people are emotionally underdeveloped, undertrained, and undereducated. And that's how they get bound.

It's no one's fault. Chances are your parents, families, teachers, and leaders had the same blind spot. How could you learn from them?

Children are told "Shh, don't cry!" and "Stop pouting!" and "You're okay!" No wonder they become adults who deny feeling anything—"Nothing's wrong. Really, I'm fine"—alongside other suffering from stiff upper lips.

And we've failed to question the absolute lunacy of this. Because everyone's doing it. Heartbreaking, when you think about it.

Research shows that emotions impact everything we do—focus, attention and memory, physical health, mental health, decision making, and relationships—and everywhere we do it, whether at home or at work.[2] And when we don't know how to handle them, we suffer, and so do the people around us.

You'll notice that when you're stressed, anxious, or angry, you're not able to pay attention or remember things as well. You have a hard time learning when you're sad. If you need to make a big decision, it's going to look radically different on a day you're burned out versus a day you're relaxed. Have you noticed that our inability to handle our negative emotions leads us to hurt the people we love the most and want to hurt the least?

On the other hand, when you know how to handle your emotions, you can harness them for creativity, energy, deeper relationships, and greater happiness and fulfillment.

We bind ourselves to our emotions and abdicate our sovereignty when we disregard our emotions, suppress them, and numb them. Ironically, by attempting to flee them, we become stuck to them: they last longer. In trying to stop feeling, we also often engage in destructive habits—as I did with food—and often end up feeling even worse.

Yet, as I mentioned in Chapter 2, reclaiming sovereignty involves (1) questioning the destructive programs that are running our lives and (2) making more life-affirming choices instead.

In this chapter, we'll discuss how we bind ourselves: all the dumb things we do that get us stuck there. Bear with me on this one! We can't get unbound if we don't know how we got ourselves tied up in knots in the first place. Saving the best for last, I'll then discuss how to gain sovereignty over our emotions.

BOUND EMOTIONS

We bind ourselves to our emotions when we suppress and numb our feelings. We're afraid of feeling uncomfortable emotions and, in the process of avoiding them, we suffer and get addicted to habits that are destructive. Ironically, the more we try to avoid our emotions, the more we're stuck with them. Yet we keep falling for flawed beliefs that keep us stuck in this cycle.

Belief That Binds You #1: Leave Your Emotions at the Door

Historically, Western society has considered feelings childish and weak. Emotions don't matter. Don't bring them into the workplace. And for goodness' sake, pull yourself together and don't let them spill out all over the place. Leave your emotions at the door.

This belief is a joke because emotions are not like shoes you can slip off. You can't take something off that's on the inside. And, ironically, the more we try to ignore our emotions and stuff them away, the more they keep us captive, sitting on the throne of our life, ruthlessly running the kingdom.

Sure, research shows some people are more emotional than others, but research also shows everyone feels emotions, and this is true regardless of gender, age, or culture.[3] Laughter, crying, sorrow, despair, stress, joy, calm, frustration, anger, peace—we've all felt them. Since they are often considered frivolous or inappropriate—especially the negative ones—you may have buried them, hidden them, swallowed them, or used any number of substances to squash them maybe even to the point that you aren't even aware of them, but they most definitely are there.

Even if you could leave emotions at the door, you'd need a lot of doors because you experience emotions every minute of the day. Right now, I hope you're interested, curious, entertained, and excited to read on, but earlier, you might have checked your phone briefly and that brief moment might have elicited an avalanche of feelings:

- An angry text from your partner stressed you out
- A request from your boss made you anxious
- A post on social media gave you FOMO
- A memory on the Photos app made you nostalgic
- A notification that you spend four hours/day on your phone depressed you

See that? Five emotions in a moment. BOOM.

It's guaranteed that our ancestors didn't have to deal with even a fraction of the number of emotions in a day we do in a few minutes, thanks to our technology.

Research by Rob Cross, professor of global leadership at Babson College, shows just how these small stressful experiences—which he appropriately calls "microstressors"[4]—can accumulate and create a toll on our minds and bodies. Although nothing really "big" happened, you are wondering why you feel like you've been through a war zone by the end of the day.

Each emotion—especially negative ones—is a micro-drain on you. It's fatiguing. And it's even more draining when you have to pretend it's not there—which we'll discuss next.

Belief That Binds You #2: Suppress Your Emotions

I've asked audiences from around the world what their society taught them to do with their big, bad negative emotions.

I invite you to think about your answer to this question before reading on.

Most audience members' answers go something like this:

- Hide feelings and pretend not to feel upset
- Bottle them up
- Stuff 'em down
- "Suck it up, buttercup!"

Stuffing emotions seems to be a quasi-universal phenomenon and expectation. I say *quasi* because an audience member once pointed out that this was not the case for his southern Italian family, where vehement emotional expression is considered good for the heart. However, even if you're from an emotionally expressive family or culture, you undoubtedly have to deal with suppressors and personal moments of suppression.

Take a minute to think about this question: How is suppression working out for you?

Tragically, although suppression is the number-one most popular technique people use to handle difficult emotions, it is also the absolute worst and most unsuccessful one. Research shows it makes you feel worse, damages your health, and, ironically, ruins the very relationships you're trying to maintain. Suppression leads to a host of unfortunate outcomes, including having fewer closer friends, more negative emotions, less social support, lower satisfaction with life, poorer memory, and elevated blood pressure.[5]

Depressing, I know, especially given how practiced we are at it.

To top it off, it doesn't work! Research shows that suppressing emotions does the opposite of helping you: it makes emotions stronger. Take anger, for example.

As it is, we know that anger increases inflammation, heart rate, and blood pressure. It activates your fight, flight, or freeze stress response. Your nervous system goes into high-alert mode, expending significant energy, straining your physiology, and increasing inflammation. No surprise that anger is correlated with heart disease.

What happens when you suppress anger? You may *look* less angry, cracking one of those stiff, tight-lipped, "everything's just peachy" smiles, but at the level of the brain we see the emotion itself gets more intense! There is greater activation in the emotion centers of the brain and in the physiology. Your heart rate and blood pressure get even higher than they already were.[6]

Suppression is the equivalent of taking a soda can and shaking it up. Everything looks the same until you pop the top and it squirts up your nose. No wonder it eventually makes you more likely to explode in a way that has onlookers wonder when you're due for your next psychiatric appointment.

An emotion is "action potential," or energy. If it isn't processed, it lands somewhere in your body or psyche—unresolved, festering, and generally causing problems. If anger (or resentment or jealousy or any negative emotion) doesn't explode, it can *implode,* showing up somatically with stomachaches, migraines, or other physical symptoms.

Being from Northern Europe—part German, English, and Finnish, cultures where burying your emotions way down deep is the norm—I have a black belt in suppression. So I was the queen of stomachaches for most of my suppressing life.

Suppressed anger can also come out as passive aggression—ouch! Anyone who has experienced passive aggression knows how it can degrade relationships over time like a slow burning fire.

In sum, emotional suppression, the world's number one most popular emotion management technique, keeps you bound. When you hide your emotion, you are stuck to it. Resisting emotions gives them free rent on prime real estate in your mind. It keeps you captive, not free.

On the other hand, full-blown emotional expression is usually not a superior option, for obvious reasons. I don't recommend temper outbursts, but I have not always found them easy to control—especially during the sleepless postpartum years when my tank was hovering near empty. Husband doesn't prefer temper outbursts. The only heated thing he appreciates is the saunas he takes to sweat out his marital stress. Thankfully he is generous in his forgiveness of my occasional fire (I have his Catholic faith to thank for that).

Belief That Binds You #3: Drown Your Emotions

If my first labor had been a movie, it would have been a drama—or maybe a comedy. I sobbed, called for my mom, and cursed like a seasick sailor. I had decided to labor with no meds like my mother had done for her four children. I was in agony. I resisted the pain, panicked at the ever-increasing speed of the unbearable contractions, and felt terribly sorry for myself.

Many of us have a hard time with physical pain. "Give me the pill, the shot, the laughing gas, the Tylenol, the steroids, put me to sleep. I don't want to feel!" *Bad,* that is. We don't want to feel bad. Ever. Justifiably! Physical pain can be excruciating and so debilitating.

My point, however, is that we feel the same about our emotional pain as about our physical pain. We try to numb that too. But unfortunately, numbing our emotions doesn't work as well as Novocain does at the dentist. What it does do, however, is get us hooked to addictive habits.

On some level, if we're honest with ourselves, we all are addicted to something. The "something" can seem so innocent: that daily glass of wine, scrolling through your phone, or reaching for a treat.

Emotions are hard to live with. So we use all sorts of tricks to try and do away with them:

- Stimulants
- Alcohol
- Food
- Sex
- Weed and other drugs
- Entertainment
- Reputation or fame

- Work
- Money
- Attention
- Social media
- Anything new! New car! New job! New house! New partner!
- And so much more

There's so much for us to choose from, isn't there? There are many ways available to numb our pain. For me, in college it was food. Later, it was workaholism. Husband looks for emotional consolation in Merino wool. Whenever he shows up with a new warm top, we know he went "sad sweater shopping."

We teach our kids early too. Cookies, candy, and screens will quiet a child.

We look to these outside resources and substances to dull the pain or give us highs. We shop or gamble, drink or binge, watch movies or porn, scroll or smoke, overwork or overexercise, over-indulge or punish ourselves. This can look like being industrious ("I work 12-hour days") or gritty ("I do an Ironman a month!"), or even saintly ("I volunteer 30 hours a week!") . . . but it's all the same thing: numbing.

Anything we're dependent on—though it might feel good for a minute or two—we have given our power away to. It drains our energy. We've handed over the remote control to our life. Given away our sovereignty. Not until we reclaim our sovereignty will we feel the true potential that we are.

What's more, numbing is like a pain med—it doesn't heal the source of the pain. It masks it temporarily at best. The emotions are right there waiting for us when we're done. They'll come raging back like the tears that rushed forth after my college binges. Only now we're exhausted, beaten up by the side effects of our drug of choice, and, sadly, in worse shape to face the pain than when we started.

We bind ourselves when we buy into the idea that the answer to our emotional pain lies outside of us. An extensive menu of modalities is at our fingertips. Convenient, easy, yummy. We just don't realize that menu is poisonous. We don't realize that the menu is filled with empty calories and junk. By selecting from it, we perpetuate our pain, make things worse, and give others control over our lives.

Numbing, because it's temporary, keeps us on a treadmill, searching for more. We become more vulnerable, weak, and manipulatable. And it's hard to resist temptation. By appealing to our need for comfort and emotional escape, others exert control over us. Think of the many entities—from pharmaceutical companies to liquor brands and entertainment companies—that are profiting from our numbing habits. We spend dollars and time and get hooked. Not to mention there are plenty of social media influencers, advertising executives, and skilled marketers who make a great livelihood on us believing their product is the solution to all our negative emotions forever.

There's a better way to handle life's challenges. We can reclaim our sovereignty.

Think about it. You deserve so much better.

SOVEREIGN EMOTIONS

Many problems would never happen if, along with reading and math, we had been taught how to regulate our emotions. But it's not too late: we *can* learn to cope with emotions effectively using simple science-backed tools.

Emotional sovereignty is learning to navigate emotions with grace. As I'll describe, you have to be willing to feel, practice, be self-aware, be honest, and be courageous. But you'll gain so much awareness, energy, and well-being in the process. I'll share techniques in the pages ahead that can make it all much easier.

Technique #1: Feel the Damn Emotion

Remember the raucous circus that was me giving birth without meds the first time? Well, believe it or not, the second time I was so relaxed, no one noticed I was giving birth, and I practically had to deliver the baby myself.

A couple of hours before I delivered, my midwife announced to everyone that, given how calm I was, I would not give birth until the next day. Then she and her assistant walked off and had a nice nap. As for Husband, he enjoyed his beauty sleep next to me. In response to my pain-induced hand squeezes, he would offer occasional closed-eyed grunts and a mild squeeze back as signs of wakeful, attentive compassion for his suffering beloved and exuberant excitement at their soon-to-pop-out pup.

During my first childbirth, I had been resistant, feeling sorry for myself and like a victim. The second time, I was sovereign.

Instead of anxiously panicking, wallowing in self-pity, and desperately trying to escape my situation, I surrendered to it. I had gone through a hypnosis program that had trained me to welcome the sensations. I rested instead of wasting my precious energy with resistance. I accepted every sensation—intense and painful as it was—as the process of helping the baby move out of my body and into the world. The labor went by easier, smoother, and faster. Despite being as physically challenging as you can imagine, it remained a peaceful experience not just for the sleeping midwives and hubby but also for me.

My childbirth story is about physical pain, but it's also a metaphor for how to handle our emotional pain successfully.

Notice how children get over emotions fast. The tantrum happens; they scream at the top of their lungs. They cry 100 percent. Two minutes later they're done. Sovereign once again.

What makes children so emotionally resilient? They let the emotions flow through them. As the saying goes, *feel it to heal it.* Emotion is energy in motion. It needs to move like a baby on its way out. And it *will* move if you let yourself feel it—observing and embracing the discomfort—without resisting, numbing, or feeding it, i.e., if you accept it rather than resisting. Fully experiencing negative emotions isn't pleasant. It often hurts like hell, but the good news is that, like childbirth, it ends with deliverance.

Note that fully *experiencing* the emotion doesn't mean fully *expressing* it during its peak. It can be damaging to our relationships when we blow up at someone. It's better to communicate once you have calmed down. The point here is that by experiencing your emotion, you process and digest it. You'll communicate better once you've taken those steps.

Brain-imaging studies have shown that using acceptance during emotional moments helps the brain's emotion centers to calm down (i.e., deactivation of the limbic area).[7]

The day of my cold-pizza epiphany back in college was the first time I realized that if I let myself fully experience my despair and sadness, the urge to binge would disappear. Surrendering to the emotion would set me free. I just needed courage and forbearance.

I say "just." Not that it's easy. But it's worth it.

The result was that I became free both from the emotion and the destructive numbing habit I was using to suppress it.

You heard me talk about the need for awareness and courage in Chapter 2 and as you can see, you'll need them here again (and you'll see these themes popping up throughout this book because they are keys to sovereignty).

Technique #2: Realize You Are Bigger than Your Feelings

You may be wondering: How do I stop suppressing? And how do I face emotional pain with full awareness? Sounds awful!

You're not alone. Whenever I've talked about the need to feel and go through your emotions on social media, I've received touchingly open, transparently honest, and refreshingly concise feedback like "F*ck off."

I get it. It's hard. Really hard. And emotions hurt. Anger, anxiety, fear, depression, and rage are unpleasant and often seem unbearable. Excruciating. Which is precisely why we fall into addictive and destructive habits in the first place. Reeducating yourself to feel is undeniably difficult, especially when you've been suppressing your emotions your whole life and you're scared as hell to face them. But you now know (and have probably for a long time experienced) that numbing, escaping, and suppressing aren't working for you.

Besides, whether it feels like it or not, you are bigger than your feelings. During a yoga teacher training I attended in Canada, our instructor would help us get through excruciatingly long abdominal exercises with these six words: *you are bigger than your body.* Emotional sovereignty requires the realization that *you are bigger than your emotions.* Although it may feel as if your emotions could take you down in a boxing match, they can't. They may hurt you, but they can never destroy you—unless you numb and resist them. Then, as we discussed earlier, they're running the show.

The difference between you as a child and you as an adult is that children are immersed in their emotion. They *are* their emotion: *I am mad!* As an adult, you can become *aware* of the mad *without* identifying with it. *I am experiencing mad.* You can observe the emotion and differentiate between you (the observer) and the emotion (pissed).

This point is critical; please let it sink in. As an adult you have the choice to become the observer of your emotions. Just like you observe a TV screen and the TV screen doesn't control you, you are also the observer of the phenomena that happen on the screen of your mind and body. You are the viewer, not the screen. You are the experiencer, not the experiences. You are the feeler, not the feelings. They don't have to control you. Ironically, it's by surrendering to them, welcoming them, and observing them run their course that you end up in control.

After the yoga teacher training where I learned the whole *bigger than your body* lesson, I traveled to India for the second part of the training. The difference in mentality was astounding. Whereas in Canada the yoga trainees were disciplined, on time, and completely focused, in India the students were relaxed, late, and totally nonchalant. Even their yoga mats were rebellious: while ours were thin plastic mats offering little to no support to our aching knees and backs, the Indian participants had four-inch-thick cotton roll-up mattresses that looked more like comfy, squishy beds that begged for a snooze.

The teachers attempted discipline by trying to enforce rules and a code of conduct. They really gave it their best, but the Indian students broke the rules every chance they got. In North America, I learned discipline and grit; in India, surrender and relaxation. I learned a lot about yoga but also about emotions during that teacher training: have the discipline, forbearance, and courage to endure the emotions, but then surrender and relax into the process to allow them to move up and out.

Counterintuitive, isn't it, that it's by surrendering to emotions you end up mastering them? That it's by being defenseless you end up winning?

Sure, emotion is sometimes an indicator that we need to do something about a situation. For example, if you're angry about some injustice that you notice happening or that recurs repeatedly in your own life, it may be a sign that it's time for you to address it. And being aware of your emotion doesn't mean that you become passive in the face of events you want to act on. But it does mean you'll probably do so from a more poised and skillful place.

Here's something else to consider: Sometimes it's not even *your* emotion. Research on emotional contagion shows that we pick up on other people's emotions. An obvious example is when there's panic in a crowd and suddenly everyone is panicking. Or when one person near you is angry and soon you find yourself mad. You may notice that when you arrive in a place buzzing with stress, like Manhattan or the Bay Area, the anxious energy in the air is palpable. All the more reason not to take emotions so seriously all the time. They may not even belong to you.

You stop identifying so strongly with emotions when you realize they may not even be yours.

Remember Stephanie from Chapter 2? The one who used drugs and alcohol for so long to suppress and numb her pain before developing a more sovereign relationship with herself? She still experiences pain, but here, in her own words, is how her relationship to it has changed. "When I'm feeling weak or fragile or emotional, I now embrace my feelings rather than avoiding them. I have learned no longer to avoid the feelings of emptiness I used to drown out with substances. I no longer avoid the void. It's in fact become a place of refuge when I'm overwhelmed and insecure. Above all, I have come to trust that the rhythmic ups and downs of life are themselves wise and intelligent guides." Stephanie gained sovereignty over her emotions by claiming, owning, accepting, and allowing their energy to course through her body. As a consequence, she gains solace in the very experience itself.

When you accept an emotion, it no longer controls you. You simply see it for what it is. You become an observer and let it wash over you. From that place, you access power. No longer a victim, you are master. Sovereign.

Technique #3: Reappraisal

So the emotions are there, and you're feeling them. And it's hard. You don't want to suppress, so what do you do?

Much of the field of emotion regulation has focused on cognitive reappraisal as the number one technique for emotion management—and so did the lab I was in as a graduate student. Reappraisal is the ability to use logic, reason, and wisdom to manage your emotional response in accordance with your goals. It involves looking at the situation from a different perspective.

I was once in the subway coming back from school in the late '80s while the HIV epidemic was at its peak. Life expectancy was extremely short for infected individuals as there was no medication available yet. I overheard two men speaking about the situation. One of them, pale, skinny, and with gray hair beyond his years, clearly had tested positive based on what he was saying. On his way out of the subway car, he held the door open for a moment, turned to his friend, and said: "But you know what, it's changed me for the better. I'm not taking a single day for granted now; every breath is a blessing." His situation was extremely challenging, but he gained sovereignty by using reappraisal to help him look at his situation as a gift.

Research also shows that perceiving stressful situations as a challenge or adventure instead of a burden helps you handle the situation much better, lowers activation in emotion centers of the brain, and even reduces harmful health markers like inflammation.[8]

It's probably no surprise that sovereignty is linked to better relationship outcomes. How we deal with conflict in a relationship and how we handle the emotions resulting from those conflicts impact the quality and longevity of the relationship[9] as well as our mental health. Being able to handle your emotions makes others around you—colleagues, family, friends, partners—happier. Colleagues and I ran a study that showed that varsity coaches who reappraise their emotions rather than suppressing them have happier, higher-performing teams.[10]

Sometimes work is stressful but home life is going well, for example. Refocusing on the things that are going well can help you snap out of the funk about what is not going well and what you can't change. It can give you the energy to handle the things that are not going well with greater forbearance. It broadens your perspective.

In China, I learned an interesting and very useful way to reappraise emotions when things are challenging. There is a Chinese expression, *chi ku shi fu,* which means "eating bitterness" (i.e., hardship) "is good fortune." But we think the cliché "no pain no gain" applies *only* to exercise and diet. It couldn't possibly be true about our emotional pain: our anxiety, fear, insecurity, anger, frustration, loneliness, depression, midlife crisis, darkest thoughts, languishing, or anxiety. Nope. When it comes to those forms of pain, we do everything possible not to feel.

Here's a proposition to help you reappraise:

What if growing pains didn't end in your teens?

What if they kept going so you could keep growing?

What if emotional pain was not useless suffering?

What if pain were your friend?

The friend who matures you, makes you stronger, fiercer, and wiser.

The friend that loves you so much they will break your heart so it can grow larger.

The friend that lures you into the darkest areas so you can see your own light shine brighter.

The friend that truly sees the beauty, strength, and magnificent potential you are.

And who will go to any length to help you become your truest, bravest, boldest self?

Sovereign.

Looking back on your own life in this light, from what life experiences have your greatest lessons emerged? Inevitably it's the divorces, deaths, sudden unemployment, health issues, cheating partners, abusive relationship, or financial difficulties. It is those hard, painful, heartbreaking, and excruciating times that have also brought forth your best self.

They have invoked resilience in you because you had no choice.

They brought forth your courage because you had to make it through.

They cultivated forbearance and steadfastness in you because you felt like you were dying, but you had to keep going.

There were tears and moments spent writhing on the floor, but you got up, had breakfast, and went to work anyway.

You witnessed the warrior within yourself.

The valor.

And you carried on.

Your hair grayed, but you grew.

Post-traumatic growth is real. The lotus really does grow from the mud. When we go through hard times, it brings about forbearance and enormous strength. It brings about wisdom because we've seen suffering. We no longer take small things for granted. Most of all, post-traumatic growth leads to compassion. Because you've seen and experienced pain, your heart has stretched. Its capacity for love is greater and its desire to help others in need is stronger.

I once worked with a veteran with trauma who had a family member die by suicide. He recounted that he'd experienced no emotional response to the death. In pathologies like post-traumatic stress, you can stop feeling emotions at all. The problem is that even your positive emotions are numbed. This veteran was in the active arm of a study we ran on a technique called SKY Breath Meditation, which helped him with his trauma (more on that in Chapter 4). He regained the ability to feel. He was telling me about the crush he had on one of our mutual friends and the ups and downs that came with that. He exclaimed to me with great joy: "Emma, I feel *good*. I feel *bad*. I *feel!*"

With no valleys, there are no peaks. If you can't feel bad, you also won't feel its opposite: good.

Technique #4: Breathe

Yeah, but. That's what I kept thinking in graduate school when reappraisal was discussed. This is all well and good and it works to "talk yourself out" of mild frustration—logic can be the master of feelings to a certain extent when things aren't too bad—but my question was: How do you reappraise when the rug gets pulled out from underneath you: you get suddenly fired, you find out your partner is unfaithful, or something else equally dramatic. Then what?

Reappraisal is a great strategy but doesn't always work.[11] It can *only happen if the emotion isn't overwhelming.* If an adult finds himself in a situation that profoundly provokes anxiety or anger, no amount of reason and logic will help.

Here's why: When all hell breaks loose, cognitive strategies are no match for big emotions. The emotion centers in the brain are so acutely activated, they trigger the stress response, and you temporarily lose the ability for reasoning and logic. We know from neuroscience research that when emotions are intense, or during periods of high stress or lack of sleep, brain areas responsible for rational thought in the prefrontal cortex are impaired.[12] That's why you can't easily talk yourself out of high anxiety, fear, or anger. Under those kinds of intense emotions, your brain's emotion centers (e.g., the amygdala) take over and the prefrontal cortex has a weakened connection[13] with other brain areas, so it is unable to properly regulate our emotions.

That's why logic and trying to talk yourself down from a situation seldom helps you regain control when emotions are intense. And this is why they say "no one in the history of calm down has ever calmed down by being told to calm down." (Now that you know the science behind its ineffectiveness, I hope you'll join me in a silent oath never to say "calm down" to yourself or anyone ever again.)

So what can help us when rational thought can't? In our cerebrally oriented life, many of us have forgotten one critical piece: the role of our body to help our mind. Because emotion is energy in motion, if we want to regain our ability to think clearly, it helps to process emotional energy through the body. And the fastest-acting way to do that is via breathing.

Jake was a Marine Corps officer in charge of the last vehicle on a convoy going across Afghanistan when he drove over a roadside bomb. When the dust cleared, he saw his legs almost completely severed below the knee. This level of shock, trauma, and excruciating pain usually results in fainting pretty quickly. But Jake actively prevented himself from going into shock with a breathing technique. It allowed him to maintain his ability to think clearly and perform his first act of duty—check on the other servicemembers in his vehicle—and his second act of duty—to give orders to call for help. It even gave him the presence of mind to tourniquet his own legs and think to prop them up before falling unconscious. He was transported urgently to Germany and then to Walter Reed Army Medical Center, where he was told that had he not done those things, he would have likely bled to death. Jake's injuries were so severe that he lost both his legs. But he is alive, has a family, and is well. All this because he knew how to calm his nervous system through breathing in a moment of acute emotion.

If Jake can remain emotionally sovereign in such dire circumstances, what can breathing not do for our (hopefully) lesser stressors? We all know how to breathe, of course. Our first act of life was an inhale and our last will be an exhale. Between those pivotal moments, we will take roughly 20,000 breaths a day. That should make us breathing experts, yet most people don't realize the profound potential the breath has for mental health.

How we breathe impacts our heart rate,[14] blood pressure,[15] emotions,[16] and memory.[17] Our breathing patterns influence the function of many critical areas of the brain.[18] Breathing influences how we perceive the world, think, pay attention, remember, and feel.[19]

Our neurons respond to the rhythm of our breath: When we alter our breathing, we can control the activity of our brain cells.[20] Research shows you can rapidly change your emotions using just your breath.[21] Different emotions are associated with different forms of breathing, and changing how we breathe can change how we feel. Actors learn these techniques—they can manipulate their breathing to evoke an emotion they need to display. They breathe long, deep, and slow to trigger relaxation and short and shallow to evoke anxiety or anger.

Slowing the rhythm of your breath—especially your exhales—can initiate relaxation.[22] It calms your heart rate and stimulates the vagus nerve, which runs from the brainstem to the abdomen and is part of the parasympathetic nervous system. You start to calm down. You feel better. And your ability to think rationally returns.

I've included a simple exercise you can try in the tools at the end of the chapter and will talk more about recommended breathing protocols in the next chapter.

Technique #5: Self-Awareness and Radical Honesty

Sovereignty is becoming radically honest and self-aware. Are you addicted to entertainment, to food, to work, to shopping, or to just being busy? So you don't have to feel bad? Sovereignty is making room for the entire human experience with eyes wide open and with courage.

We've talked about the critical importance of self-awareness. I have a brilliant academic colleague who is a recovering addict.

When I asked whether she is on social media, she gave me this highly self-aware answer: "I don't do social media. I can't risk getting involved in any activity that might give me a high." Social media is not alcohol or drugs, but it can give us a buzz that gets us hooked on likes, comments, and follower count—another addiction-forming habit that you can use for getting high and numbing out. Self-awareness made my colleague sovereign. She recognizes where and how she can fall into the traps of captivity and skillfully avoids them.

How do you develop self-awareness? A straightforward technique, as I described in my story about the eating disorder epiphany, is meditation. Even a single dose of meditation for people who have never meditated before alters brain activity and helps increase self-awareness.[23]

Mark lost his mother at age 15. His suffering led him to drinking. A lot. Eventually he became an alcoholic. After years of struggle, it was through meditation that Mark finally became sober.

While alcohol numbs your awareness (which is why you don't drink and drive), meditation cultivates it. A number of studies show that meditation increases brain volume.[24] It also strengthens areas of the brain that promote the opposite of addiction: self-control, self-awareness, and emotion regulation.[25] Perhaps this is because you process more thoughts and feelings when you are meditating than when you are doing some other relaxing activity.[26]

(Alcohol does the opposite. Research on more than 36,000 adults found that even drinking less than one alcoholic beverage a day—the equivalent of about half a beer—reduces brain volume. Going from one to two drinks a day is linked to changes in the brain equivalent to aging two years.[27] Even a single drink permanently alters the morphology of neurons, making you more likely to crave more alcohol and fall into addiction.[28])

Meditation cultivates your awareness, but you also need radical honesty in that self-awareness. Because if you're not honest, your relationships will make that glaringly obvious to you, as Mark discovered.

Though he had married the girl of his dreams after getting sober, in only a short time Mark's marriage fell apart. Angry and feeling sorry for himself, he met a psychologist who told him to stop being a victim. "I just broke. He was the tipping point. I said 'F*ck you, man. I do the meditation. I do all the things. Why me? Why? Why? Why?'"

A light bulb went off in Mark's head, though. He realized that it was his unprocessed anger that had destroyed his marriage. He had quit the act of drinking but never processed his emotions or taken responsibility for them. "I was wearing sobriety like a badge of honor but still feeling sorry for myself, angry, and righteous. I felt entitled and like a victim of circumstance. I was not being honest with myself," Mark shared with me.

"I finally understood I needed to take responsibility for my feelings. If I get angry at someone, it's not their fault. *I*'m the one experiencing anger. *I* play a role in that. Just because I meditate doesn't mean that I can be an asshole and yell and scream and demand things. I have to clean up my side of the street: I'm responsible for my emotions, thoughts, speech, actions, beliefs—all of it. I can't blame anyone else."

As I mentioned, our emotions are contagious, and they impact the environment and the people around us. You can think of emotions as pollution. Or perfume. When we take care of our emotional well-being, we spray perfume wherever we go. Or at least a neutral scent. When we don't, we create toxicity.

And as we'll discuss at greater length in Chapter 5 on sovereign relationships, we cannot expect to have good results in our relationships, workplace, or health if we don't learn to work through our emotions. If we don't learn to let go of anger. If we don't learn to release grief. If we don't learn to forgive. If we don't learn to be grateful and to celebrate the good.

It's not easy to be self-aware and radically honest with yourself. You may witness parts of yourself you're not proud of, as Mark did. But it's the key to healing and to emotional sovereignty. Mark shared with me how much happier he is now. He views his life and his challenges as a gift that helped him heal.

When you love someone, it's because there's love in your heart. When you are kind to someone, it's because there is kindness in your heart. When you're angry with someone, it's because there is anger in your heart. It all comes down to you. Perhaps the world, with all its stories and dramas, its ups and its downs, is just an excuse for you to come back to you and heal your own heart.

Technique #6: Creative Expression

Creativity can be a healthy form of release for a strong emotion. My five-year-old son had to have surgery, and he and I traveled out of town for it. My sister came to support us for two of the three weeks we were there. On the day she left, my son was devastated. "Now we're all alone here," he cried and started sobbing. Suddenly, he yelped, "I need paper!" He drew and drew until all his love and grief had spilled onto a beautiful drawing of himself with his aunt, complete with the giant bun she wore on her head during our time together. And the emotion was processed.

Several years ago, I found myself using creativity in a similar way. After moving to a new area for a demanding job that left me little time for myself or for socializing, I found myself in a painful state of loneliness. I didn't know what to do, so I did one thing I knew how to do: I wrote. Specifically, I wrote an article on how to overcome loneliness. To this day I receive e-mails from readers who say the article helps them. I had no idea expressing my pain creatively and from direct experience would come to someone else's aid. I've written about what to do when you're angry when I was dealing with someone who was very angry, when you're dealing with passive-aggressive people when I was dealing with passive-aggressive people, and when you're the target of a nasty office rumor when I was. Creative expression can be a place of true transformation for self and other, a way to absorb and process emotions. The energy of the emotion, painful as it is, can be transmuted into healing for yourself and solace for another. Like the debris that gets caught in the delicate insides of a mollusk and becomes a pearl, the emotion can be processed from raw pain to real beauty.

But you don't need to create something for an audience. The process of expressing your emotions alone can be beneficial.[29] Psychologist James Pennebaker has shown that just the act of writing about emotional difficulties—a technique he called "expressive writing"—can deeply benefit your well-being and mental health.[30]

Engaging in the arts as a spectator or listener can also help you move the energy. There is a hub in our brain that responds to music, emotion, and memory, and some people are particularly affected by different music, such as yours truly.[31] (Husband is careful not to play piano music in the car to avoid the spontaneous tear deluge that overcomes me when I feel moved.) A college student who babysits my children shared with me that she puts on music and dances freestyle to help release painful feelings when they start to interfere with her life.

Technique #7: Move and Ground

Speaking of movement, when you think of emotion as energy in motion, then of course moving the energy, burning energy, and altering your energy will shift you. Sometimes anxiety has you shaking or anger has your blood boiling. Sitting around with this energy can often lead to overthinking or getting yourself tied up into knots. Instead of exploding or numbing or stuffing it, do an angry kitchen cleanup, bust out 100 sun salutations, challenge yourself to a CrossFit class, do a lying-down meditation (yoga nidra), or snap yourself back into the present moment with a cold shower. Even if you haven't fully calmed down the emotion, you'll have spent some of that energy and you'll have a clean kitchen countertop, a fresher disposition, and greater physical well-being. No wonder research shows exercise is linked to not only better physical and mental health but also better emotion regulation.[32]

Exercise is always a good idea as it also fills you with endorphins and feelings of accomplishment. It can give you a fresh outlook on a situation and has immediate benefits for depression and anxiety, research shows.[33] However, don't let it become an addiction in itself. If you spend two to three hours a day training your jiujitsu moves to the detriment of your relationship, then just make sure you're not using exercise as another way to numb, suppress, or escape your emotions.

Ideally, go outside, preferably in a natural environment. Nature or even just a broader horizon offers you a new perspective. Within the four walls of our room or the restricted boundaries of our virtual communication with people, we can get caught up in narrow-minded perspectives. We forget to see how relative our problems are in the grand scheme of things. Going into a natural environment or even just stepping outside, no matter where you are, can help you see the bigger picture. No wonder research shows that exposure to nature benefits mental health and that you can improve your mood in even a short walk outside.[34] More on that in Chapter 7.

Emotions—when they are strong—can often make us feel slightly disembodied. We're caught up in our thoughts and feelings and we lack steadiness. Exercise can help bring you back into your body. So can being in a natural environment like the woods or the beach. Sit on a rock. Take your shoes off and be barefoot on the earth—a practice known as "grounding," which research shows reduces inflammation, promotes immunity and wound healing, and benefits mental health.[35]

Some techniques may work better than others, depending on the situation and emotion. When you're highly anxious, soothing activities will be better than high-intensity ones like running, which, though it might pump you with endorphins, also puts further stress on your heart and activates your sympathetic nervous system. Choose a breathing exercise, a slow walk in nature, or a gentle yoga class in those situations.

The Transformative Power of Emotion

Sovereignty means facing all that life offers—the good and the painful—and growing stronger and wiser for it. Your emotions, when observed with compassion and patience, pass faster. You're happier, braver, stronger, and freer. You've already been through tough times. You can do this. Knowing you can stand in the face of anything and come out the other side, you become sovereign.

Besides, according to Elisabeth Kübler-Ross, who spent her career supporting people on their deathbeds: "The most beautiful people we have known are those who have known defeat, known suffering, known struggle, known loss, and have found their way out of the depths. These people have an appreciation, a sensitivity, and an understanding of life that fills them with compassion, gentleness, and a deep loving concern. Beautiful people do not just happen." It's life's challenges that mold the human spirit into its greatest beauty.

It's a normal part of life to come unhinged and unhappy and uncentered at times. The ground comes out from under us—trauma, loss, shock, sudden transitions, life-or-death situations, sheer exhaustion. It's what develops our understanding and compassion for others who are suffering, and it's what makes us value the good times so much more.

I once worked in a research lab whose culture was known for its toxicity. The members of the lab were not particularly friendly, except for two people. The two Black women there—one a scientist and the other an administrator—always went out of their way to be warm and welcoming to me. They smiled and joked, and we always stopped to talk. They made me feel safe. They stand out in my memory, and I'm grateful to them to this day for having made my experience there so much better than it otherwise would have been. After I left the lab, I shared my gratitude with one of them. She said to me: "Don't you find it fascinating that the two people who showered you with kindness, love, and community were two Black women? It's because we know what it's like not to experience any of those." As awful as their life experience had been, they made a remarkable decision: to flip that pain into an intention that others not go through the same suffering. What would the world look like if we all set that intention?

SIDE EFFECTS OF SOVEREIGN EMOTIONS ⚠

Better physical and mental health: Suppressing emotions damages our mental health and can lead to physical health challenges too. As you learn to process rather than suppress your emotions, both your mind and your body will benefit.

Better relationships: Others may be surprised by the fact that you no longer suppress your emotions—maybe even a little uncomfortable with it at first. After all, it's a change! There will be shifting dynamics in how you relate to others. But your relationships will improve. Because as you learn to process your own emotions and recognize that others too must do so, you become more understanding and compassionate. You judge them less.

Lightness: When you learn to process your emotions, you don't hang on to them for as long. No longer bearing the weight of suppressed feelings, you feel lighter. It's easy to be happier and more joyful.

Courage: It takes guts to feel your emotions fully. I'm not going to lie. But the more you do it, the stronger your forbearance and endurance. You cultivate valor.

SOVEREIGN EMOTIONS TOOL KIT

Remember: When you run from your feelings, you run from your healing.

When you're highly stressed, anger, anxiety, or fear will be your fight, flight, or freeze stress response. Notice if you want to escape that state. Part of the panic that arises when we have strong emotions is a feeling of lack of safety. Our system is hijacked by the stress. That is why we look to numb ourselves to get away from the pain. When you notice the need to numb yourself, take that as a cue that you need to feel safe.

Take care of your basic needs.

Remember the points we discussed in Chapter 2, "Sovereign Self." This is where it can help to take care of yourself. As you work through accepting your emotion, it helps to make sure your basic needs are met: Are you sleeping enough, eating well, exercising, and taking care of yourself? The fuller your tank, the more sovereign you'll be as you manage your emotions.

If possible, go to a location where you feel at ease, or if not, imagine yourself there. Take rest, nourish, and hydrate yourself with care. As you start to fill your tank back up, you'll notice everything is more manageable. When our life force is stronger, everything feels better.

Feel instead of suppressing.

Remember the only way out is through. You will undoubtedly notice a strong desire to escape your emotion and to resist it, because you're not comfortable being uncomfortable, let alone in pain. This is where you need patience and profound acceptance, surrender, and self-compassion. And forbearance. If it helps, think of it as labor, like in childbirth. You're delivering the emotion and will be free from it soon. And as you allow yourself to feel it, you'll allow yourself to heal it.

Let the emotions wash over you like a wave that comes, keeps you underwater for a bit, but eventually passes so you can resurface and take a breath of fresh air.

Remember these two mantras.

- **You are bigger than your feelings.** Come back to a place of observation: you are the experiencer, not the experience.

  It's helpful to remember that you've been through challenges and difficult experiences before. No matter how awful you felt then, you got to the other side of this. You did it. You might even have learned a few things along the way. You can do it again.

- **Emotions are energy in motion.** What will you do with that energy? You can breathe, as I describe below, but you can also shift the energy in other ways. Do something creative: Write out your frustration or your fear, or draw it, or play music. You can move your body, exercise, stretch, or dance. Clean the house or organize your shelves. Going outside can really help as well—and going out in a natural environment is the cherry on top as it helps with anxiety and depression (more on that in Chapter 7). Walk barefoot for the added benefit of grounding I mentioned earlier. If emotion is energy, you can channel it.

Breathe.

We talked about Jake's story of survival and the science of how your breath is connected to your emotions. Breathwork has now become popular, with many techniques taught on YouTube or various apps. I can't vouch for those techniques. What I can recommend is what we know works from research. Here's a technique that will slow your heart rate in minutes and help you shift your state of mind: Breathe in until your lungs are completely full (to a count of four, for example), and then on the exhale try to breathe out for longer than you breathed in—ideally a time and a half or two times as long (to a count of six or eight). Do this for five minutes and notice the aftereffects. You'll probably feel more calm, with your mind clearer and more present. The next chapter will describe a breathing protocol we have researched and found to be very beneficial for mental health and well-being.

Reappraise.

Once you have calmed down—and remember this *only* works once you've calmed down, because emotions skew our vision—look at the situation from a different perspective. You might remember how past challenges helped you grow stronger and wiser, for example. Maybe you learned something from the situation. Embrace all the feelings. If we can learn to celebrate our ability to feel—as that veteran did who had lost the ability to feel—our whole experience of life shifts. Though emotions can be so hard, it's the difficult moments that have molded us into who we are today, often for the better.

Use radical honesty.

If you find yourself blaming others, remember to be radically honest, as Mark learned to be. Sometimes it takes two to tango—Mark took responsibility for his anger and his actions. He learned that he needed to clean up his side of the street. Again, the point is not to blame yourself here, as we learned in Chapter 2, but to observe what happened, how it happened, and how you can let go of it by not hanging on to anger at someone. We all make mistakes; so do others.

Practice.

When I first stopped consciously suppressing, I was like a toddler with his first coloring book. Let's just say I did not know how to color within the lines.

There was one time when I expressed myself a little too intensely. But here's what was interesting: I meditated shortly after the experiences and felt almost blissful peace.

To clarify, the high I experienced was not due to the outburst; that made me feel remorse. The giddiness was from the freedom of finally having let out what I had painstakingly been suppressing for so long. The steam had finally blown off. There are way more graceful and less hurtful ways of expressing an emotion, but the relief I felt does exemplify how, when we completely experience an emotion and let it move through us, we become free: sovereign.

Ideally, feeling the emotion doesn't have to equate to chaos and disruption. It doesn't mean you live your entire life like a volcanic eruption spewing lava all over everyone. But it's important to remember we're all toddler-like when we try something for the first time: awkward and far from perfect. Practice is essential, and practice, by definition, is filled with trial and error and failure. That's how you learn. Be patient with yourself (and others). It does take some time to relearn how to handle emotions, especially in relation to other people.

Bookmark and reread this tool kit whenever you need to. Practice these tools and remember that it's normal to make mistakes when we practice. You might find yourself no longer suppressing but expressing a little too much.

Be patient and kind with yourself. You may have spent a life suppressing or reaching for comfort through distraction, entertainment, food, and so on. It will take practice to unlearn those habits.

That's okay, we only learn through experience. Allow yourself the time to build new habits and ways of interacting with your emotions—it doesn't happen overnight.

Take action (if you need to) once you are feeling more centered.

You will see things from a different perspective. And if you need to do something about the situation that sets off the emotion, you may need to communicate your feelings to someone. You will do so in a much more constructive way when your own state of mind is more settled. Then, in fact, communicating about your feelings skillfully can lead to a deeper bond with another person instead of a rift

For additional tools and ideas, visit my website at www.iamsov.com.

Whole and Complete

You were made to be ashamed.
Of your actions
And therefore, of yourself.

Not okay as you are.
Not okay to make mistakes.
Not okay to feel what you're feeling.
Angry or upset or jealous or sad.
There's something wrong with you.

And in that process
Bit by bit,
You divorced yourself.
From yourself.

Hidden in a shell.
That you tried to make look perfect.
You become perfect outside.
And were crying inside.
Like a fraud.

Your job is to pick up the pieces.
All the lost pieces of yourself one by one
And softly blow life back into them.
Whispering

"You're okay, little one.
I got you."
And to love them
Slowly
And surely
Back to life.

Those parts of you,
Numb, cold, and anesthetized away
Become warm once again.
In the constant and steady embrace
of your own acceptance and love

And your self-love will be the
Glue that brings the puzzle of you
Back together.
Whole and complete.
Healed.

CHAPTER 4

SOVEREIGN MIND

I was blown away when I first met Starr, an executive who came through our Yale Women's Leadership Program. Starr is charismatic, brilliant, and passionate. It was obvious to me—and all her classmates—that she is a powerful leader with enormous potential. It wasn't quite as obvious to her, though, because of an old belief that she was harboring.

"As a Black woman," she explained, "I believed the most important thing was to feel safe . . . and for good reason. Black women have all heard stories of other Black women that perhaps reached too high, hoped for too much, were cut down literally and figuratively simply for being, shown no mercy, no grace. So I was constantly searching for a safe space. Layer this with a sentiment heard often in the Black community, likely heard in some other form in other marginalized communities, 'You have to be twice as good to get half as much.' So I found myself sitting in what was a 'safe space' being 'twice as good' and getting half as much. The problem is that it's so embedded in me that if I make a mistake, I believe I deserve every bad thing that comes my way. I go from 0 to 100. You had a typo, you deserve to be fired because you're not twice as good. I'm afraid that something is going to happen to me, and it becomes self-fulfilling because I have so much anxiety that I'm not focusing on what I'm supposed to be focusing on. And here's the rub . . . if you're feeling all that . . . you're NOT SAFE."

The belief Starr held had kept her in a secure position as a lawyer working for the government for 13 years. She notes it wasn't all bad. After all, an advocate sent her to the Yale women's leadership course—no small feat on a government training budget. But her soul yearned to stretch and expand into bigger roles she knew she was capable of, and that she deserved.

What Starr is describing is an imprint. Research shows our brain is deeply influenced by what we've seen, heard, or learned in the past. Many of our experiences are recorded in memory, conscious or unconscious, resulting in beliefs, concepts, or assumptions with which we navigate our worlds. These experiences leave a mark, an impression that programs your mind to think a certain way, interpret situations a certain way, or judge yourself and others. Imprints shape our perception of what's going on in the present and sometimes completely distort it.

Some imprints are positive or neutral, but when they limit your perspective, harm you, or restrict you from accessing your fullest potential—as they did with Starr—they are problematic.

During the breaks in our weeklong program at Yale, Starr would often be in deep thought. She was questioning her old beliefs. Here's how she described it: "I'm in a reprogramming battle with myself." She went on to say: "Something in me is saying no. This program that I need to be twice as good is the stupidest thing ever, and it's so toxic. I don't have to be twice as good. I can be Starr. I can be human."

A few months after our program, I got a text from Starr. She had not only applied for jobs in the private sector (a bold move and not easy after a long career in the government) but also received multiple offers. Not just anywhere. At a Fortune 100 company.

Turns out that once Starr saw what her belief was doing to her, she refused to let it control her any longer. In fact, in stretching her comfort zone, she went above just moving jobs and sectors. When her current company offered her several positions—one as legal counsel (staying relatively "safe" in her comfort zone as a lawyer) and another as a vice president doing something she'd never done before that would involve a steep learning curve, guess which one she chose. The latter, of course. And she's thriving. Sovereign.

To be clear, Starr wasn't at fault for the limiting beliefs she had held; her imprint was the result of trauma. The point for her was to understand what she can do now, in the present, so her imprint doesn't keep her from being who she really wants to be. And that's what this chapter is about: seeing through imprints and clearing them so you can, like Starr, have mental sovereignty. First, I'll talk about the kinds of imprints that bind us, and then I'll talk about how we can attain sovereignty.

BOUND MIND

We are constantly accumulating imprints in our minds. Think about it: whatever you focus on, you become. After seeing a movie, for example, you'll notice the images and story linger with you for a few hours (or a few days if you're like me!).

Imprints are in part social conditioning: the religious, political, and philosophical viewpoints of our family, ancestry, and community; the ones we learned from our culture and that were shaped by our socioeconomic status, gender, ethnicity, and race. But we also accumulate imprints through our life experiences: significant relationships and events. Some you'll remember your whole life; others will dissipate over time. Some are positive or neutral. Others are destructive—like the imprint that confined Starr for so long.

And since imprints are like glasses through which we make sense of the world, they shape the way we interpret our life and interact with others. In that way, they are like a program running us. They are destructive when they get in the way of our song, our magic, our ability to shine as ourselves. Which they almost did for Starr, until they didn't.

How do you know if an imprint is destructive? When it creates constriction: undue fear, anxiety, anger, or discomfort despite not being in a life-or-death situation. For example, if you're terrified before public speaking or a first date, it's probably due to an imprint. If, like Starr, you're keeping yourself confined in a job, relationship, housing situation, or anything that you know you've outgrown or that makes you suffer, chances are an imprint is running the show. A false belief has you in its grip, confining you and getting in the way of your sovereignty.

A decade ago I was soaring high as an academic with dual appointments at Yale and Stanford; a speaker at multiple TEDx events; a well-being expert who appeared on *Good Morning America* 10 times; a psychologist whose *Psychology Today* column had received over 5 million views; and an author whose first book, *The Happiness Track,* sold more than 50,000 copies in the U.S. and across the world, translated into dozens of languages. External markers of success, perhaps, but . . .

Physically, I was withering. My health was at an all-time low, and I had to spend most of my time resting. My heart broke daily because I was not able to take care of my newborn and toddler. I was operating at a small percentage of what I was capable of previously. Although I was sustained by the practices and principles I described in *The Happiness Track,* I was still missing something key. And that was sovereignty. I was buying into imprints that were destructive. And I was paying for it.

Trauma Imprints

There are two kinds of imprints: those we learn through our life experiences and those we acquire through media and messaging.

Some of our deepest imprints result, of course, from difficult moments in our past. The more emotional an event—especially a highly negative one—the more likely our brain is to remember it and hold on to it. If it's a deeply disturbing event, it can stay there for a lifetime. For example, if you were born before 9/11, you probably remember where you were on that day. Trauma is nothing but a deep imprint. An undigested experience.

A life-or-death situation can also create a debilitating imprint. I was walking with a group of friends, and we were about to cross a bridge when sweat started pearling on Jose's forehead. He had been in the Army during the Iraq war and had survived an explosion on a bridge. His logic knew nothing was wrong in this moment, but the *bridge = danger* imprint was more powerful than his mind could control.

We may not have a post-traumatic stress diagnosis, but almost all of us have been through difficult experiences like car accidents, sudden losses, divorces, failures, rejections, and so on that can live on as imprints in our mind, keeping us hooked to the past with a ball and chain.

That's why if you've ever failed or embarrassed yourself, that imprint can stay with you as debilitating fear of failure despite external proof of success. Annelies was a ballet dancer at the New York City Metropolitan Opera Ballet. Despite her success as a dancer, she had a profound fear of failure. Adrenaline coursed through her body prior to performances and she was unable to eat all day. After a performance, she was self-critical, ruminating on all the mistakes she had made. No matter how successful she was, her mind and body were trapped in a vicious pattern of fear followed by self-criticism. Her success was not sufficient to heal an imprint that was destroying her ability to enjoy her hard-won career despite dancing on one of the most famous stages in the world.

Cultural Imprints

I grew up in Paris, which sounds glamorous—but the philosophy on the streets makes you think things are always going to hell in a handbasket. You bond with others through moaning and complaining. You've heard the French phrase *oh là là*! In the U.S., it's used for something positive, like when someone looks fabulous, but in France it usually accompanies bad news. Oh là là, the weather! Oh là là, the traffic! Oh là là, politics! Oh là là, les Américains! Oh là là, life!

Even when you pose for photographs, you don't smile—models in French ads are considered beautiful when they look slightly depressed. The sexy pout. For a kid in school, grading is harsh.

No one ever gets a perfect score, and you learn you're just never good enough. In fact, you're probably hopeless. There's a saying when you dare make any kind of optimistic plan or dream: *ça ne marchera jamais*—meaning "it's never going to work out." Talk about demoralizing.

When I moved to the U.S., I was introduced to a radically different and more enlivening perspective: *you can do anything if you put your mind to it* (which is why America is home to inventions like Slugbot, a slug-eating robot for your garden, or the Parihug, a WiFi-enabled teddy bear that hugs your loved ones from afar). French people would say that's naïve and perhaps it is a bit, but I gratefully traded cynicism for hope. That perspective was more energizing and served me better.

For the longest time, I wasn't sure if the French cynicism imprints were just me, but then I heard my high school classmate Justin Guilbert on a podcast:

"As a French dude, you live in this world where nothing is really doable and that's the culture . . . everything is hard and challenging and you stay in your stasis . . . and then you come to the U.S. and people are just like, 'Let's just do it.' And you wonder, 'What? You just do it? You just get up and do it?' And it happens."[1] And it does. As founder of Harmless Harvest and Bravo Sierra, he is now a successful serial entrepreneur running businesses that have social impact.

Don't get me wrong. It was obviously a privilege to grow up in France. Its history, literature, poetry, art, beauty, and bread also offered me extraordinarily beneficial imprints. As for the U.S., it wasn't all perfect—the common U.S. imprint, a belief that you are what you do and that you should work yourself to the bone—took me a while to deprogram. *Do it! Do it right! And do it right now!* The productivity and perfectionist imprints will drive you bananas if you let them run you (ask Husband).

My point is we carry cultural imprints we're not aware of and they shape how we see the world. I wasn't aware of my cynical French mindset until I came to the U.S. and saw its opposite.

Because here's the first secret to unbinding yourself from harmful imprints: awareness. That theme is appearing again and again because it is one of the core keys of sovereignty. Once you're *aware* that the imprint is there, like Starr was or like I became after moving to the U.S., it loses its power. Once you see an imprint for what it is, you can choose not to fall for it.

It's only mind control if you're not aware.

I'll soon share other ways of deprogramming imprints.

Should Imprints

A subset of cultural imprints are *should* imprints that keep us bound.

Scrolling through a Yale alumni group on Facebook, I was shocked to see the sad answers submitted to an admin's innocent discussion prompt: "What is your profession and how would you advise someone who wants to work in that field?" Most comments were from physicians and lawyers who did *not* actually answer the question. Instead, they wrote about how they had thought they should choose a career for financial success and prestige and how they now hated their job. Having presumably ruined their lives in the pursuit of material success, they pleaded with younger alumni not to choose careers for money or status.

So what if you've succumbed to all the *shoulds* in your life, have done everything "correctly," and become a big deal if you hate your life?

Women suffer because they *should* look like they are 17 for the rest of their lives. Men suffer because they *should* not appear weak or vulnerable. Kids suffer because they *should* always be "good." These imprints are torture—unrealistic and unhealthy.

I was once confiding in my mother about a difficult coworker. I needed to assert some stronger boundaries with the person but was worried that what I had to do wasn't very nice. At which point my mother asked: "Why do you have to be *nice* all the time?" Hmm, I hadn't considered that. She was right. In the U.S., it's pretty much imprinted on us to be nice, especially if we're women, even at the expense of ourselves. My mother lives in Paris, and Parisian women do not suffer from this problem (as anyone who's been there on vacation can attest).

In France, I learned I should be humble and obedient and try to fit in, so when I arrived in the U.S. and learned I should be proud of myself, stand out, and toot my horn, I was thrown. *Should* is so relative. It's not absolute truth. It's perspective. Opinion.

As my endearing tell-it-like-it-is friend Moria puts it so simply: *should is sh*t.*

This whole *should* imprint business is no one's fault, by the way. We all fall for *should*s. If you think about a child under age 10, they are wide-eyed. Not just with innocence and cuteness, but because they are stretching their eyes open to *take it all in.* They are making sense of this world by absorbing *everything.* Their brains are developing at lightning speed to learn as much about life as possible as fast as they can. Whatever they're rewarded for, they'll remember. It's not surprising that as adults, we then continue to adapt and conform to society's expectations—sometimes at our own detriment.

Media

Most people don't realize we mass-consume imprints *voluntarily*—upward of 60,000 GB of information per day across all our media channels (TV, podcast, social media, messaging, entertainment, etc.),[2] which is sufficient to crash a small computer in a week. Whether news or entertainment, much of it is empty and filled with expertly crafted messages designed to suck you in. After all, that's what makes you click and consume.

You know those moments where you get lost scrolling online news, random tutorials, or TikTok dance clips instead of finishing work, paying attention to your kids, exercising, making dinner, or watering the poor dehydrated plants? The tech's got you. Bound. Whoops.

Consider this: Your smartphone is mostly just other people's agenda for you. For example, the urge to check social media is even stronger than the urge for sex, research suggests.[3] Some of the brightest minds, armed with the most sophisticated knowledge of how our brains work, have designed these experiences to exert control over your attention and be maximally addictive.

Talented scientists run behavioral studies that demonstrate what gets people most hooked based on some of the research I mentioned in Chapter 3—the addiction cycle our brain gets locked into. Tech companies then design products accordingly. Why? So they can sell ad space. Ugh.

Same goes for entertainment. Former CBS and NBC programming president Jeff Sagansky said, "The number one priority in television is not to transmit quality programming to viewers but to deliver consumers to advertisers."[4]

Let *that* sink in for a moment.

And, unaware, we click right into our roles as obedient consumers. Indian friends of mine whose family followed a 20th-century Indian mystic said he gave this haunting prediction: "In 50 years, you'll hold the cause of your misery in the palm of your hand." Hard not to think he was referring to our digital devices. Looking from the outside in, we appear controlled by our technology, walking around, heads down and attention locked onto a device, letting its messages imprint on our minds 24/7. By choice! It's like something out of a sci-fi movie.

Fun fact: research shows most people don't prefer overtly violent or sexual content in movies. So why is there so much of it? Advertisers believe viewers prefer it, so they are more likely to buy ads during highly violent or sexual parts. So producers make more of it—for the advertisers![5]

And meanwhile, viewers' brains absorb violent imprints, leading to more aggression, especially in younger viewers who can go on to become more aggressive adults.[6] Violent media has also been shown to increase anxiety in adolescents.[7]

I was once at a party where a mixed martial arts fight was being broadcast. While the adults were talking, my heart broke for the host's five-year-old, who was standing inches from the TV, absorbing what he was seeing with all his senses: two vicious-looking grown men beating each other up while an audience cheered. What were the messages he was absorbing?

News Imprints

When the Iraq war started, I was in France visiting my parents. The U.S. and Iraq were enemies while France and Iraq were allies. Accordingly, headlines in the two countries were strikingly different. While the U.S. newspaper showed moving photos of Iraqi grandmothers warmly welcoming American soldiers with open arms, the French paper *Le Figaro* showed a heartbreaking picture of a massive explosion with a gloomy headline, "Bombs over Baghdad." Same facts. Different opinion. Different framing. Completely different news.

In 1983, 50 companies owned most of the media in the U.S. Now it's only six shaping and honing most of the information you receive due to companies consolidating.[8] There are some independent news agencies out there, but you have to seek them out. And understand their perspective. News articles may report factual events, but the articles themselves are interpretations. Opinion pieces.

The point here is not that the media is evil or that there's a news monopoly. The point is awareness—if we wish to be sovereign. Be a discerning consumer, see through and beyond the messaging and imprints you are taking in. Appreciate them for what they are—carefully curated perspectives that someone is profiting from.

I lived in China from 1999 to 2001. Every time I picked up the *South China Morning Times* or another Chinese newspaper, it was mostly positive headlines. Everything seemed to be going just peachy all the time. During breaks from our Mandarin class, the other international students and I would drink tea and laugh at the Pollyannaish headlines.

However, heading back to France and the U.S., the news coverage there suddenly seemed similar—only in reverse. Every murder and act of child abuse was covered in excruciating detail, making it feel like heinous crimes were the norm.

Which news source is "true," the Chinese or the American? Probably neither. Which one is mind conditioning? Both. They are doing the same thing: spotlighting one thing (the overly optimistic or the overly terrifying) and thereby imprinting specific perspectives on the viewers' minds.

I have a neighbor who is glued to U.S. news. She's constantly scared sick. By focusing on rare atrocities that are the exception and not the norm, news reports make you think there's more danger out there than there actually is. You're freaked out. No wonder research shows that consuming high-intensity news can lead to a higher probability of developing post-traumatic stress.[9]

When you're watching a musical and the spotlight is only on one actor, you think they're the only one on stage. But if you know there's a lighting professional controlling the spotlight and keeping the rest of the stage in the dark, you're aware that there's a lot more than meets the eye. Sovereign.

Without awareness, we don't realize how stuck we are in our media's messaging. Especially since we're absorbed in the messaging alongside others who are stuck in it. It feels normal. But by confining our human experience to limited and controlled views, stimulation, entertainment, consumption, and fear-based messaging, we deprive ourselves of the higher states of consciousness, awareness, and happiness the brain is wired for. We unknowingly find ourselves bound. We abandon our own sovereignty. But there's a way out, as we'll discuss soon!

Imprints: The Power of Negativity

What you fill your mind with is what's going to haunt you. I had a friend who constantly suffered from intrusive sexual thoughts. Every 15 minutes, to be exact. (Not sure how he got any work done.) When a mutual friend asked him whether he engaged with a lot of porn, the answer was yes. For sure. A lot. "You are what you eat" is also true of mental imprints.

It's one thing if the media you ingest is inspiring and uplifting; it's another if it makes you want more stuff or it's filled with negativity or is evoking fear, insecurity, anxiety, desire, or anger. Because then you're stuck, disturbed, and miserable. Bound.

Why does our news tend to focus on negative events—murders, calamities, atrocities? Fear triggers your sympathetic nervous system, causing stress, which is stimulating, grabs your attention, and keeps you hooked (and consuming advertisement).

A colleague at Yale once came to me and confessed he couldn't sleep. He looked exhausted and stressed. I felt so bad for him. I asked him what his bedtime routine looked like. He told me he fell asleep watching the news every night. How can you sleep in peace when, night after night, you set off your internal alarm system by focusing on the sad and the scary? Whatever you hear or read as you're drifting to sleep is going to leave the deepest impression on your mind. After all, research shows we remember items we learned right before sleep much better the next day.[10] How are you choosing to condition your mind before bed?

Neuroscience research also shows that negative information impacts our brain's ability to think, reason, and perform on cognitive tasks.[11] Considering how much negative information we take in through news and otherwise every day, how much better would we be at performing and thinking if we did not?

Also, sadly, the more we see awful things, the more likely we are to carry them out. When German poet and author Goethe published a book in 1774 whose hero took his own life after a heartbreak, it spurred a trend of copycat suicides throughout Europe. Two centuries later, psychologist David Phillips showed that the more a suicide is covered in the media, the greater the rise in suicide in the area where that media was consumed.[12] Sadly, we are seeing this now with social media's influence on teen self-harm.

Living in China provided a period of remarkable deconditioning for me. It's extraordinary to spend several years surrounded by media not aimed at you (e.g., a supplement to grow *taller*, cream to make your skin *whiter*). You're like an alien on a planet where nobody is trying to influence, persuade, or brainwash you. My mind was sovereign: true to itself and so much more at ease. There was a sense of mental freedom.

Poet and activist Maya Angelou is a sovereign wisdom keeper worth learning from. She says, "I simply refuse to have my life narrowed and proscribed."[13] Nothing can bind you, if you choose for it not to do so. And that's sovereignty.

SOVEREIGN MIND

The good news is that imprints can be released, and that's what we'll talk about in the rest of this chapter. Because if they're not released, they can eat away at you. Ever noticed how some people are young in years but seem old? They've stopped smiling and look beaten down or lifeless? And then you see others, like my 75-year-old mother, who sparkle with enthusiasm, joy, and mischief (like the time she was talking to an ultra-conservative Christian family and brought up penis tattoos—something she seems to know a lot about—because why not?).

What's the difference between these two types of people? Harmful imprints—have you accumulated them and let them weigh you down or have you managed to free yourself from them?

Our mind is like a mirror. It reflects what we put in front of it. If it hasn't received regular cleanings, it's grimy with the dust of past events and information accumulated over years. Sovereignty involves dusting off the mirror by releasing those imprints and developing greater awareness, discernment, and clarity of mind. And then nourishing it with high-quality imprints that feed your sovereignty.

Deprogramming Imprints

Layers and layers of imprints have filled our minds since childhood. We clean our bodies, houses, and computer screens. But we forget to do the same with our minds.

There are many ways to shed impressions. First, I'll share a few time-tested research-backed methods. Second, I'll make suggestions for curating what you allow in.

Awareness of Internal Imprints

When I talked to Starr about how she gained sovereignty over the belief that had been confining her all those years, she shared this: "You need to call out the limiting belief, name it, tell the truth about it, and identify the virus. Then you take power away from it. It's hard, but you have to face it with courage. The worst thing you can do is ignore it, because that gives it power. Shed a light on it and know that it's not true."

See that? The topics of awareness and courage that you've seen in the previous chapters. It's a simple equation, really: **Awareness + Courage = Sovereignty.** This equation is true for every aspect of sovereignty in this book.

You need to engage in a staring contest with self-loathing tendencies to gain a sovereign self (Chapter 2), with your emotions to free yourself from suppression and addictive habits to gain emotional sovereignty (Chapter 3), and with your imprints to gain a sovereign mind. Not always comfortable, but always key to sovereignty.

Because if you're not aware of imprints, they rule you. In Starr's words: "How do power-packed, incredibly intelligent, highly qualified individuals suddenly think they can't do something? Where does this delusion come from? Why does our mind create delusions that are not true? Creating this whole fantasy or nightmare in our own minds that isn't even true? Eighty-five percent of things people worry about never happen. What is it that is holding us back? If we're in a prison, we have to ask if the prison walls are real." It's when you become aware that an imprint like Starr's is *just an imprint* that is ruling you that you can start to take back the reins as she did.

How do you develop awareness of your imprints so you can deprogram them? After all, it's sometimes difficult to know that you're under the influence of an imprint. How many years did Starr operate under the need to be safe without realizing she was being controlled by that fear?

As you start reflecting on what your own harmful imprints might be, think about what keeps you feeling confined or constricted: A belief that others are out to get you or that you don't have enough or that you're not good enough or that you don't belong or that you are in danger? Look at what you crave: Attention? Approval? Money? Sex? Power? Think about your fears: Fear of humiliation? Or rejection? Or the dark? Or something you've seen in a movie or on the news? There are countless imprints a person could have.

Practices like meditation can help build awareness.

The good news is that this releasing imprints and attaining mental sovereignty business has been researched in many parts of Asia. You know how they say it takes 10,000 hours to become an expert in something? Well, India has 10,000 years of experience on how to decondition the mind. Thank goodness we don't have to reinvent the wheel—though we've tried in the field of psychology with some limited results.

Traditions like Hinduism and Buddhism, unlike other faith-based traditions such as Judeo-Christian ones, involve awareness and self-study. The Buddha famously said something to the effect of "Don't believe anything I say unless it's a product of your own experience." The goal of contemplative activities like yoga, breathing exercises, and meditation, for example, is sovereignty. Observe your mind and imprints. Treat your mind like a scientist: investigate it objectively. You are in your very own lab.

Breathing Out Trauma Imprints

Traumatic imprints are difficult to remove with pure awareness and cognitive strategies (like the ones suggested in talk therapy) alone because of an important difference: they are often lodged in the body. Remember Jose? He knew there was no danger on the bridge we were crossing that day, but his body reacted like there was. The traumatic imprint in his body was more powerful than his mind. That's where body-based practices like those involving breathing are key.

While I was a postdoc at the University of Wisconsin–Madison, research was showing that traditional treatments (pharmaceutical and therapeutic) were failing many veterans with post-traumatic stress. So my colleagues and I ran a randomized controlled trial to test the effects of a breathing protocol called SKY Breath Meditation on veterans returning from Iraq and Afghanistan with trauma. We partnered with a nonprofit called Project Welcome Home Troops that offers SKY to veterans and military at no cost (SKY Breath Meditation is taught by a nonprofit called Art of Living Foundation to nonmilitary).

Many of the veterans in our study had post-traumatic stress so severe that they were bunkered up in their basements, smoking pot and drinking. Jose, who was afraid of bridges, was one of them. Many couldn't finish school, and even those who could hold down a job often had failing marriages due to uncontrollable anger outbursts or the alcohol and drugs they used to sedate themselves to sleep. Others were medicated so heavily they could not function properly.

We found that, after one week of practicing SKY Breath Meditation, the veterans' anxiety dropped to normal levels compared to the control group that received no intervention. We even saw a reduction in anxiety at the physiological level—the vets weren't just telling us they felt better, their bodies were also showing greater ease and less stress.[14] I'll never forget the day Jose turned to me after learning SKY and said, "I didn't need any weed to get to sleep last night." It had been the first time since returning from Iraq that he was able to sleep without substances.

What surprised us most was that the veterans still had normalized levels of anxiety one year later, suggesting long-term recovery. In fact, many no longer qualified as having PTSD at all—even though most did not continue to practice.

A few years later, I collaborated with the Palo Alto veterans' hospital on a larger version of this study, comparing SKY to a gold-standard PTSD therapy (cognitive processing therapy). SKY not only had similar benefits as the therapy on PTSD but also showed greater improvements in emotion regulation.[15]

If you'd rather not talk through your trauma or therapy isn't working for you, breathing may be the answer. Many of the veterans in our studies went through such horrific experiences that the last thing they want to do is talk about them. Remember Maya from the opening chapter—the one who was in the National Guard and whose boss prostituted her during the war in Iraq? She appreciated that she could breathe without having to revisit her trauma: "With the breathing exercises, I learned to release my dark emotions without having to confront them directly. It was like loosening the soul, letting go without needing to attend to those emotions."

I personally discovered the impact of SKY on trauma shortly after 9/11. I was attending graduate school in Manhattan at the time and witnessed the second plane crash into the Twin Towers from my rooftop. After that day, I shook with anxiety every morning. I tried many things. Mindfulness triggered full-blown panic attacks. Hot yoga gave me glowing skin, a six-pack, and probably much-needed lymphatic drainage to detox post-9/11 Manhattan pollution, but no long-lasting peace. I even attempted to attain inner peace by osmosis, attending countless talks by Buddhist monks at New York City's Tibet House, but I'd inevitably find myself back at square one, sitting on the floor of my tiny 34th-floor studio apartment wondering what the heck I could do to stop shaking.

One day, I stumbled into a SKY Breath Meditation and finally experienced calm again. Twenty years later, I haven't missed a day of my SKY practice.

One of the most appealing aspects of a breathing practice is that you're helping yourself. You're not dependent on someone else. You're in charge of your own healing. You've got this. You've got sovereignty.

Remember Annelies, the ballerina with debilitating stage fright? She was the one who taught me SKY Breath Meditation at Columbia. She started teaching SKY Breath Meditation soon after she discovered it helped her with her stage fright. Just as she had trained her physical body for athletic sovereignty, she had now found a way to train her nervous system for emotional sovereignty.

Annelies realized her imprint was fully healed on a night she had to stand in for a sick dancer at the last minute. The opera that night was *Julius Caesar.* The set was a huge Roman building that nearly scraped the ceiling of the MET. The other dancers had quickly filled her in that she was to walk behind it and then make a sharp right to dance onto the stage. She followed their instructions but soon after making the sharp right found that she couldn't move! Horrified, she strained forward. Her dress was caught in the set! As she forcefully pulled at it one more time to get on with her performance, she dragged that entire sky-high Roman building forward across one of the biggest stages in New York City in front of thousands of onlookers.

Before learning SKY, Annelies would have been devastated and afraid to go to rehearsal ever again. Instead, as soon as she got backstage, she exploded with held-back laughter instead of shame. Sovereign, not crushed.

As a scientist, it's nice to see an intervention work, but you ask yourself how it measures up side-by-side with other well-known interventions. To test this, we randomly assigned stressed Yale undergraduates to one of three well-being interventions—SKY Breath Meditation, mindfulness meditation, or emotional intelligence—or a control group. The SKY Breath Meditation group showed more statistically significant benefits for mental health and well-being compared to the control group than the other interventions.[16] One reason for these results may be that mindfulness and emotional intelligence are mostly cognitive exercises, while breathing doesn't just bring ease to the mind, it also deeply calms the physiology.

Michael Goldstein at the University of Arizona ran a very similar study (comparing SKY to stress management training) that showed almost the same results as ours. In addition, he showed the results were maintained three months later for SKY.[17] My favorite part of his study was that he placed participants in a high-pressure performance situation to see if he could experimentally test their ability to withstand stress.

Compared to the stress management group, the SKY breathing group held steady in terms of breathing and heart rate, suggesting the program had instilled in them a buffer against the anxiety typically associated with anticipating a stressful situation—like Annelies, who overcame her stage fright! This is stress resilience, psychological sovereignty. From what our research has shown, the SKY Breath Meditation builds a stronger foundation for stress resilience in the nervous system—thereby creating more sovereignty.

Removing imprints makes you sovereign. Things and situations can't push your buttons if your buttons are gone. No situation is inherently stressful; situations are a function of how you perceive them. New York City hadn't changed, I had. Performances hadn't changed, Annelies had. Bridges hadn't changed, Jose had.

Epigenetics research shows that trauma can be passed down over several generations[18] when they're not healed. Children of parents who have gone through traumatic life experiences or have post-traumatic stress may be more likely to develop post-traumatic stress, depression, and anxiety. Their genetic profile is more sensitive and vulnerable. That's why it's so important to heal ourselves so we don't pass it on. In healing yourself, you heal the future generations coming after you. If not for yourself, do it for them.

Meditation

After learning the SKY Breath Meditation breathing technique, I was calm enough to practice other forms of meditation. As I mentioned in Chapter 3, meditation and other contemplative activities—by turning you into the observer of your thoughts rather than their captive audience—help you see your imprints for what they are: just thoughts, memories, emotions, and judgments. When you stare that imprint down without reacting, engaging, or feeding it, its power dissipates. Meditation is key to developing awareness.

It's a pretty radical act in our modern age to sit there and do nothing. It certainly goes against the grain of nonstop productivity, stimulation, and media consumption we're used to.

It's also no surprise meditation has become so popular in a high-tech, high-speed, high-consumption world. Our mind—clogged with imprints and the constant flow of notifications and information—is longing for slow, our mind is longing for silence, our mind is longing for peace.

To claim sovereignty over your mind in an age of imprint overload and distraction, meditation allows you to make time for the opposite: silence.

The benefits of being voluntarily peaceful and still on a daily (or regular) basis while your mind releases imprints are tremendous, research shows. Meditation benefits anxiety, depression, emotion regulation, happiness, attention, memory, creativity, compassion, and social connection.[19]

There are many forms of meditation, but the one that has received the most attention in the West is mindfulness because it has been researched more than other techniques—probably because it appeals to researchers since it takes a scientific approach: (1) observe your thoughts, (2) objectively and (3) without judgment.

As I mentioned earlier, it was not the right fit when I was suffering post-9/11 anxiety. Willoughby Britton, a professor at Brown, explored mindfulness's potential drawbacks in the case of trauma.[20] Once my trauma was resolved, mindfulness was no longer problematic, but I found it kept me in the heady mind space I already spent so much time in as a research scientist and writer. I prefer techniques that are less cognitive. I found that mantra meditation (*sahaj samadhi*) or a guided meditation (I use the Sattva app) helps quiet my thoughts more and brings me to a place of peace, which suits me better. This goes to show that if you try meditation and it doesn't work for you, it may not be meditation that didn't work for you but the technique you tried. Find the right fit for you.

Silence

There once was a time when no virtual world tugged at me. When I would wake up to the sound of birdsong and feel the vast stretch of time laid out before me . . . time in which I could be fully awake to my life, immersed in observation of nature, deep in a book for hours, in wonderment at the sky, or fully immersed in my work or studies and more present in my relationships. That was all there was. Perhaps you also remember a time like this—at least from childhood, if your childhood didn't involve cell phones.

Now I have to consciously carve out silence. I go on three-day silent meditation retreats. What's most interesting about these retreats is how busy your mind feels during the retreat. It's like a ball of imprints that was wound tight and is finally unraveling. In fact, I was so unnerved by this unraveling process, that I ran away from my first retreat. The second time, I would have run away, but this was pre-Uber and I couldn't find a ride. When the retreat was over, however, I felt so much peace and bliss that I immediately signed up for the next one being offered. Now I do one quarterly.

I come back not only refreshed but also with greater awareness of the impact that different messaging has on my mind and well-being, a greater ability to be present with my family and immediate surroundings. Most importantly, I have more discernment: about what I do and do not want to allow into my mind.

In that way, meditation and silence give you mental sovereignty. Despite all the noise.

X-Ray Scanning Media

Awareness allows you to step back whenever you are consuming any media or information or message from anyone—and decipher the intention behind it. See through what you're told and what you're sold.

When the audio-based social media app Clubhouse came out, it was obvious to me as a psychologist that the developers were using well-known persuasion and influence principles to get people hooked. For example, the psychological principle of *scarcity*: People want something more if there are limited resources and it's hard to get. The name *Clubhouse* itself made it sound exclusive and hard-to-get. At the time of launch, Clubhouse members could join only if they were invited, making the platform seem even more desirable. Another principle is *social proof* (i.e., we look to others to decide what we should do) and *authority* (i.e., we trust and follow people we believe know what they're doing). So Clubhouse's first members were celebrities, making the platform seem even more attractive. Sheer manipulation and it worked. Clubhouse launched very successfully (at least at first).

So how do you resist manipulative messaging? I asked a lieutenant colonel in the Army whose job it was to create messaging designed to manipulate the enemy. See that? It was his job to create imprints and condition minds. We had a fascinating conversation in which he relayed that whatever he reads—news, media, or any type of information—he automatically scans for intent: what does the content creator want the consumer to think, feel, and do? Awareness—that sovereignty skill—allows you to do this too.

He shared this fun anecdote about how he's teaching his kids to develop mental sovereignty. When he's at the store shopping for groceries and his child wants an unhealthy cereal brand, he'll ask the child this: "Why do you want that cereal?"

"Because it's colorful."

"So tell me, why do you think it's colorful?"

"Because it looks fun."

"Why do you think they made it look fun?"

"So kids would like it?"

And so on.

Nothing like getting parenting tips on mental sovereignty from a high-level military commander who is in the business of creating imprints! He is training his kids to arrest manipulation before it can even happen. May we all be that perceptive. You may remember that in high school English class, you learned to discern the intention behind an author's words: What do they want the reader to feel and to believe? It's a good idea to keep doing that with any media we consume.

Curating Content: A Shield for Manipulation

Again, your mind is like a mirror—it reflects back to you what you put in it.

Ultimately, you know best what content energizes, inspires, and uplifts you and what brings you down.

Silicon Valley tech entrepreneur Premal Shah, co-founder of Kiva.org, shared with me: "The White House has a 'no-fly zone' that restricts aircrafts coming into its airspace. I've been thinking of that metaphor for my own brain—a 'no-fly zone' where I'm more careful about what I let in." He started by removing electronics from his bedroom.

I took social media off my phone, which freed up so much mental space. But when I took e-mail off it too, it felt like someone gave me my life back. I'm more present and have more space to think. If I want to look at any of it, I go and power up my laptop. I realized I don't need to check my e-mail 24/7. A couple times a day on my laptop is plenty. If there's an emergency, that's what texting is for. Some people protest that they need to be available all the time. But I know CEOs of companies with major responsibilities who have started doing the same thing. "If there's an emergency, people can call me," one of them shared with me. "But meanwhile, I have more time to think with greater clarity than if I am constantly interrupting myself to check my device."

As for social media, I don't check it daily, but when I do it's for no more than 5 to 10 minutes a day. And I check it on the computer, where it's less easy to consume mindlessly. I also don't scroll, which sets me up to see all sorts of things I may not want in my mind space. Instead, I select accounts I want to visit.

Bryant Wood is a social media influencer with over half a million followers. I asked him for advice on good boundaries with social media, given that it's his profession. He explained, "When on social media, the rule of thumb is to be a creator not a consumer. You want to share wisdom and content for the greatest good of others not consume information all the time. Otherwise, you lose your identity in the programming of the social space."

Losing your identity in the programming of the social space. No thanks. Creating content for good and following those who inspire you—now that's worth it. If you enjoy social media or have to use it for work, have fun creating inspiring content—and not too much of it. That's what I try to do.

Cultivate Wisdom

We've talked a lot about clearing our mind of imprints, but what then? That's not all.

A major key to sovereignty is not just ridding your mind of harmful imprints but nourishing your mind with input that will enliven you, energize you, inspire you, uplift you, and make you more aware and sovereign.

Our world is filled with a rambunctious cacophony of meaningless or unsettling information, devoid of substance and sustenance. Empty calories. Education teaches you how to think and analyze and learn technical skills but nothing about how to sail through life's curveballs. Wisdom isn't just downplayed, it's nonexistent in popular social discourse.

Cultivating your mind with wisdom will both help you clear out more imprints and fill your mind with sovereignty tools.

Finiteness

On our way back from a ski trip in Vermont during my last year of college, a college friend, Etelle, and I were driving uphill through a snowstorm, behind a semitruck, in a 1980s Volvo with a stick shift. As you might be able to predict, it didn't end well. I lost control of the wheel; we skidded across the oncoming lane and rolled the car three times. It finally came to a stop upside down. By some miracle, we were okay. But changed. For a full 24 hours, Etelle and I were on a high difficult to describe in words. We couldn't understand why classmates were stressed about finals; we were overjoyed to be alive! So grateful! If there is a seventh heaven, we were in it. Completely liberated from all things that weighed down the mind, in a state of freedom, joy, and inner peace. We experienced total mental sovereignty.

That's why certain wisdom traditions, like Tibetan Buddhist traditions and the Stoic philosophy of ancient Greece, made it a habit to contemplate death and impermanence. Sounds gloomy but it's not. Really understanding how short life is gives you mental sovereignty. You become really clear on what's important and what's not.

You realize it's possible to go through the ups and downs of life without being weighed down. Not because you are naïve or have blinders on, but because you gain wisdom. You become simultaneously aware both of the painfulness of life and of its beauty, of its difficulties and of its delights, of its reality and of its impermanence.

The Vermont trip set me on a trajectory to seek inner sovereignty. It's why I went into psychology, why I was drawn to elderly people in China and Tibet who seemed mentally emancipated despite hard lives, why I completed a master's in Indo-Tibetan Buddhism, why I conducted research on the benefits of breathing, why I have meditated for 20 years and regularly attend silent meditation retreats, and why I continue to immerse myself in wisdom. And all these paths have allowed me to re-access and cultivate the state of freedom I was once in, for 24 hours, on that fateful day after the car accident.

In the realm of science, we focus so much on what we know, we don't talk about the fact that what we know is, in actual truth, minuscule. Where were we before we were born? Where do we go after we die? What is this universe? And who the heck are we in the first place? In truth, we have no idea. It's a freaking mystery!

Wisdom is *making room for the unknown*. The mystical. The creative. As you do that, your mind enters a state of wonder and contemplation. Instead of being weighed down by small petty concerns, it opens up and gains perspective.

It wasn't until I attended graduate school at Columbia that I took a class with a professor of Indo-Tibetan studies who discussed these issues: Robert Thurman—"Buddha Bob"—who also happens to be Uma Thurman's dad (thus her name, which is also the name of an Indo-Tibetan goddess).

The film *The Matrix* had just come out, and Bob explained that it was based on an ancient Vedic text called *The Yoga Vashishta. The Yoga Vasistha* is a really wild ride with stories within stories that don't seem to make sense yet paint a picture of reality not far removed from the ones you see in movies like *Inception*. When I read it, I felt like I was getting deprogrammed. I walked out of Buddha Bob's classes with a feeling of intense freedom. I still have it by my bedside.

According to Vedic and Buddhist cultures, we are all living in a matrix; it wasn't a Hollywood invention after all. Caught up in our imprints and stories, we live life as if it would go on forever, on an eternal hamster wheel chasing what we want and fleeing what we fear. We are focused on ourselves, the star of our own movie, and blind to how deeply connected we all are to each other. The secret, Bob told us, was to see through that matrix by observing our thoughts, emotions, and imprints instead of being at their mercy; deeply understanding the impermanence of all things; and filling our minds with wisdom and our hearts with compassion.

It doesn't matter what path of wisdom you pursue. Find the one that speaks to you. Whatever path brings you serenity, peace, strength, and perspective will allow you to truly savor life when things are good and to prevail with fortitude when things are hard.

After learning SKY Breath Meditation, I met its originator, Gurudev Sri Sri Ravi Shankar. I had my doubts about gurus but was also deeply appreciative for SKY Breath Meditation, which had helped me and the veterans in our studies gain more mental sovereignty. Whether I listen to him on YouTube or in live talks, I notice that Gurudev's wisdom does not crowd my mind with more imprints but quietens it, releases stress, and opens my perspective.

One teaching related to mental sovereignty that Gurudev often underscores is that "the state of your mind determines the quality of your life." What does this mean? Think back to those moments in your life when things were going extremely well—maybe you were on vacation or financially successful—but you were *still* miserable. Similarly, there were times that were externally hard—maybe during the pandemic—but still, you found yourself happy. The situation is often irrelevant. It's the state of your mind that runs the show and that's good news. Because there's only so much we can do about our circumstances—taxes! health! relationships! uncertainty!—but there's a lot we can do to improve our state of mind. And that's mental sovereignty.

In all the centuries that have passed before us, wisdom flowed through various philosophical schools and religions: Native American wisdom, Indigenous traditions from around the world, the Stoics, Sufis, Humanists, Daoists, Hindus, Buddhists. Ancient teachers like Plato or Rumi or more contemporary ones like Thich Nhat Hanh, Ram Dass, Eckart Tolle, or Maya Angelou—whatever touches you and elevates or lifts your spirits. Most religious traditions have both a spiritual component and a philosophical one. You don't have to be religious or spiritual to dive into the deeper questions of life. Geniuses like Einstein were deeply contemplative and knew to read widely, including Vedic philosophical texts like the Bhagavad Gita. You can find wisdom in poetry, art, or music. And you can find it in the elders among us. Often cast aside by a busy society that doesn't honor them (at least in the West), they are often treasure troves of experience and knowledge. Sometimes they are sages with much to teach.

Wisdom can systematically free you from the thoughts, emotions, and destructive programming that don't serve you while opening you up to what does.

Gratitude

An essential part of the 24 hours after my car accident experience of enlightenment was gratitude. Gratitude is one of the most important tenets of wisdom. It sets you free.

My mother always showed me the power that gratitude can have. Although she had a traumatic childhood and suffered as a single working mother on the brink of poverty for many years, she's done her fair share of healing imprints through therapy. Defiant of her severe chronic pain, my mother laughs age in the face and cuts down her own trees with a chainsaw. And she's not overloading herself with new imprints either. She's almost never online or watching or reading the news. She's certainly not on her phone. Instead, she's cracking jokes with strangers, taking saunas, spending most of her day outdoors, skinny polar plunging, reading books, eating cheese, telling rude jokes, and feeding the local foxes with fresh sausages (although she's vegetarian) until they follow her around her well-maintained garden and into her house like faithful dogs. The most powerful practice she has, though, is gratitude. She is so grateful for the life she now has that every day is a celebration—pain or no pain. Gratitude is a powerful psychological shield. Very few new negative imprints can take hold of her.

I saw this when I lived in Shanghai in the late '90s. People weren't allowed heat in their homes at the time. While I felt sorry for myself (alone in my cold studio with the scrawny street kitten I'd rescued, the fleas it hosted, and the cockroaches its food attracted), they lived three generations together in spaces no larger than mine, with broken windows. They wore big ski jackets just to stay warm in the freezing winter months. They didn't have running toilets or hot water. But they were so grateful—grateful for a roof over their heads, grateful for each other, grateful to be alive.

I learned gratitude from those who have nothing but are grateful for everything. They are so much wealthier than those who have everything but are grateful for nothing.

Gratitude doesn't mean you are complacent or stop having dreams and ambitions or stop fighting for what's good and right. But what it does do is give you a state of mind that is more deeply able to find joy in life, optimism, and resilience.[21]

Gratitude is a lifeboat.

Nourishing Your Mind

Compared to all the junk food media out there, wisdom is high-nutrient nourishment. Junk food can be a nice treat once in a while, but it's the healthy stuff that keeps you strong, resilient, and healthy.

A teacher shared a story of running with an elementary school child who had a lung defect. He asked the boy, "How can you run when it hurts to breathe?" The little boy responded, "I run *past* the pain."

Wisdom allows you to do the same thing. It's not that you don't experience pain and suffering, but you don't sink in it. You remain buoyant.

When you've immersed yourself in meditation, silence, breathing, and wisdom, then you'll find it is so much easier not to get caught up in the noise of the world, the agendas, stories, and opinions. And even when you do get caught, you're rarely fully entangled because there's a part of you that notices you're getting caught. So you can extricate yourself more easily.

To take care of your body:

Stay *aware* of your needs.
Keep it *clean*.
Give it *good nutrition*.
Rest it regularly.

The same thing goes for the mind:

Stay *aware* of your imprints.
Keep it *clean* with activities like breathing and meditation.
Give it *quality input* like wisdom.
Bring it for *periodic servicing* and *rest* like silence.

SIDE EFFECTS OF A SOVEREIGN MIND ⚠

- **Calmness:** You have a less busy and frantic mind because you release imprints daily through meditation or other contemplative practices.
- **Energy:** You're less distracted and less likely to be overtaken by the many messages coming your way.
- **Centeredness:** You consciously work to heal your trauma imprints, so you are less reactive to the world. You're less swayed by events around you because you know how to come back to center.
- **Awareness:** You see through messaging and are less easily manipulated by what's coming your way.

SOVEREIGN MIND TOOL KIT

We carry imprints from our culture, personal history, trauma, news and media messaging, and more. But we also have something more powerful than the imprints themselves: awareness. That sovereignty skill again.

Here's how to cultivate awareness and remove imprints.

Observe and discern.

What you can see can't trap you. Start to observe the messaging coming at you with discernment. Rather than diving right in and letting it have its way with you, step back and observe: What are the intentions behind the messaging? Is it giving you freedom or binding you in fear? Do you wish to engage with it?

Identify your imprints.

Journal or reflect on these questions:

- What areas of your life have you felt most constricted in? Was it relationships? Work? Family? What were the beliefs you held in those spaces?
- Are you worried about losing your safety, like Starr was? Are you afraid of failing, like Annelies was? Are you emotionally triggered in certain situations, like Jose was?
- Think about what your greatest fears are. Fear of not having enough money? Anger and argument? Abandonment?
- Now consider your cravings. What do you pursue most feverishly? Success? Attention?

Remember that some imprints are perfectly healthy. For example, the need to connect or belong. As you think through your imprints, remember it's the ones that are confining and hurting you that are the harmful ones. Meditation can be a key practice to get to know your imprints because it makes you familiar with your mind and thoughts.

The next chapter will give you further insight into how relationships can help you discover your imprints.

Sovereign mornings, sovereign nights.

What's the first thing you condition your mind with in the morning? How do you set up your day? Do you immediately go on social media? To look at what other people are doing? To look at what other people are selling you? To give attention to people who want your attention? Or do you give attention to yourself and condition your mind with things that bring you joy and peace? Perhaps it's your family or your pet, perhaps it's looking at the trees, perhaps it's prayer or meditating or a quiet run outside.

What do you do in the last hour of your day? Do you give it away? Or do you reclaim it as yours, no longer taking in information from others but settling into a quiet time with yourself, for your mind to unravel, for your thoughts to dissipate, as you come back to yourself?

Breathe.

Our research shows that SKY Breath Meditation is effective for trauma imprints. You can learn SKY from a trained instructor online (or in person) through the Art of Living Foundation (www.artofliving.org). This is the technique we studied with veterans and students[22] and that I personally practice daily. Veterans, active military, and their families can learn it at no cost from Project Welcome Home Troops (www.pwht.org). There are various breathing techniques called SKY on YouTube; I can't vouch for those, as we haven't studied them. Best to go with a trained teacher. The silent retreats I take are also offered through the Art of Living Foundation.

Consciously release daily imprints.

While practices like breathing and meditation can help you release old imprints, there is a Jain practice that a Jain friend shared with me designed to release daily imprints. At the end of the day, consider everything that happened to you. In this practice, you review the day as if you were rewinding it. Go over each event from the moment you were just in to the moment you woke up. As you do so, set the intention to release any harmful imprints that were formed.

Create boundaries around your media.

Notice the media on your feed or phone that doesn't serve you. Consider completely removing apps that take up more of your mind space than need be. Maybe set aside times of the day—say, between 7 P.M. and 7 A.M.—when you don't engage with your media at all.

Cultivate wisdom.

Wisdom from around the world is at our fingertips. It's up to us to choose to consume it in whatever way we wish. Whether it's poetry or ancient philosophical texts, the world is your oyster. What would it feel like if you conditioned your mind not with fear messaging or marketing and advertising but with food for your soul? With inspiring knowledge that lightens your load, eases your stress, fills your heart, and turns you into a sage? It would feel sovereign. Learn about different philosophical paths and choose the one that speaks to you. Dive deep into it and see what pearls you can find there.

Reflect.

Here's a question worth pondering, put so eloquently by Charles Bukowski: "Can you remember who you were, before the world told you who you should be?"[23] Think back on when you were a child. What was important to you? Think back on your deepest values. List them. Remember who you are before the shoulds and all the other imprints flood your mind.

Meditate.

I've talked about meditation repeatedly and across chapters. That's because it's benefit cannot be overstated. This is the ultimate awareness-building exercise. Just as when the night falls and you see the stars, you suddenly get wrenched out of your little world as you stare into the vast and infinite universe, when you meditate you start to transcend the limited everyday affairs of your thoughts and feelings as you stare into the vast, magnanimous, and infinite space within. That is the inner space of sovereignty.

Meditate daily. The best way to start is to commit to 40 days. That way you can see its impact for yourself. The impact is cumulative, and you are most likely to notice its benefits when you commit to a daily practice for a specific amount of time.

For additional tools and ideas, visit my website at www.iamsov.com.

A Good Thing to Remember

Most of us identify
with what's
going on
inside our head.
We take it
to be
truth.
And yet,
often,
it's not.
Especially,
When it makes us feel
small,
afraid,
less than.
Confined,
Controlled,
Constricted,
Conflicted.
Then it's
Usually
A lie.
That's
A good thing
to
remember.

CHAPTER 5

SOVEREIGN RELATIONSHIPS

As I mentioned in Chapter 2, decades of research show that social connection is our greatest need and a powerful predictor of both psychological and physical health. We crave connection. The root cause of why people do most things—have children, join communities, seek romantic partners, try to be successful or attractive—is that they think it will lead to positive, life-supportive relationships with other people. That it will lead to love, connection, and belonging. At our core, we share the same deeply vulnerable need: to be seen, heard, and valued. We want to feel safe, and we want to feel we can trust people around us.

Yet relationships are another realm—like emotion—where we never received formal training. And because no one prepares us for how to navigate them successfully, they can cause a lot of grief. Learning the secret of relational sovereignty, however, can prevent much of it.

Etelle Higonnet—the same friend from the college car accident in Chapter 4—went on to do extraordinary work as a human rights lawyer and environmental activist. She can be found doing investigations on deforestation and child labor in the jungles and forests of Africa and South America, often risking her own life, as nearly happened on a mission in an African country where she was working to stop a rubber company from illegally cutting down trees.

As Etelle was about to leave for the airport, which was three hours away, her driver mysteriously disappeared. The local officials suspiciously insisted she set off for the airport with two threatening-looking, muscle-strapped strangers in military apparel. The safety concerns were obvious: The rubber company Etelle was investigating for illegal deforestation had built close financial ties with the country's leaders. Her activism was a potential threat to the kickbacks the leaders were receiving. Still, she had no other choice than to get into that car.

In those three momentous hours in the car with her would-be hitmen, Etelle worked a miracle. She connected with her handlers in such a way that they not only safely escorted her to the airport, but also shared their snacks with her and—get this—even held up a little sheet to give her privacy while she relieved herself by the side of the road.

When they safely dropped her at the airport, Etelle received confirmation that they had been ordered to kill her. They warned her that she was not safe in their country and that she shouldn't ever come back, but that, if she did anyway, she should travel over a land border and under their protection. And that she should stay with them.

How did Etelle turn her hitmen into protectors?

She didn't threaten them, seduce them, or pay them. She didn't need to. Because Etelle has something much more powerful than that: positive relational energy. It's what makes her what I call *socially sovereign*, and it's what we're going to talk about in this chapter. Social sovereignty is having a relationship with oneself and others that is deeply life-supportive. The result is nothing short of extraordinary, as Etelle's story demonstrates.

THE SCIENCE OF POSITIVE RELATIONAL ENERGY

Kim Cameron at the University of Michigan's Ross School of Business, together with his colleagues, discovered the fascinating science of relational energy while studying organizations. He noticed that among these large networks of people, certain subgroups stood out as anomalous. They had significantly higher levels of productivity than other groups at the company. Not just a little higher, much higher. What was going on here?

When Kim and his team of scientists looked further into what could be causing this extraordinary productivity, it seemed that one person at the center of this subgroup was causing the effect. And—though it didn't sound scientific—the best way the researchers found to describe this person was that they had contagious positive energy.

Kim and I collaborated on several articles about positive leadership, and he also wrote a book called *Positively Energizing Leadership* about this phenomenon and these life-giving individuals.

Kim explains positively energizing leadership by comparing it to the heliotropic effect—the fact that plants are drawn to the sun because it is life-giving. Similarly, we are drawn to life-giving people—they are inspiring, uplifting, and energizing.

Kim and his colleagues also noticed that there were certain individuals who had the opposite effect. They were de-energizing. Being around them made people feel less motivated, less enthusiastic, and less alive. Thinking back on your own life, you've probably experienced that some friendships and work relationships are draining while others are enlivening.

If you've noticed so far, in every chapter in this book we talk about energy. You can have an energizing or de-energizing relationship with yourself, as described in Chapter 2. Same with your emotions, which are energy in motion, as we saw in Chapter 3. You can suppress them or fall for addictive behaviors, all of which deplete you, or you can let them move through you in various ways, allowing them to energize rather than drain you. Same with the mind, as described in Chapter 4. Negative imprints can de-energize you, while clearing your mind of imprints and filling it with nourishing imprints energizes you.

Relationships are also an exchange of energy. You can either fill someone's tank or empty it, as my kids' favorite book, *How Full Is Your Bucket? for Kids*, describes. But this isn't a fairy tale. It's serious empirical research. Companies whose leaders have mastered relational energy simply do better. Companies with more de-energizing leaders fail. And the same can be said in any community, family, friendship, or romantic relationship.

And the good news is that positive relational energy—which is key to social sovereignty—can be learned. Etelle, before our near-fatal car accident, was already an activist. She was organizing peacekeeping conferences on campus and working hard to make a difference even then. But it was from a place of frustration and indignation. And she was a little intense to be around. She would unknowingly push people away from her with her well-intentioned but angry activism.

After her brush with death, however, her entire mindset shifted. Filled with wisdom and gratitude, she began to relate to others with positive relational energy. She completely turned around her messaging and focused on the positive. Instead of confronting people with a depressing message like "Do you know how many African kids die working as slaves in diamond mines every year?" she would invite them with a message of hope and possibility: "Do you know how many African kids' lives could be saved if we only imported ethical diamonds?" Her entire tone shifted. So did her success rate as an activist both in college and beyond.

As anyone who knows Etelle can say, being around her is indeed uplifting, enlivening, and inspiring. Her ability to relate to others helps her accomplish extraordinary things. The French government, in fact, knighted her while I was writing this book, awarding her the National Order of Merit for her life's work.[1] Did I mention she's only in her 40s?

It's not hard to become a positive Energizer. Kim and his colleagues are turning around failing companies by training previously de-energizing leaders to become positive Energizers. And that means we can learn it too. Because it is both extraordinary and absolutely ordinary, as we will see.

The 6 Keys of Positive Relational Energy

Positive Energizers relate to others in such a way that they are a catalyst for those around them to get in touch with and reach their fullest potential. They raise their own energy *and* that of others. Both the giver and the receiver leave the interaction uplifted. These Energizers live a fulfilling and productive life and are magnetic.

What makes someone a positively energizing person? Based on Kim's research[2] it involves six things:

1. **Caring for, being interested in, and seeing the best in others**—their qualities and skills, their attributes and gifts. In so doing, you meet their fundamental need to be seen, heard, and valued. To feel safe and to trust. You let others know that you appreciate them for who they are and that they matter and that you have their back.[3]

2. **Providing support for one another, including offering kindness and compassion** when others are going through a hard time. Everyone has moments of struggle, and when someone knows you genuinely are there for them during those times, it automatically deepens your relationship. Think about someone who was there for you unconditionally when you were going through a hard period in your life—perhaps it was a mentor or a friend, a teacher or a boss. If that person were to call you right now and ask for help, you'd probably drop everything to do what you could to help. That's the kind of loyalty that grows out of a deeply supportive relationship.

3. **Avoiding blame and forgiving mistakes**, not holding on to grudges. As we discussed in Chapter 2, making mistakes is a basic part of the human condition. It's how we learn. I'll talk about the science of forgiveness in greater depth later in

this chapter. It both benefits the relationship and increases your own well-being.

4. **Inspiring one another and focusing on what's going right.** As I talked about in Chapter 4, many of the messages we receive are negative. It's easy to be negative, criticize, and complain, but it's also de-energizing and depleting—both for yourself and others. Positive Energizers don't just focus on what's going right, they make a point to emphasize it and celebrate it. Gratitude, for example—which we discussed in Chapter 4—is a tenet of wisdom. It is energizing and enlivening both for yourself and others. Research shows it strengthens relationships.[4]
5. **Emphasizing meaningfulness.** Whether you're parenting children together or working on a group project at your job or in a community, focusing on the impact and benefit of what you are doing is a powerful motivator. It reminds others of the impact they have. In one of my favorite studies, workers at a university alumni call center doubled their productivity after they heard a student talk about the difference financial aid had made in her life.[5] Feeling that you are contributing in some way and making a difference is automatically energizing and inspiring.
6. **Treating others with basic human values like respect, gratitude, trust, honesty, humility, kindness, and integrity.** Think about it. When you know someone has those kinds of values, you automatically feel trust and safety around them. You can relax and let your guard down. You know they will do the right thing, so you appreciate them. These are the type of people you want to be around and want to be like. They are uplifting.

How are positive energizers, like Etelle, able to show up in that way? They have a great relationship with themselves (as described in Chapter 2), they know how to handle their emotions and fill their own tank (Chapters 2 and 3), and they have healed or are in the process of healing their imprints (Chapter 4).

The 3 Types of Energizers

Some people are De-energizers—you can likely think of a few in your own community, workplace, or family. You may even—if you're truly honest with yourself—think of times, places, or relationships in which you held this role as a De-energizer.

The good news is that anyone can become a positive Energizer, but—and here's the catch—not always the kind that drive the best results. There are three types of Energizers, but only one of those can help both themselves and their families, communities, and organizations reach their fullest potential. I have named them as follows: Crushers, Sacrificers, and Stars.

- **Type 1: Crushers.** These Energizers can be extremely captivating, charming, and inspiring. From the outside, they're literally "crushing it" and often deeply beloved by some. They can drive positive change and carry out innovative and beneficial work. They can attain high positions of power, fame, and reputation. Patrick is a famous scientist whose work is celebrated all over the world. The press gushes over his data and his books are bestsellers. He's been nominated as one of the most influential people in his field for his groundbreaking research. In this way, Crushers are energizing to themselves and others.

  Yet when you dig a little deeper and ask Patrick's colleagues and lab members about him, you'll find that the culture in his research facilities is miserable and backstabbing.

Here's the problem: Crushers (often unknowingly) also "crush" their own people underfoot. Their imprints (often of not being good enough) lead them to desperately seek attention, discarding others in their wake. This great need for attention and adulation, which helps drive them, also keeps them trapped in a self-centered and self-aggrandizing mission. While they may be motivated by human values, and their work can break new ground, paradoxically they also reap destruction.

In most cases, their behavior leads them to be less successful than they would have been otherwise. In some cases, it can destroy them.

Though Patrick provided tremendous energy to the audience he inspired, he drained and depleted his own staff by focusing on himself, taking credit for their work, forgetting to mentor them, and failing to support them in their own professional development. Imagine what heights he could have climbed if his team and the people "below" him had been on his side.

- **Type 2: Sacrificers.** These Energizers are also inspiring and can accomplish great things. Like Crushers, they can carry out great work and are beloved and admired by friends, outsiders, and colleagues alike. Sacrificers do not trample others underfoot. To the contrary: They tend to lift others up and share the limelight. They are truly noble—but there's a hitch.

  Johane, a Haitian-born immigrant who came to the U.S. in her teens, became a passionate and award-winning school principal after seeing how much she could contribute to improve the U.S. educational system, especially for poor and at-risk youth. She gave so much of herself, however, that she eventually burned out to the point of landing in the hospital.

> Here's the problem: In an attempt to give of themselves, Sacrificers don't know their own limits, so they drain themselves. Their imprint—also, ironically, often of not being good enough or of needing to do more than they are able to—leads them to perform while destroying themselves.
>
> They often have poor boundaries with others and themselves and are easily depleted. In many ways, they are their own worst enemy. In some cases, Sacrificers, like Crushers, are also intent on proving their significance, only they don't sacrifice others. They sacrifice themselves.
>
> While they can be extremely successful, they often will have to pay the price for their profound self-neglect at some point (often through mental health problems, physical health concerns, and/or burnout) and do not reach the pinnacle of success they otherwise would.
>
> Thankfully, Johane did learn to take care of herself and thrive—using many of the techniques described in Chapter 4. She continues to be a successful and inspiring principal. She is also working on a Ph.D. in leadership—something she knows a thing or two about! And she continues to inspire others to attain their highest potential. But she's not burning out. Why? Because she went from being a Sacrificer to a Star—the third type, which I'll describe next.

Though I've given mostly work examples here, you can see how Crusher's and Sacrificer's ways of relating to others might play out in a relationship. You may have witnessed or even personally experienced what it's like when a Crusher dates a Sacrificer, for example. It's a match seemingly made in heaven that turns out to be hell. You can also think about how this applies in a smaller system such as a family, a community, or a friend group.

Now let's talk about the Stars.

- **Type 3: Stars.** These Energizers, like Etelle, have all the positive traits of Crushers and Sacrificers, but they have learned how to make the best of their traits while not falling prey to selfish or sacrificial tendencies. They have worked on becoming more self-aware of their imprints and have a healthy and supportive relationship with themselves and others.

  Stars become highly successful in a sustained and sustainable way. They have deep humanity when relating to others. They are humble, they are compassionate, they are caring, they are forgiving and trustworthy. Stars display attitudes and behaviors that highlight the positive aspects of difficult circumstances. They focus more on what is right or what can be learned than on what is wrong and what is missing. Stars demonstrate gratitude, compassion, humility, forgiveness, and trustworthiness. They focus on helping others flourish rather than on themselves alone. In the process, they themselves thrive.

  Stars who are leaders in organizations, for example, outperform competition at significantly higher levels. Compared to industry averages, profitability, productivity, quality innovation, customer satisfaction, and employee engagement under Stars' leadership are through the roof.

  The fascinating paradox of being able to strike the balance of energizing both themselves and others simultaneously is the key to their success. They can be both outwardly focused and inwardly focused and do so with grace.

  It's not that Energizers are naïve or saccharine-sweet, by the way. Etelle is brilliant and bold and has brought major organizations to their knees on issues of deforestation and child labor. As one person, she routinely addresses the entire legal counsel of major companies—even when they try to intimidate her with their size and power. She shows them who's boss. She's a badass making a significant positive difference to the planet—thus her recent knighthood.

Stars are not just do-gooders who let others step all over them. They are not Pollyannish. They have profound self-respect, good boundaries, and self-awareness. They care for themselves and know how to fill their own tank. They rely on a very strong inner platform, be it their values, spiritual orientation, contemplative practices, or commitment to service.

They are also authentic and real. Deeply familiar with their own weaknesses, they are humble, honest, and open about them. They are deeply human—both highly relatable and inspiring. Simply put, they are badasses. Irresistible.

BOUND RELATIONSHIPS

A bound state, in relationships, is when people are engaging in either Crusher-type or Sacrificer-type relationships with other people. There are a number of ways to de-energize both oneself and others in relationships and most of them have to do with imprints. We have not yet developed self-awareness of our imprints or done the necessary healing work to mature past them. Either way, we're leaking energy and making others and ourselves suffer in the process.

Imprints

I once entered a relationship with a person with serious anger issues.

In hindsight it was obvious why: I had met a perfect match for my imprints. My destructive and depleting relationship with him was a direct reflection of my destructive and depleting relationship with myself. He was treating me like I was treating me. Poorly. I tended to be a Sacrificer, and the relationship held up a perfect mirror to my self-loathing imprint. It was therefore an opportunity to either stay in the relationship and the imprint or heal the imprint for good and no longer put up with abuse from my then partner—or anyone, really.

Everyone is walking around with imprints, as we discussed in Chapter 4. Like a little kid who, under his big kid outfit, is hiding big purple bruises: imprints of fears, anxieties, and so on. Relationships can evoke love and joy and many other wonderful things, but also involve bumping up against each other's bruises—and that hurts. (And that's also why a dear friend of mine in his late 40s explains why he would rather stay single in this way: "One mind full of imprints is hard enough to deal with, let alone two.")

When someone (friend, romantic partner, family member, colleague) bumps up against your bruises and you have an unusually strong reaction, you can either play the blame game or—and this is the more sovereign approach—see it as a powerful opportunity for self-awareness. "Wow, that's quite an imprint I still have there."

There are situations of abuse that may, of course, not be tied to your imprints. But in my case, if I was really honest with myself, it was that I needed to respect and honor myself more. The relationship was not healthy and needed to end, but so did the self-neglect and self-denial programs I was running. The end of that relationship was the beginning of a brand-new and much more positive relationship with myself.

We often blame our partner when a relationship doesn't work out. We try to find someone new and better. Finding a new partner, however, won't usually help if you haven't resolved your imprints. Research shows you bring the same dynamics into new relationships and can end up with the same type.[6] Ever had a déjà vu in a relationship? I know the first person I dated after the destructive relationship was basically another version of the same guy. Thankfully I only dated my ex's brother from another mother for about five minutes, but I still encountered varying degrees of the same scenario in workplaces and even friendships until I really woke up. Things don't change until we change.

I once had a conversation with a young woman named Kristy. She was an actress in Los Angeles in her early 30s. We met at a party where she was describing to me how she had just escaped a frightful relationship with someone who tried to kill her. She had had to lock herself in the bathroom and call 911. It sounded horrendous, but then she told me something even more shocking: This wasn't the first time a partner had almost killed her. It was the seventh! The relationships always seemed to be wonderful at the beginning, but they would inevitably end in terror. The first couple of times she found herself in these dramatic situations, she blamed her partners (who were obviously disturbed and dangerous people). But when it kept happening, she realized there was a self-destructive part of her that attracted her to these kinds of partners.

To clarify, I'm not victim-blaming here. There are horrendous situations in which people are being victimized every day and it is obviously not their fault.

The point is, relationships—good or bad—can be opportunities for self-awareness. We are all swimming in our own homemade soup of imprints, interpreting the world accordingly, and spilling our imprints out all over our relationships—or not. And while other people may indeed be jerks, the battles we face are also battles with ourselves. And that's why relationships are opportunities for healing, growth, and, ultimately, sovereignty.

Your Triggers Can Reveal Your Imprints

Reading the last chapter, you might have wondered how to find out what your imprints are. One very easy way to do that is to look at your triggers in relationships. They are mirrors for your imprints.

The relationships I just described were not healthy ones. Your relationships are, I hope, happy and healthy ones, but *regardless* they will still reveal imprints to you. When something feels personally assaulting (i.e., it triggers you), for example, more often than not it's not the other person. It's your imprints.

If your imprint is that people don't like you, for example, then when someone—your partner or really anyone—pushes that button by being rude, you may have a reaction that is wildly out of proportion to what actually happened. Because it's bringing up all the pain you've felt your whole life about this one imprint. And you may risk unleashing all the anger on whoever it was you feel did not respect you. And to them your temper comes out of left field. Because it's not actually about them. It's about you.

I was in a week-long workshop a few years ago where we sat in small groups and shared how we felt we were viewed by others. A sweet elderly gentleman whom I had spent the workshop week with said, "I feel like I am annoying." The weird thing is that over the course of the week, I had in fact felt he was annoying, but for *no* logical reason. He was perfectly respectful and even adorable as the eldest gentleman in our group, trying hard to keep up with the rest. Yet I'd been mildly irritated by him all week. When he uttered those words, it hit me: he was projecting his belief—an imprint he had picked up along the way about himself—that he was annoying, and I was registering it though it made no factual sense. Inevitably, he would then pick up cues from people like me and others that yes, he really is annoying, even though it was a self-fulfilling prophecy he was manifesting. And it was de-energizing for all involved.

That's why, when you feel unlovable, others will mirror that back to you—or you will imagine that they do. If you are hard on yourself, you may assume others are just as hard on you, and you will feel insecure. Sure, in some cases, people really aren't kind or don't like us—that happens even when no imprint is there on your side. However, it's still critical to be self-aware, especially if you notice repetitive patterns in your relationships.

To give another example, many people have some degree of rejection sensitivity—a term psychologists use to describe being highly sensitive to rejection cues and having a particularly strong emotional response to rejection—probably because it evokes an unhealed imprint of being rejected at some point earlier in life.

How intense is your reaction to a colleague dismissing you? A friend criticizing you? A romantic interest breaking up with you? Is it just a bummer or highly debilitating? Do you get over it quickly or does it stay for a painfully long time? Does it trigger searing emotional pain? Or are you able to let it go, understanding that the other person's opinion may have nothing to do with you at all?

Self-awareness involves looking at those big reactions, identifying the bruise, and, when you feel yourself getting triggered, turning that into a moment of self-reflection rather than blame. Awareness, as we've now repeatedly seen, is the key to sovereignty.

That's why taking care of ourselves to the best of our ability is always key. Because when we're stressed and our self-awareness or peace of mind is low—which naturally happens to all of us at times—imprints start to run the show, and we no longer see things clearly. That's when we tend to assume everything is the fault of the other person. They caused all this annoyance in you, after all! They may have done something objectively annoying (and if they're abusive, they do need to go), but at the same time, *you* are annoyed because they pushed *your* buttons. If your button is a biggie, even a five-year-old can trigger it. Either way, when you blame them, both of you are de-energized and unhappy. When you stay aware and take responsibility for what's yours, you grow and your relationships improve.

The Victim Imprint

African American writer and poet James Baldwin said: "It's not the world that was my oppressor, because what the world does to you, if the world does it to you long enough and effectively enough, you begin to do to yourself. You become a collaborator, an accomplice of your own murderers, because you believe the same things they do."[7] While he was speaking of the oppression of people of color, his wisdom holds lessons for everyone. We internalize destructive imprints from social conditioning or past perpetration—and the more we fall for and identify with those imprints, the more we allow them to bind us.

You may have been a victim of violence or abuse or neglect or swindling or any other kind of perpetration. That's a fact. But *identifying* as a victim for a long period of time, or even for life, *once the abuse is over* is profoundly disempowering and de-energizing for you.

Here's why: Victimhood makes *you* become your own perpetrator *in the present.* It continues the abuse. You remain at the scene of the crime despite your perpetrator being long gone. The past is past, but you continue to torture yourself about it now, robbing yourself of the present. Your perpetrators continue to take up prime real estate in your mind, squatting there large and in charge. Victimhood evokes anger and fear that keep you in fight, flight, or freeze mode. Your perspective is skewed, and your brain, because it is under stress, functions suboptimally.

And that's how you lose your sovereignty.

A 25-year-old veteran from Wisconsin who had severe post-traumatic stress after his time in Fallujah, one of the deadliest battles of the Iraq war, wrote these extraordinary words: "They call you a victim of war. I AM NOT A VICTIM." He held onto his sovereignty even in the face of his suffering and trauma. Like Maya, whom I described in the first chapter, he showed me that no one can take your sovereignty away if you choose to claim it. Despite his challenges, he was fully empowered.

I know this may be hard—maybe even frustrating—to read. I'm not trying to downplay trauma at all. Trauma healing often needs to take place before you can fully let go of the difficult experiences. And that's where using some of the techniques described in Chapter 4 on releasing trauma imprints and healing from them is an essential step.

But when I say step out of victimhood, I'm saying it out of compassion. Because it sets you free and gives you back your sovereignty. How about instead of identifying as a victim, you identified as a warrior?

The Myth of Needing Others to Complete Us

A popular social imprint is the idea that we need others—friends, children, partners—to complete us. We look at relationships as a way to gain something, fill a hole, or quench loneliness. A bit like a commodity. Others as the source of our happiness.

This myth is perpetuated in entertainment. Our eldest son's little friend watches way too many Disney movies. When she is with him, she pretends he's a prince, and she plays out the whole drama, singing songs of woe to him. He has no idea what's going on and doesn't understand what all the wailing and pouting is about when all he wants to do is just go down the slide together. Our youngest watched the movie *Bolt*, whose main character is a girl called Penny. He goes to sleep at night telling me: "I can't live without Penny. You know I'm falling in love with her." He's five years old. And we don't even have a TV, do screens, or watch movies regularly—just a couple times a year. The myth that you need another person to complete you can be programmed in early and easily.

Porn often propagates a similar message—sexuality as a performance in which you get something from the other, with little emotion, love, or kindness and often with brutality. Many college students I taught had been addicted to porn from their adolescence. It was their introduction to sexuality. A painful addiction that modeled sexuality as a selfish performance rather than the romantic intimacy they actually wanted. They told me that their first intimate experiences were disappointing, hurtful, and sad when compared to the performances they had watched for so long. Another of the many ways media imprints can destroy the happy and healthy relationships we actually long for.

When we believe we will find completion in our partners or friends, we set ourselves up for heartbreak. Here again, *we* are the ones who break *our own* hearts by binding ourselves to the myth that someone *else* can complete us.

Loving someone because you want something from them is no different than a business transaction. What's more, when both people in a romantic relationship are coming from a place of deficiency and of wanting something from the other, research shows this dynamic can end up damaging the relationship through aggression,[8] violence,[9] and passivity.[10] It can lead to unhappiness, conflict in the relationship, and feelings of uncertainty and anxiety.[11]

That's also how we become De-energizers and become bound. It's draining to be with someone who looks to you as the solution for their problems and the answer to their dreams, who believes you should complete them and give them what they want. Inevitably, they will be disappointed. They fail to realize that others can't fill your tank. Only you can do that. And when you do, you'll be a much better partner yourself.

That's why research shows that the healthiest and happiest relationships are ones where both partners *feel* a high sense of personal power.[12] See that? Two sovereign people make for a happier relationship. Makes sense.

The Myth of Separation

The final and perhaps most profound way we bind ourselves is through the imprint that we are separate. We self-identify narrowly with things like our religion, race, and so on, artificially creating boundaries. Of course, we are all different, but categorizing ourselves and putting ourselves and other people in boxes creates pain for everyone. We believe we are on one side, while they are on the other. We judge, criticize, and fight. The media and politicians stir the pot because they capitalize on this division. Divisiveness is an imprint that makes everyone suffer.

I was in second grade with my best friend George. We were sitting at a desk in our classroom working on something. At that moment an adult said to me, "He's black, you know." Planting the imprint of difference and division where before there had been none. Like a thorn that tore ruthlessly through our hearts.

Because while there are indeed many ethnicities, religions, and cultures, at our core we are one race—the human race; one family—the human family. We may feel separate but we're not.

We may feel different but our genes are 99.6 percent identical to the genes of the next human.[13] One fragile people who all want the same thing: love, peace, harmony. We need each other, we have so much to learn from each other, and so much diversity to celebrate among one other. Children get this. Adults often need to relearn it.

I've attended several World Culture Festivals, which are put on to bring home the message that we are one world family. Ten thousand artists performed over a weekend from 100 different countries and cultures; a celebration of unity within diversity. Witnessing the unique beauty that has emerged from every human culture and civilization on this small planet brought tears to my eyes. There was such a sense of belonging and love. And real hope for humanity.

The latest one I attended was on the National Mall of Washington, DC, with the Capitol in the background and more than a million people in attendance over three days. The DC police said they'd never seen such a large event with no violence. It is possible. Peace is within reach. It just needs to be kindled—when we are reminded that we are one family.

We kill our own selves when we move to one side. We break our own hearts when we judge and divide. Separated, we're weak. United, we're sovereign. Think about it: wars declared by leaders can't happen if no one shows up to fight them.

How can we bust the myth of separation? It starts with developing sovereign relationships.

SOVEREIGN RELATIONSHIPS

Sovereignty is understanding relationships as valuable opportunities to heal yourself and respect yourself on the one hand, but also invaluable opportunities to give and support others on the other.

Just as we can deplete ourselves and others by relating to others through our imprints, the good news is that by healing our imprints and understanding the principles of relational sovereignty, we can turn our relationships into energizing ones.

Every relational exchange is an exchange of energy. And those who have mastered this energetic exchange know how to enhance energy and well-being in themselves and those around them, primarily because they have a great relationship with themselves. They prioritize filling their own tank so they have the energy to relate to others in an uplifting way based in human values. As a consequence, they energize others while re-energizing themselves through their relationships—a positive feedback loop.

A Positive Feedback Loop of Energy

Remember my dark postpartum years? Annelies, the former ballerina I mentioned in Chapter 4, would periodically stay at our house while she was working in the area. The moment she walked into the room, I would feel more energized. And it wasn't just because she was a dear friend—after all, I had other friends visiting me from time to time. It was her presence. Even Husband, who was slightly irritated to have Annelies's favorite snacks crowding his well-organized kitchen cupboard, would remark: "She's uplifting to be around." If you ever have the good fortune of spending time with Annelies, it basically feels like you're a cell phone that's just been placed on a charger.

Kim Cameron and his colleagues saw how leaders who are positively energizing transfer life-giving energy to those around them, creating superproductive work units. But here's the kicker: usually energy depletes with use. Take physical energy, for example. You're tired after you work out. That's not true of relational energy. The leaders who deploy positive relational energy in turn get re-energized by their interactions, creating a positive feedback loop. Annelies inspires, uplifts, and energizes the people she works with and teaches, and in so doing she is re-energizing herself. By enlivening others, she re-enlivens herself.

We might believe that Energizers have to be extroverts. But that's not necessarily the case at all. Annelies would self-describe as an introvert. She loves spending time alone. What makes her an Energizer is how she fills her tank: She eats healthy vegetarian food; gets good amounts of sleep; does a yoga, breathwork, and meditation routine twice a day; engages in community service; listens to wisdom; and spends time in nature. She works a lot, but she fits fun activities into her busy schedule when she can.

She works with some difficult people, but as she tends to focus on the best in others, she also brings that out in them. The colleagues around her are happy, productive, and upbeat. She has the ability to inspire and create a culture of genuine joy and hard work at the same time.

As I mentioned earlier, positive Energizers relate to others with human values. When you talk to Annelies, you know she has your back and she really cares. She's compassionate, honest, and kind. She also doesn't shy away from telling you what she thinks, and she is not a pushover. She's strong and forthright and street smart and doesn't take any nonsense, but she remains positive and uplifting and caring and forgiving at the same time.

When I once asked her husband what it's like to be married to her, he laughed and said: "It's great! Every time we argue, she's over it after her next meditation." (Given that she meditates twice a day, that makes for a happy marriage and a lucky guy!)

Neuroscience research shows that what people give to—rather than receive from—a relationship is what makes them happiest.[14] Service, compassion, forgiveness, trust, and kindness don't just make relationships better; they make you happier and healthier.

The greatest source of happiness and fulfillment lies in service to others. We know that compassion, kindness, and service increase well-being much more and for longer periods than other things we believe bring us happiness, like pleasure, money, or fame. Think about those times you were there for someone else, helping them through a difficult period. The feeling is indescribable. You are uplifted, empowered, and energized. Alive! It leads to a fulfilling life and research shows it benefits your physical health, mental health, and longevity.[15] It even decreases inflammation at the cellular level (a precursor to diseases like cancer and diabetes).[16]

My favorite study showed that in a group of people who had gone through a severe life stressor such as war, acts of service were a protective factor ensuring their longevity.[17] We know that people who have lived through extreme stress tend to live shorter lives. The stress wears and tears on the body. However, among a group of people who had gone through such extreme stress, a subgroup lived long and healthy lives. What was protecting them? It was that they were engaged in altruistic activities in their life. In other words, acting in service to others erases the impact that a severe life stressor may have had on your health and body. When you show compassion to others, it saves your own life.

Of course, you don't want to be of service at a cost to yourself, but if your tank is full, the best way to capitalize on that is to offer your services to others in whatever capacity works for you. You create a positive feedback loop that is energizing for all involved as well as inspiring.

Self-Compassion

As I mentioned earlier, I saw a pattern in my personal and work relationships—an invitation to heal myself. The recurring theme was showing me what I needed to work on. I needed to develop a healthier and more respectful relationship with myself. And when I finally did, the recurring theme disappeared. Self-compassion involves doing the healing work so you can show up from a place of fullness in your relationships.

When we are in a healthier relationship with ourselves, we are more likely to be in a healthier relationship with others. When we have more self-compassion and make sure to take care of our needs and well-being, research shows we are more likely to have better relationship outcomes.[18] Because it's not always imprints causing the depletion in relationships. Sometimes it could also be fatigue and self-neglect.

During one of my first research jobs, we had a colleague who pushed everyone's buttons. Everyone's, that is, except mine. I didn't find him as irritating as everyone else did. Then one day, I went to work without doing my morning practice, which is the backbone of my self-care (yoga, SKY Breathing, and meditation), and discovered that this postdoc was indeed irritating as hell. He was, in fact, infuriating! They were right, I decided. I finally understood what everyone was talking about.

Or did I? When I came back into the office the next day with a more sovereign state of mind after doing my morning practice, the guy no longer bugged me. He wasn't different, but my state of mind was. You'll notice that on some days you will be triggered by someone cutting you off in traffic, while on other days you won't. On some days your significant other/children/co-workers set you off, and on others they don't. What's the difference? Your. State. Of. Mind. You've either cultivated a sovereign state of mind, or you haven't, and you are tired, wiped, your tank is empty. In the former case, you've stayed sovereign. In the latter, you're de-energizing yourself and others. No one can make you feel bad if you don't feel bad.

It wasn't until I developed a more self-compassionate and loving relationship with myself (which we discussed in Chapter 2) and a more sovereign emotional and mental state (discussed in Chapters 3 and 4) that my relationships improved. It wasn't the other people who changed. It was me. My newer and healthier relationships with others reflected a newer and healthier relationship with myself.

When your tank is full, you can approach others with generosity. Two people coming together from a place of fullness, rather than from emptiness, makes the whole (the relationship) greater than the sum of the parts (two individuals). Both partners have something to offer each other, and they can interact from a place of kindness and patience, love, and compassion.

Instead of being demanding, you become authentically grateful for the other person, further benefiting the relationship.[19] You are no longer in taker mode. The relationship becomes about "we" and "us," which research shows leads to a more successful relationship.[20]

Not that work isn't needed in a relationship—even between two positive Energizers. But it's much easier to figure things out when both people have a full tank, both have worked to become aware of and heal their imprints, and both are coming from a place of kindness, honesty, forgiveness, and integrity.

Boundaries

A key aspect of self-compassion is boundaries. To master relational energetics, being aware of your boundaries—and those of others—is critical. And that's why the data shows that being true to ourselves leads to better relationships.[21]

Relational boundaries can be strong and obvious or very subtle. Take your cell phone, for example. It connects you energetically to everyone you're in touch with in a subtly invasive way. Think about it. Your boss can reach you while you're in the bathroom in your underwear. Talk about no boundaries.

I can wake up feeling sovereign, but as soon as I turn the phone on, I can feel myself energetically connecting to anyone who has reached out. It can energize me or—more often than not—deplete my energy reserves. Same with e-mail. Your inbox is often filled with other people's to-dos for you. Same with whatever else you look at, be it news or sports or anything. It's as if filaments of our attention and energy are constantly dispersing in micro-drains.

Boundaries often depend on having good awareness—that sovereign skill again! When I performed clinical interviews with veterans for one of my research studies, I heard traumatic stories day after day. I had never done this type of interview before and went in wide open, taking in all their stories of suffering. At the end of the day when I got home, I had to lie down on the floor. I couldn't move. I was drained and sad and had nothing left in the tank. Compassion fatigue is a thing. And it wasn't helpful to them or me. It was a lesson in building boundaries so I could be there for them without going downhill myself.

I did simple things, like setting an intention to have an invisible barrier around me protecting me so I could be there with all my heart but not allow their pain to become mine. I washed my hands with soap between one interview and the next, symbolically letting go of the last one and preparing for the next. It was more about the ritual and intention than the acts themselves. Sometimes I would step outside for a moment, letting go of all I had seen and heard. There is a lot of suffering on this planet. We can be so much more resilient and useful to others when we're whole rather than in pieces.

Developing boundaries takes practice and courage when people are really pushing up against them. I was having trouble getting one of my research studies published. That's when a professor stepped in and said, "Let me help you. I really just care about this research." Now, I knew he was up for tenure and his situation was precarious—a situation in which more publications could be very helpful. His request was strategic. He didn't "just care" about the research as he had said, he cared about being an author on the study. I had no choice but to accept, given the situation in my lab, in which politics had stopped me from publishing the study. With this professor's help, the study was published, for which I was grateful.

And then it came. The moment I was anticipating. Just as we were about to submit the final draft for publication, he e-mailed me, copying his colleague, the director of my lab, saying: "I'd like us to be co-first authors." He had helped edit the final draft of the paper and get it out the door, but I had spent five years raising the funds for the study, recruiting the participants, interviewing the participants, running them through the study, organizing the intervention, training the research assistants, analyzing the data, and drafting the paper. I had already placed him as second author, giving him precedence over others who had spent much more time on the study than he had. When I discussed with my lab director how problematic this request seemed to me, the director replied that he had no problem with this professor getting co-authorship. In other words, he did not have my back at all as a junior female scientist in his lab whom he was meant to be mentoring. I felt shocked, deflated, and betrayed. Talk about a de-energizing experience.

I could have chosen the victim route. I certainly did feel abandoned by my director and devastated by my colleague's manipulation. It was like a déjà vu of other times when people had taken credit for the work I had done.

Yet there was a part of me that no longer wanted to play into that imprint. I was done rolling over. As much as I wanted to break the pattern, however, I was simultaneously anxious. It's nerve-wracking to suddenly exercise strong boundaries, especially when you're not used to it and it's in the face of people with more power than you. It takes courage—that sovereign skill that you've read about in previous chapters. Reaching for sovereignty can feel daunting and scary. I ended up mustering up the boldness to hold on to my sovereignty in the face of these two men, who were much higher on the totem pole than I was as a mere junior scientist. I sent them both a one-sentence e-mail: "I respectfully decline your request."

To my surprise, it worked.

Later in my career, a well-known academic invited me to join her lab to run a research study. She tried to get me to take on more than I was comfortable with by saying, "You'll be university faculty" instead of "just a contractor." I was still willing to take the opportunity, but *on my own terms*. I said thank you very much, I'll be a contractor. Later, others in her lab asked me how I had had such good boundaries with her. I'd been there, done that, and wasn't willing to sacrifice my sovereignty again.

Letting Go: Forgiveness

Another key aspect of self-compassion in relationships is the ability to let go and forgive. Energy in relationships doesn't just come from positive interactions but also from the ability not to waste energy on resentment.

My husband and I went to a marriage retreat when things were difficult. We didn't realize all the couples there were on the verge of separation. We were having challenges, but we were nowhere near that point. The fascinating thing was that the entire retreat was led by couples who had been to real hell and back (affairs, alcoholism, loss of a child, severe mental-health issues). One couple shared how one partner had had an affair with someone he became obsessed with. He couldn't let the person go, even though he tried, and the wife suffered through years of pain. Finally, they came out the other side and began the healing journey.

At that point, the wife said something remarkable: "I was a wreck, and he was guilt-ridden. But we weren't going to heal with me constantly bleeding all over him." It was striking to hear those words and to see her—the victim in this story—taking responsibility for her own emotions. She understood that keeping him in a cycle of blame and guilt would stand in the way of healing the relationship. It would be de-energizing for both. In that seminar room, it felt like you could cut the air; it was so thick with love.

Forgiveness is one of the key aspects of being a positive Energizer. *Let bygones be bygones. Forgive and forget.* That sounds good in theory. What you may not know, however, is that forgiveness is primarily a gift to yourself.[22] It's a profound act of self-compassion and can help you move past trauma and victimhood and release imprints so they don't bog you down or your future relationships. Most importantly, forgiveness restores your energy.

Studies show that forgiveness is associated with:[23]

- **Decreased resentment and stress.** We all know what it feels like to be angry at someone: unpleasant. As we discussed in Chapter 3, studies show that holding on to resentment and anger not only makes you feel terrible but also increases your blood pressure and heart rate—all physiological signs of stress that can deteriorate your health. Forgiveness lowers your blood pressure. It even lowers the blood pressure of the person you are forgiving! Likely because it's setting you both free.
- **Improved well-being.** Forgiveness is linked to higher satisfaction with life and more positive moods.
- **Better physical health.** One study even showed that forgiveness is linked to less medication usage, improved sleep, and lower fatigue and pain.

- **Improved relationships.** No surprise, people who tend to forgive (rather than be vengeful) have less conflict and negative emotions and are more willing to work on a relationship.
- **Kindness.** Studies show that forgiveness makes people kinder and more generous, increasing the likelihood that they will donate to charity.
- **Better mental health.** Higher levels of forgiveness significantly reduce negative emotions and stress and help build stress resilience and may even protect against depression.
- **Resilience in general.** Research shows that forgiveness helps you move on with your life!

My favorite forgiveness study showed that people who learn to forgive perceive hills as less steep and are able to jump higher.[24] Anger and resentment can feel like a burden; in forgiveness, by letting that go, you lighten your load. Forgiveness psychologically and physically unburdens you. See that? Holding grudges is draining and binds you, forgiveness is energizing and makes you sovereign.

Not that you don't hold people accountable, set up good boundaries, and act with self-respect. You do! But forgiveness allows whatever happened in the past to stay there while you move on with a lighter heart. You haven't let the situations that made you a victim in the past steal your future away from you too.

Wonderfulness

As I write this, a dear friend, a Star by the name of Diego, is lying in the hospital with a fatal diagnosis. He may only have days left. Humble, kind, and always ready with a smile and a word of encouragement, he lived his life quietly but was of service to everyone—especially the children he taught with all his heart in at-risk schools. He filled his tank with a true dedication to yoga (108 sun salutations every morning!), meditation, and community service and poured it out in love, joy, and kindness to others. Every time I met him, I felt uplifted by the sparkle in his eye; his humble benevolence; and warm, encouraging, and positive attitude. As he lies in his hospital bed, an outpouring of love is coming to him from friends all over the world: videos, texts, and voice messages sent to his sister to share with him—testaments of the positively energizing relationships he had with hundreds of people. Too weak to talk much, he's still positive: giving thumbs ups and smiling in response to the messages.

We are taught to strive to be "successful" in our work, parenting, athletics, and so on. The other day, I challenged the idea of "success" in an undergraduate class I was teaching. I asked my students, "What are the qualities of the most *wonderful* person you know?" Think for a moment about who the most wonderful people in your life are. Make a list of at least three people. What are the characteristics that they have? How do they make you feel? It's likely they are positive Energizers and perhaps they are even Stars.

The adjectives that came to mind for my students were *loving, caring,* and *present.* I then asked, "Would you say that this person has had a 'successful' impact on your life?" There was silence. They had never even considered this definition of *success* before.

And yet isn't it the wonderful people, the generous, kind, and compassionate ones, who actually do the heavy lifting? Isn't it they who carry us through life? They are there when we have fallen, they love us when we don't love ourselves, they care when no one else does, they show a depth of empathy that inspires us to be better people, they laugh from a place of wisdom and peace, they share with us a kindness we don't find elsewhere. It's the wonderful people who are the most successful and impactful influences on all our lives, and we are fortunate to know them. If we are indeed "successful," it's in large part because there were wonderful people along the way giving us a hand.

And as Kim Cameron's research shows, that's what makes up a Star. Long-lasting fulfillment comes from being there for others, helping where we can, loving one another despite our differences, and making others smile. Yes, follow your ambitions, dreams, and professional goals—why not? They too can bring great satisfaction and a sense of purpose. But remember what also leads to your deepest happiness. You already know what you will know on your deathbed: that a life well lived is a life in which you have shared an abundance of love. With others and yourself.

***

Think back to my college friend Etelle. As extraordinary as she is, what Kim Cameron's research shows is that we all have the ability to relate to others in positively energizing ways. It's within our grasp. It sets us on the trajectory of becoming our best self, our greatest potential. Etelle is a force for goodness for everyone who has the good fortune to meet her, and we can all be that too.

Every interaction you have, whether with a loved one or a stranger, is an opportunity to uplift another person. And in so doing, you uplift yourself.

SIDE EFFECTS OF SOVEREIGN RELATIONSHIPS ⚠

Energy: As you learn to be a positive Energizer, you will energize others around you and, in so doing, you will re-energize yourself, creating an uplifting positive feedback loop. The human values you deploy, like compassion and kindness, will in turn benefit both your physical and mental health.

Awareness: Your relationships will teach you to get to know yourself like you never have before. You will see all your imprints show up in the guise of triggered emotions like anxiety, fear, and anger.

Healthy boundaries: You may feel awkward setting boundaries at first and those close to you may feel surprised when you do so, but the long-term benefits will outweigh short-term discomfort. Boundary setting is the most useful skill you'll build because it allows you to respect both yourself and others.

Power: Your personal power will grow as you learn to both energize others and set good boundaries while taking care to fill your own tank.

SOVEREIGN RELATIONSHIPS TOOL KIT

Remember the 6 keys of positive relational energy.

1. Caring for and being interested in others
2. Providing support for one another, including offering kindness and compassion when others are going through a hard time
3. Avoiding blame and forgiving mistakes
4. Inspiring one another and focusing on what's going right
5. Emphasizing meaningfulness
6. Treating others with basic human values like respect, gratitude, trust, honesty, humility, kindness, and integrity, while maintaining healthy boundaries and self-care

Use relationships as opportunities for healing.

- Understand your relationships as mirrors of your relationship with yourself and of your imprints. Reflect or journal on the following:
  - What are some ways my past and current relationships can help me understand my imprints better? For example, what are my biggest triggers?
  - Are there repeating patterns across time and relationships? What can they teach me about my imprints?
- Self-awareness exercise: Are there times in your life, areas of your life (e.g., work), or relationships in your life in which you show up (or have shown up) as a De-energizer for others? How did that make you

feel? How did that show up in your relationships? What were the consequences of this type of relating?

- Which type of positive Energizer do you most identify with: Crusher, Sacrificer, or Star? Don't just ask yourself, have your friends or partner read the descriptions and give you their thoughts. What are areas where you're leaking energy, and how can you improve that?

Heal relationship insecurity and rejection sensitivity.

Do you tend to feel insecure in relationships? Insecurity in relationships is oh so common and often runs deep. As we discussed earlier, we are deathly afraid of rejection. But you can heal rejection sensitivity by deprogramming it. If you give yourself affirmation, you won't need it as much from others. Exercises like the Reflected Best Self, in which you gather feedback on your best self from people who know you well (described in the Tool Kit in Chapter 2, page 41), can help a lot here too. It is a way to collect objective information that directly contradicts any insecure feelings you might have.

As I mentioned in Chapter 2, my colleague Cendri Hutcherson and I ran a study on loving-kindness meditation (a meditation that helps you experience unconditional love) and found that the more sensitive people felt to rejection, the more they benefited from this meditation because it helped them recall the love they receive from others while also giving them the benefit of extending love to others. It conditions you for connection to yourself and others.

Fill your tank to be a star Energizer.

Remember not to fall for the idea that you need others to *complete* you. No one can complete you. Only you can do that. If you are true to yourself, heal the wounds you carry, and find inner fulfillment, you can be a great friend, wife, son, mother, and so on. What are some ways in which you are currently not filling your tank? And how could you find more fulfillment in your life? When you love, honor, and value yourself, you can create extraordinary relationships that enhance your life and the lives of others, creating a continuous feedback loop of energy and positivity.

True sovereignty is learning how essential self-care is for good relationships, and that part of self-care are the tools we have learned in Chapters 2, 3, and 4, but also:

- Not falling for the victim trap (remember this doesn't deny that you experienced trauma)
- Practicing forgiveness (which lightens *your* load and increases *your* well-being)
- Establishing good boundaries

Make sure to take note of where you are energetically each day (is your tank full or empty), especially before you interact with others. It will help you gauge how you will show up. There are moments when I must alert Husband to the fact that I'm running low and need extra support. In those moments, I hope his tank is running high. If not, we have to figure out what we'll do so we can show up at our best for each other and our kids.

Practice boundary setting.

Practice asserting your needs, asking for what you deserve, and pushing back when others aren't respectful. If you're not used to asserting your boundaries, it may feel scary at first and you may feel awkward doing so, but it can also work. So what if you mess up a couple times? It's okay. The world moves on. Every time your boundaries are crossed is an opportunity to build and strengthen them.

When you first start developing stronger boundaries, you can throw them up a little high or lay it on a little strong. Your words can come out too intensely because you're not practiced. I know because I did that. It can feel nerve-wracking. I once was helping one of my best friends when she came home after a surgery. While I was there, her partner was disrespectful and condescending. He was also a man three times my size with a personality to match his stature—intimidating, to say the least. But I was going to stand my own. Though I was trembling when I said it, I told him that he was condescending and that I didn't need to be there cleaning his dishes. Well, he was respectful after that. The more you practice—awkward as it might seem at first—the more skilled you become, until it's second nature.

Compassion.

After studying the science of happiness for two decades now, I can honestly say that the people who live the happiest and most fulfilled lives (as well as the healthiest and longest ones!) are those who live lives characterized by compassion. For all the reasons I mentioned in this chapter, it benefits your physical and mental health as well as your longevity—when balanced with self-compassion. Remember that every time you uplift, help, or support another person, you in turn are also getting benefited. It's a win-win. A well-kept secret.

If you don't have much time, then micromoments of upliftment—whether it be with the cashier at a store or your romantic partner—can serve as catalysts of well-being for both you and the other party. If you have more time, think about how your particular skillset can be of service to others.

For additional tools and resources, visit my website at www.iamsov.com.

How Do You Feel about You?

I chose to be in a destructive
relationship.
And then
I chose to stay in it.
That's a lot of choosing,
isn't it?
I'm not blaming myself.

Not blaming my then-
partner either.
Just reflecting that
the place I placed myself
was a direct reflection
of how I felt
about
me.
If you don't like yourself,
your relationships may be
ones
in which your partners
don't treat you with the
kindness you deserve.
Neither do you
treat you
kindly.
There was a mirroring
in our interactions
of my own self-worth.

The world is a mirror for
our mind.

That is how
you create the world,
your reality
with your mind.

How are your circumstances
showing you
how you feel about
you?

CHAPTER 6

SOVEREIGN INTUITION

Kushal, an ambitious and successful young New York City trader, had just gotten to work on 9/11. He entered one of the Twin Towers, where his office was located, just as the building was hit. Orders were being given for everyone to stay in the building. Kushal hesitated for a moment, then went with his gut instead, rushing out of the building minutes before it collapsed. That fateful day changed his life, and he lived to tell the story in his book *On a Wing and a Prayer.*

You know the time you knew you shouldn't speed, but still did and got caught? Or the time you knew the relationship was over, but it took you 5 years to break up (or 20, ouch)? You've known when you shouldn't do something. Your gut knew. Speeding and getting caught is one thing; marrying someone you feel you shouldn't is another. We can claim innocence but deep down, yeah, we knew.

Like our animal counterparts, humans have intuition—a hidden dimension of intelligence for which the brain is wired. But intuition has a bad rap—we think good decisions always have to be reasoned. What we don't realize, however, is that intuition is a form of cognition that is instinctual and can improve your decision making. It's an elegant, fine-tuned, and incredibly rapid form of perception that research shows can help strengthen sovereignty.

Our body is a more sophisticated communication device than any that technology has ever developed. Our brain is complex, and there are forms of cognition and awareness that modern science has yet to understand more deeply and that many of us have yet to fully tune in to.

Intuition is an instinct—a form of cognition meant to guide us, to alert us to things we might not otherwise be able to see. We bind ourselves when we completely ignore this instinct and we gain sovereignty when we learn to harness its wisdom.

Sovereignty is allowing yourself to make informed choices based on all the information you gather and process, both with reason and with intuition. The result is that you become more creative, more insightful, and more aware. It can save your life—as it did for Kushal.

INTUITION

What is intuition? You can think of it as an instinct or gut feeling. A *knowing* or inner wisdom. The internal compass that guides you. Our instincts are meant to keep us away from danger and near safety in a complex world.

And our world is indeed so complex. We take in so much information, as we've discussed in the chapters so far.

- The external physical world that we engage in with all our senses: seeing, smelling, touching, tasting, and hearing what is going on around us
- The internal physiological world with its experiences, needs, and demands; its hungers and aches and wants and energy levels
- The internal mental world of constantly flowing thoughts and ideas, imprints of various types
- The internal emotional world, with its varied landscape of feelings rising and rocking our world

- The many virtual worlds tugging at us: social media, phones, messaging, advertising, entertainment, artificial intelligence, and more

Worlds upon worlds of information are coming at us in a constant flux. It's a lot to take in and a lot to navigate. Our attention is constantly in demand from all sides.

We've talked about the hidden messaging in media and advertising that we sometimes don't discern. But there is so much more information that we do not see and are not aware of.

The word *understand* reflects this phenomenon. It comes from the Old English *understandan,*[1] which can be translated as "stand in the midst of." We can only perceive that which we can grasp within the limitations of our five senses, that which we stand "in the midst of." However, there is a whole world out there that is beyond what our physical senses can perceive yet still exists: the thousands of microbes crawling on your skin, the particles floating in the air, the Wi-Fi network, your partner's anxiety, the traffic in a city far away. The many smells and colors that flies and cats and hawks can see but that we cannot. There are worlds upon worlds of information inside and around us that our five senses are not privy to. There is so much we are not able to see, feel, hear, taste, smell, touch, or otherwise know.

We forget what we can't perceive. We think it's not there. But it is.

Intuition is a cognitive skill that allows us to navigate the complexity of our lives in a way our sensory and logical mind—which is limited and much slower—cannot. It's something you can think of as *inner*-standing.

Why talk about intuition with regard to sovereignty? Because most of us have been trained out of listening to our own instincts, despite the fact that research shows we are physiologically wired for intuition and can train it to help interpret our world, make better decisions, pick up valuable information, and even save our own lives. I'm going to use the terms *intuition, gut feeling,* and *instinct* interchangeably here because those are all names that have been given to similar phenomena of rapidly perceiving information by means other than the intellect alone. In this chapter, we'll look at different ways the military, scientists, and artists have conceived of intuition. We'll look at how we bind our intuition and what we can do to capitalize on it for greater sovereignty.

BOUND INTUITION

We all have an inner compass, but we often ignore it or override it, just like animals who lose their survival instincts in captivity. If these animals are brought back into the wild, they will most likely not survive.[2] The same has happened to many of us humans. We have often disempowered ourselves from the gifts our intuition has to offer by tuning it out or shutting it down, drastically restricting and narrowing our perception, potential for insights, and innovative thinking.

It's common to meet the idea of intuition with an eyeroll. As I mentioned in Chapter 4, "Sovereign Mind," we tend to value reason over everything else, using expressions like "think before you act," "think twice," and "look before you leap." We don't trust intuition. In fact, we believe it's flawed and magical thinking, either vaguely crazy or downright stupid.

Why do we pooh-pooh intuitions and gut feelings?

We're trained to rely on outside sources of information, not internal ones. As we discussed in Chapter 4, outside sources and imprints shape our thinking. We depend, trust, and rely exclusively on information coming from outside of us, shutting down a valuable additional resource: our inner knowings. This binds us through a limited perspective that doesn't take advantage of other forms of cognition to which we could have access.

"Many Indigenous communities in the Americas and in Africa have relied on intuition for survival—intuition of the environment, of the earth, of threats to humanity," says Dr. Dena Simmons, education scholar, author, and founder of LiberatED. "It's too bad that this wisdom isn't respected more and that we do not look to the knowledge of those before us as a guide."

We overemphasize reason over other forms of cognition. Our education has conditioned us to dismiss gut feelings, instincts, and intuition as superstition. We are rational and reasoned, and that can make us very sensible but sometimes also narrow-minded and unaware because we rely on intellect at the cost of other modes of perception. We try to figure things out and categorize, analyze, and critique. We often forget to even consult, let alone give any weight to, our inner feelings on a matter. Unfortunately overreliance on the intellect leaves us unnaturally disconnected from the intelligence of the gut and weakens intuitive forms of perception that can help us come up with creative solutions, access information, and, as I've said, even save our lives. We are thereby binding our fullest potential.

I'm a scientist with huge respect for reason. I like a good logical argument (and try to write that way too!) and have a hard time respecting arguments that aren't sound. But we should not allow the pursuit of reason, logic, and proof to shame us into dimming other sources of insight. Intelligence is understanding that we have processing mechanisms other than our intellect. And it's having humility about what we do and do not know and an openness to the idea that there is still much to discover—especially about how the human brain works.

To quote neuroscientist Dr. Thomas Insel, founding director of the Center for Behavioral Neuroscience at Emory University: "I can't tell you—nor can anyone else—how the brain functions as an information processing organ. How does it do it? What is meaning, how is it stored, where does it exist, what does it look like in the brain? We really don't have a sense of how the brain works."[3] If Insel, a renowned neuroscientist who was also the director of the National Institute of Mental Health for 13 years, can't tell how the brain functions—we know there is much still that we do not know!

Who are we to dismiss something we haven't even thoroughly researched and don't know all that much about?

Intuition Research

One of psychology's best known and most respected social psychologists, Daryl Bem, was fascinated by the idea of intuition. It was the subject of the last paper he published, in 2011, for which he spent almost a decade collecting data with hundreds of participants and methods considered rigorous at the time.[4]

He looked, for example, at whether participants could predict where images would be before they appeared (and before, in fact, the program would randomly assign the picture to appear). In the majority of experiments he ran, Bem found that participants were able to correctly intuit the future with greater accuracy than could be accounted for by chance alone.

His findings created an explosion of both enthusiasm and ridicule in the field. His methods were questioned. This happened to be a time (which continues to this day) when all of psychological research was stood on its head and subject to question—for good reason—because of flaws in research methods. But another reason for the explosion of backlash Bem received was that his statements also flew in the face of psychology's way of understanding the mind—in particular, the tenet that a cause has to come before an effect and that you can't predict things ahead of time.

Flaws in methodology and prejudice against certain ideas can exist at the same time.[5] Our field has preconceptions that pooh-pooh this alternate form of cognition and label it—just as society does—as nuts. When I was a graduate student, there was a rumor that a pot of money existed in the department for anyone who wanted to research extrasensory perception. It had supposedly been gifted to the department for that exact purpose. Although everyone wants money in research—after all, we need the resources to get our studies up and running—no one dared to touch it for fear of being ridiculed.

Interesting, isn't it, how scientists, who are supposed to be open-minded so they can discover new phenomena, can close themselves off from new discoveries because of peer pressure, preconceptions, and biases about what will and will not work and about what is and is not worthy of study. It's wild when you think about it. And not very objective, discovery-oriented, or scientific.

I once heard that there are two types of scientists: cynical ones and skeptical ones. The cynical ones will say "That will never work" and not do the experiment. The skeptical ones will say "That will never work" and do the experiment. Only the second type is open to possibility and the potential of being wrong, and therefore to new discovery.

There was a time when psychologists considered meditation a fringe research topic—not a safe one or well-regarded. In fact, in my second year of graduate school, two professors who served as my mentors warned me: "You don't want to be pigeonholed as a meditation researcher. You have to do research on other things." Turns out that, 15 years later, meditation is now a huge field of research with thousands of papers published on the topic every year. The paper my colleague Cendri Hutcherson and I published on meditation that year has now been cited hundreds of times in peer-reviewed journals and over a thousand times in other books and articles.[6] I have no doubt that intuition will soon become another hot research topic.

SOVEREIGN INTUITION

Sovereignty is becoming aware of the level of conditioning that we have received that divorces us from our own inner voice, intuition, and creativity and nips it in the bud. It is getting back in touch with our own innate intelligence, which includes both our reason *as well as* our instincts, gut feelings, and intuitions. It's acknowledging that we *have* these gut feelings and intuitions, an inner compass or instinct that you can add to the mix of information when deliberating how to resolve a problem, which direction to go in, and what to do.

Lynn Tilton lost her father in her teenage years and experienced firsthand what the loss of the main income provider can do to a family. She got herself into Yale, her tuition paid by a tennis grant, married while at Yale, then became pregnant shortly after graduation. It was the 80's and she launched into a career on Wall Street to support her child as a young single mother. She was successful but sexually harassed daily. After making enough money to support herself and her daughter, she briefly considered retiring, until she had a dream—a vision that came to her as an intuition—that changed the course of her life. In her dream, her late father appeared to her and said, "This is not what I had in mind for you."

She realized that she needed to make her life about more than herself and to dedicate the rest of her career to making sure others would not have to go through the kind of suffering she and her family had when her father, the family's primary provider, died. She started Patriarch Partners, a company that bought organizations on the brink of bankruptcy—companies that consulting firms and others had completely given up on—and turned them around.

Because she followed her intuition instead of allowing her logical mind to squelch it as "magical" or "irrational" thinking, the Turnaround Queen, as she came to be known, saved hundreds of thousands of jobs. She also became the owner of the largest woman-owned business in America, overseeing 700,000 employees. Although many (including the government) tried to sue her, figuring she was doing something illegal given her wild success, she refused to settle, spending millions in legal fees and taking on a lot of stress but knowing that she was going to prove that her business was clean and honest. She is sovereign.

When I interviewed Lynn for this book, she shared: "I definitely move from my intuition. But intuition without intellect is like buying a plane without any propulsion. I do the analysis, but my decision comes from my place of knowing. You can't shut off your intuition. If you have to shut off much of yourself to do what you're doing, eventually you just find yourself unhappy." And because she followed her intuition, she saved hundreds of thousands of working class families from succumbing to unemployment.

She's not the only leader to do so. Research shows that a majority of CEOs (85 percent) tend to use intuition when making decisions.[7]

Military Research on Intuition

The U.S. military—always trying to find ways to maximize human performance—has been investigating intuition for decades under various names. You may have heard of "remote viewing," a form of intuitive training the military and CIA researched that was later made fun of in the comedy *Men Who Stare at Goats*. Though the military dropped that program, there were so many accounts of soldiers returning from the Afghanistan and Iraq wars reporting how gut feelings helped them save lives that the military continues to research the phenomenon to this day. The Department of Defense has opened up several new research projects under different names like the Navy's "sensemaking"[8] to look at this phenomenon.

Commander Joseph Cohn, research psychologist at the Office of Naval Research, describes why soldiers' experiences inspired the military to continue researching intuition: "Reports from the field often detailed a 'sixth sense' or 'Spidey sense' that alerted them to an impending attack or IED or that allowed them to respond to a novel situation without consciously analyzing the situation."[9] And that's sovereignty. We don't always have time for lengthy deliberation, especially in critical or life-and-death situations. We sometimes need access to information in a lightning-fast way.

There are many accounts of military members who have described moments of intuition and how they saved their own lives with it. Retired Navy SEAL commander and podcast host Mark Divine was walking with colleagues during a training exercise when he felt a sudden urgent instinct to stop in his footsteps. Seconds later he felt the wind of a bullet just miss his ear. Had he not stopped, the bullet would have hit him in the head.[10]

Staff Sergeant Martin Ritchburg was at an Internet café on a military base in Iraq, speaking to his wife back home, when he got a weird feeling about a man who walked into the café. Ritchburg saved the lives of 17 people that day because his hunch was right and the man had planted a bomb.[11]

Intuition as Conscious Awareness

As we discussed in the preceding chapters, awareness is key to sovereignty in all its forms. It is crucial for intuition too. The most cognitive form of intuition is a form of hyperawareness. Marine Corps officer Maurice "Chipp" Naylon, author of *The New Ministry of Truth*, described his experiences in Afghanistan.[12] He shared with me that the U.S. Marine Corps Combat Hunter training is a way the Marine Corps has formalized the instruction of honing into your gut. It involves becoming an acute observer. You train your observation skills for deviations from the norm in your environment. When Chipp was in Afghanistan patrolling, for example, noticing that a usually busy playground was empty would indicate a deviation from the norm and be a sign of potential danger.

"For us in a foreign country, Afghanistan," Chipp shared, "we will never understand the cultural norms, so one way we could get a baseline level of our environment like locals was to make sure we had local soldiers patrolling with us. That way if something deviated from their baseline that we couldn't pick up because we're not local, we could observe that in the Afghan soldiers. If they were hanging around, smiling, joking, smoking cigarettes, we knew things were relatively normal. But if they stopped smiling, started stressing out, two hands on their weapon, we knew something was off."

He also shared the dangers of not picking up on those cues: "We once had eight to ten Afghan soldiers with us that suddenly left without explanation. Several minutes later, we got hit by a suicide bomber. That was a deviation from baseline that we failed to pick up quickly enough."

The Combat Hunter training[13] is a form of intuition that is attention-based. You are fine-tuning your observation skills. Before you dismiss it as a highly specialized training for elite Marines, consider that it has to do mostly with that one thing we've been talking about again and again: awareness. That skill we have repeatedly discussed as a key to sovereignty. And it is accessible, when you have trained your nervous system to be calm and your mind to be present—see that? It's built on much of what we've discussed so far: **Awareness + Courage + A Full Tank = Sovereignty.**

The techniques I have been sharing with you in the preceding chapters, like breath training and meditation, hone your awareness because they calm the nervous system, sharpen your attention, and bring the mind back into the present moment. There it becomes ready and available to receive information. After all, our mind is usually wandering—from 10 percent to as much as 60 percent of the time, research shows.[14]

Navy SEALs train themselves to be calm even in stressful situations so they can think on their feet better. We can do the same without going through bootcamp. When you are calmer, your eyes literally perceive more things in the environment.[15] No wonder military scientists are studying the benefits of meditation[16]—which trains your nervous system to be calmer and more aware—for military training.

Intuition as Physiological Information

Have you ever felt off around a person and couldn't figure out why? You just want to back away and get out of there but logically you can't find any reason for your impulse?

This form of intuition is more internal—it's physiological and empathic. Psychologists define *empathy* as "the ability to feel or experience what another person is feeling." It's what we also call psychological resonance. Our body is like a sophisticated sounding board. It can register another person's physiological and emotional state, which is why emotion is often contagious and you can feel stressed around someone who's stressed or relaxed around someone who is at ease. We receive critical noncognitive information through our bodies all the time.

Let's go back to suppression, the emotion regulation technique discussed in Chapter 3 that most people use but that doesn't do us any favors. If someone you're talking with is suppressing anger (i.e., feeling anger but not showing it on their face), here's what happens to your heart rate: it increases. Your intellect hasn't caught on to any funny business yet, but your body has registered that something potentially unsafe is going on—the other person is hiding something—and your fight, flight, or freeze instinct kicks in. You can't figure out why you don't feel comfortable, since your mind hasn't caught on yet—but your nervous system has. Your heart rate is up and you want to get out of there. Simply put: your body registers inauthenticity as a threat.

You see this instinctual response in the animal world as well. In equine-facilitated therapy, the patient will do a therapy session with a therapist and a horse. If the patient fears the horse but pretends everything's cool and they're not scared, the horse is visibly anxious, moving all around. Yet as soon as the patient admits, "I'm scared," the horse calms down. Why? The horse doesn't understand English! But—like our human instincts—the horse's instincts are finely attuned to noncognitive signals that could signify danger. Physiologically, both an animal's body and ours register inauthenticity as dangerous because the other person is hiding something. And that throws up a red flag.

Our mind is slow at picking up what's going on, but our body has, through its senses, registered information that our intellect is not privy to. That's probably why we call it a "gut" feeling—it's a different and much more rapid form of intelligence and perception than the one we can access with the mind alone. It's physiological. On the flip side, when we feel safe with someone, our heart rate syncs with theirs and so does our breathing and brain activity.[17]

Again, here awareness is key. The more present you are, the more you will perceive and the more your body will pick up cues. Perhaps most importantly, the more in tune you are with your body's messages, the more you'll gain valuable insights and information to guide you.

Intuition as Emotion

Sylvie Guillem was the closest thing to a superstar that the world of ballet has ever known, in part because she knew to follow her gut. Acclaimed all over the world, her performances radiated a rare power and beauty. I was fortunate to attend several of her performances, and you could hear the entire audience gasp when she came onstage. Her energy was electric. She exuded sovereignty by living and performing at her fullest potential and, as such, woke the audience up to their own.

She was the youngest dancer to ever be made an *étoile* by the Paris Opera Ballet. (*Étoile* is the French equivalent of principal dancer—one of the best dancers in a company, who performs the starring roles.) She then shocked the whole of France when she became the youngest étoile to ever voluntarily leave the Paris Opera Ballet. Why? Because she felt they exerted too much control over her. She was one to live life sovereign, i.e., *on her own terms.* Unsurprisingly, she was known as "Mademoiselle Non" (or "Ms. No") by the English, who subsequently hosted her at the Royal Ballet in London.

When interviewed about how she made big decisions in her life, such as leaving the Paris Opera Ballet, she said, "I work with instinct." She went on to say that was why she had no regrets—a powerful statement. And when asked where one feels instinct, she replied, "In your whole body!"[18] And that's how she danced too, to the beat of her own internal drum, living her life to the fullest as a dancer, performing artist, and human, inspiring thousands the world over.

Joseph Mikels, professor of psychology at DePaul University, studies intuition as an emotional process. After all, when we speak about our intuition, we often talk of it as a feeling. Something "feels" off, though we can't necessarily explain why. Kushal, the one who was in one of the Twin Towers on 9/11, didn't have time to deliberate rationally about what he should do. He had to make a decision and fast—it *felt* right to run out of the building.

We've all had gut feelings that we can't explain. Sometimes a decision you're making *seems* like a reasonable decision but doesn't *feel* right. On the flip side, you may be compelled to do something that *seems* unreasonable but *feels* right.

Mikels has researched intuition as an emotional process that can lead to better decision making, especially when matters are complex. His research shows that, when you're making a complex decision with lots of information to weigh, you're more likely to choose the right path if you consult your intuition—your *feelings*—rather than debating the matter with reason.[19] This is not the case for simple decisions, but for the more complicated ones, it's in your favor to consult your emotions. He found this to be especially true for older adults whose cognitive faculties might not always be as sharp as younger people's, showing that intuition is even more important with age.[20]

Like Joe Mikels, Joel Pearson and Chris Donkin, psychologists at the University of New South Wales, ran a study[21] that showed that our emotions can provide information even below our awareness. In their study, participants were meant to decide whether a dot would appear on the left or the right of the screen. What they did not know is that an image (either positive, like a cute animal, or negative, like a car wreck) would appear before the dot appeared. The image flashed so quickly that the participants could not consciously see it, but their brain registered it as positive or negative subconsciously. Whenever the image was positive, the dot would appear to the right, and when it was negative, to the left. Soon, despite not consciously seeing the images, the participants became very accurate at predicting when a dot would be on the left or the right with the information they were subconsciously receiving in the subliminal images. Joel Pearson claims that "with our work, we have shown strong evidence that unconscious feelings and emotions can combine with conscious feelings, and we can use it to make better decisions." But he also clarifies that "intuition is only as good as the information you rely on,"[22] suggesting that if we don't have sufficient information or accurate information, our gut instincts could lead us astray.

Intuition as Subconscious Processing

Some psychologists hypothesize[23] that intuition is more subconscious. It comes about when your brain connects the dots between things in the background—information is getting processed below your awareness.

People with expertise in their field—for example, physicians or art collectors—may have a strong intuition due to being highly trained in that specialty. Research shows that experienced dentists who rely on intuition when they have to make quick decisions will make better choices than if they depended on reason alone.[24] Doug Woodham, former president of Christie's America, shares a similar experience: "You're able to stand in front of the work of art knowing lots of other work by that artist and be able to sense whether it's real or not."[25] I'm no expert in Gothic architecture, but when I first landed on the Yale campus—many of whose buildings are built in Gothic style—after growing up in France, I kept having this feeling: "This place *looks* old but doesn't *feel* old." Having grown up around buildings that have the same style but are centuries older, I couldn't describe to you why the Yale ones didn't feel as ancient, but they just didn't.

Intuition as Innovation and Creativity

A more abstract way of conceiving of intuition is to think of it as receptivity. One of the greatest geniuses of our time, Albert Einstein, credited intuition as the source of scientific discovery: "All great achievements of science must start from intuitive knowledge. I believe in intuition and inspiration. . . . At times I feel certain I am right while not knowing the reason."[26] He goes on to say that "the theory of relativity occurred to me by intuition."

To his point, when you look at where our best ideas come from, it's often from intuition, not reason. Ask yourself this question before reading on: When you're trying to figure out how to resolve a problem in your work or personal life, when is it that you come up with solutions? What kind of activities are you doing when you suddenly get a-ha! moments, insights, or answers to questions you have? If you're anything like the audiences I've posed this question to, you'll say something like this: in the shower, while walking the dog, in the morning before the day has started, at night before bed, or when driving.

Neuroscience research shows we are most likely to get creative insights or a-ha! moments when the brain is in alpha wave mode. It's that relaxed space—neither intensely focused nor lethargic—you could call it a meditative state of mind. Research by

Jonathan Schooler shows that sudden moments of insight tend to occur when you're in a relaxed and unfocused state[27] like when you're in the shower, taking a walk, or doing another laid-back activity. Because it's when your brain is in alpha wave mode—neither fully focused nor completely relaxed but somewhere in between. That's when it seems to be in active problem-solving mode in the background, firing up solutions to your problems. (And that's why a friend of mine who studies creativity and is always looking for ideas jokes that he takes multiple showers a day!)

Einstein claimed to gain access to his intuition via the arts: "Music is the driving force behind this intuition. My parents had me study the violin from the time I was six. My new discovery is the result of musical perception."[28] And research specifically bears this out, showing that some music—Mozart's but not Beethoven's, for example—elicits alpha wave frequencies in the brain, which are linked to both attention and cognition.[29]

You could think of it as a time when your subconscious connects dots, or—as many artists and scientists who, like Einstein, get their a-ha! insights in those moments—as a place of receptivity. The book you are reading right now—like my last book—came to me mostly while on walks in the woods, on hikes, or during meditation. It felt like I heard many of the sentences and just wrote them down.

My husband and I once found ourselves without childcare quite suddenly. We were desperate. I needed someone I could trust starting the next day so we could go to work. Exhausted, I gave up thinking about this problem and went to meditate, as I usually do twice a day. At the very end of the meditation, just as I was about to get up, I heard: "Mali's mom." That's right, Mali's mother is incredible. Having had eight kids of her own, and having infinite patience and warmth, she was the perfect person. When I called her, it turned out she was looking to leave her current job. She became a part of our family the very next day. Go figure.

Here's a question to consider. Why are children often so creative and perceptive? They build castles out of cardboard boxes, forts out of pillows, cars out of sticks and stones. Children are in alpha wave a lot more than we are because they are in the present moment, in play, and in periods of rest or daydreaming (unless they are distracted and focused on a screen).

As adults, we can access the alpha wave mode where our mind is more likely to attune to gut feelings. However, we are often robbing ourselves of it by giving our attention away in the ways we've discussed in Chapter 4.

In this attention economy, where everyone wants your eyes on their product or perspective or social media profile or TV show, we can spend all day without ever tapping into alpha wave mode. In our go-go-go society, where we value *doing* so much more than *being*, we inadvertently stop ourselves from accessing our creative genius. As we discussed in Chapters 3 and 4, our attention is monopolized by distraction in the form of technology, media, entertainment, high stress, busyness, and countless addictive and pleasurable activities. These keep us bound rather than in the alpha wave state that is so conducive to more intuitive and innovative ways of thinking about things.

We passively consume entertainment (YouTube, TV,[30] social media, video games) keeping ourselves in a focused state of mind.[31] Think about it, you could be on a screen all day from the moment you wake up, roll over, and grab a hold of your phone. Children and adults are so used to entertainment being created for them that they lose touch with their own innate intuition and creativity. Children who are used to iPads sometimes forget "how" to play when they are not on a screen. Coupled with an education system that emphasizes reason and logic over creative pursuits, no wonder there has been a sharp decline in children's creativity over the last decade. Creativity researcher Kyung Hee Kim at the College of William and Mary found that 85 percent of children are less creative than children in the 1980s.[32]

We no longer make space in our lives for fun, for irrelevant activities, for unproductive moments, for plain and simple *joie de vivre*—stimulators of the alpha wave state—and as a consequence we've lost touch with our own inner problem-solving and also our inner compass.

Yet a more sovereign lifestyle embraces the ability for downtime and relaxation *in the day to day*. It understands that a more relaxed body and mind is also far more energized, creative, innovative,[33] and intuitive—because it is joyful.[34] It invites cognitive downtime, childlike playfulness,[35] wonder[36] and exploration leading to novel insights and broader perspective.[37]

The result is a brain that is more likely to see things outside the box, to understand things from a broader point of view, and to intuit solutions to complex problems—because it is not lost in the tension and narrow-sightedness of a stressed and linear perspective.[38] Like that of a child, it remains curious.[39] As a consequence, you can come up with innovative solutions that benefit both your personal life and your work.

Innovation is what every company wants. According to a Boston Consulting Group survey,[40] it's among most companies' top three priorities. If you can create something better, smarter, faster, then you can beat the competition. How many companies understand that, in order to bring out innovative thinking in their employees, they need to curb the stress and invite their staff to spend more time in a relaxed frame of mind? Unsurprisingly, one study showed that going into nature for three days, completely unplugged from devices, increases creativity by 50 percent—most likely because nature increases well-being, reduces stress, and therefore places people in alpha wave mode.[41] How much more successful would companies be if they took this approach to innovation?

In short, binding our intuition stops us from accessing key moments of insight and creative genius that could deeply benefit our lives.

Uncharted Intuition

The most abstract form of intuition is the kind we don't have a category for yet.

In researching this chapter, I met a man called Mihir, having heard that his daughters had used intuition to help find a child. A middle schooler had run away from home in Toronto, where Mihir and his daughters live. The parents of the missing child—having heard of Mihir's daughters' gifts—called him to see if his girls could help. Mihir's daughters went into meditation and were able to describe the location of the missing girl, down to details of the area where she was and the shed behind which she slept at night. I interviewed one of the daughters about this—I'll call her Deana. She said: "The street names were fuzzy, but we could see which landmarks were in that area of the city, so we knew in which neighborhood of Toronto she was located." Thanks to the girls' intuition, the missing child was found and safely returned home to her parents.

Mihir explained to me that his daughters had both trained in the Intuition Process, a course offered to children through the Art of Living Foundation, the same place I learned breathing and meditation. The idea is that intuition is a cognitive skill you can train and that children can learn it most easily.

I was curious about this two-day Intuition Process class, so I decided to sign up my five-year-old. The class is only four hours long, two hours on each day. On the second day, halfway through the class, parents can come in and observe the kids doing a blindfolded activity. In front of each child were two coloring pages with a teddy bear on them. One page was in color, and the other was in black and white. The children were instructed to color the black-and-white one in the same colors as the colored one. They had not seen the images before putting on their blindfold.

I stood next to a tiny five-year-old. When I saw him start to choose the exact right colors and carefully color within the lines of the teddy bear's ears as if his eyes were open—all with a heavy-duty blindfold on—tears spontaneously rolled down my face. I'm not sure if it was because of how unbelievable it was and therefore somehow shocking and moving or because it was such a tiny human demonstrating this extraordinary ability—which may be an ability we all have at our fullest potential and with the right training and access to our intuition.

Will these children grow into teenagers, like Deana, who are able to navigate their world with greater insight into what is and isn't beneficial for them? Will they make better choices? The research is still out on this.

When I went over to my son, he didn't accurately color into the corners the way that first child did, but he did choose the right colors. I have no scientific explanation to offer for this kind of intuition other than that it's a form of cognition we have yet to discover and research further. And there is much that we still do not know about how our minds and brains work.

The most moving evidence of the utility of intuition training I saw was in schools for the blind in India that are offering the Intuition Process. Devoid of sight, the children are able to accurately recognize pictures and colors by using their intuition alone. They developed vision through means other than their eyes—nothing short of extraordinary, especially if you think of the applicability of this to other blind populations or elderly populations that are losing their eyesight.

The Intuition Process class is only offered for children at the moment, perhaps because they don't second-guess their intuition as adults, who are conditioned by their education and restrictive beliefs about what they feel is and isn't possible, tend to do. They may be more in tune. At the end of the class, the kids make a group pledge to only use their intuition for good, not to crack codes, intuit credit card numbers, cheat on tests, or gamble.

I haven't been so good at getting my son to keep up with the daily intuition practices he is meant to do, but he has developed an uncanny ability to tell what people need. One night, during our bedtime routine, he said: "Mama, your body needs sleep and vitamin C and D. Also, you need a liver cleanse and should avoid fats for a while. Also, you need chamomile tea. Mixed with lavender." He's often right on the money, but, as his mom, I am of course totally biased, and my son does have a lot of data points on me! Sometimes he'll want to eat some junk food, and I've gotten into the habit of saying: "You're old enough to make your own decisions now. Ask your intuition." To my surprise, he'll often turn down the junk after that or say yes to the vegetables he didn't want prior to checking with his intuition. It doesn't mean he always listens to the guidance. The other day he said, "I don't want to check with my intuition because I know what it will say, and I just want to eat the cookies anyway."

We don't have much information about this powerful and moving form of intuition that Deana and the blind children display and that appears to be trained in the Intuition Process class. We don't yet have research on how it works. It's way beyond anything we have studied in psychology—yet some colleagues and I are interested in possibly exploring this form of cognition more deeply, especially because of the fascinating possibility that it could help people navigate the world with greater sovereignty.

***

So what is intuition at the end of the day? It's probably a complex combination of all the cognitive skills we discussed. It can take the form of focused awareness, subconscious processing, emotion, physiology resonance, and other forms of receptivity we haven't fully understood yet. On the one end of the spectrum, it is extreme awareness turned outwardly watching and listening for what's there; on the other, it is relaxed awareness turned inwardly harking for internal cues. Either way, the brain is receiving, perceiving, and processing information that is leading us to gain insights and information our logical mind doesn't always understand or have access to.

Sovereignty is getting back in touch with the innate intelligence derived from our instinct, gut feelings, and intuitions. It can be trained. It is a muscle like any other. It is heard and felt, not researched or deliberated intellectually. It is perceived in silence, not noise. During times of rest.

Practices I've already discussed—like meditation, technology fasts, silent retreats, and nature immersions—can help us get back in touch with our own inner knowing and compass. We regain access to innate wisdom in addition to a storehouse of creativity and innovative insights.

Being Brave

It takes bravery to follow your gut. And as we've seen time and again, sovereignty implies courage. For one, it's sometimes hard to tell the differences between an intuition and something else. What baggage or imprints, if any, may be giving us heebie-jeebies because we're actually just in a fear imprint. In fact, feeling anxious or depressed can impair our ability to access our intuition, research shows.[42] You are probably more accurate when you are able to calm your mind—thus my repeated emphasis on the importance of breathing, meditation, and other activities that allow you to access a sovereign state of mind. Discernment is key so you can distinguish between accurate inner signals and inaccurate ones.

Another reason you need bravery is that it's scary to disappoint people's expectations of you or to do what does not appear logical or rational in other people's eyes. But are you going to live your life according to other people's road map or your own inner compass? And here's something to question: Why, when something doesn't appear logical, should it automatically be labeled as crazy?

There's a big push to follow the crowd in our society, but being sovereign means you can do something differently. Even if it doesn't look right for everyone else, it can look right for you—and you can own that.

Should you always follow your intuition? Joe Mikels gives good advice similar to that Lynn Tilton gives. Given his research on intuition and how it can help you make a better decision in complex situations, he says he makes sure to "consult" it and take it into consideration along with all the other information he has.

Combining logic with intuition seems like a wise, poised, and grounded approach. Reason obviously plays an important role, and intuition provides additional information to throw into the mix. Einstein said it best: "The intuitive mind is a sacred gift, and the rational mind is a faithful servant. We have created a society that honors the servant and has forgotten the gift."

Think of what would have happened to Kushal, Sylvie, and Lynn if they hadn't had the courage to follow their intuition. Instead, Kushal went on to not only live but thrive as a successful social entrepreneur who has embraced a life of much greater happiness than before. Sylvie became the closest thing to a rock star the ballet world has ever seen. And Lynn saved the jobs of over 700,000 people. Think of those people in the Twin Towers alongside Kushal who had the same intuition to run but listened to orders instead of running. It's both amazing and frightening that we can actually lose our lives because we are too afraid to listen to our inner voice.

Allow yourself to tap into underutilized parts of your own intelligence. Make time to connect with the many forms of cognition, perception, and creative genius you are wired for. As it did for Kushal, it might just save your life.

SIDE EFFECTS OF SOVEREIGN INTUITION ⚠

Insight: We've talked about awareness throughout the book since it is key to sovereignty. As you start to make room for intuitive insights, you'll find your awareness deepens further. By making time and space for intuition to arise, you'll have greater insight into yourself and the world.

Creativity: By making time to consult your innerstanding, you will come up with ideas and insights you've never had before. This will enrich your life and that of others.

Better decision making: By using multiple sources of information and using both logic and intuition, you will make superior decisions.

Independence: As you realize the amount of insight you have within yourself, you will start to trust yourself more and need to rely less on other people's opinions and perspectives. You'll be the captain of your own ship, guided by your own inner compass. You might push people's buttons in doing so, but you'll stay true to the most important person in your life: yourself.

SOVEREIGN INTUITION TOOL KIT

Contemplate.

Sovereignty is becoming aware of the level of conditioning that divorces us from our own inner voice. Think back on decisions you made in which you ignored your gut feelings. What were the consequences of those decisions? What about times in which you did follow your gut? How did you feel about it—was it scary? How did others feel about it? What were the consequences? What did you learn? Journal or reflect on these questions:

- How often have I betrayed my own inner knowing to fit in? And then paid the price later?
- For how much of my life have I allowed outside sources to tell me how to think and behave?
- Have I tuned into my own instincts and knowings, or do I tend to shut them down? How often do I actually consult my gut?
- To what extent do I depend on reason alone?

Consult your gut feelings.

When you need to make decisions, make it a habit to also consult your feelings on the matter. Start with small, inconsequential decisions to practice getting the hang of it. It's of course wise to think about things rationally and try to understand them, but see if your feelings—your *inner*standing—are aligned with your logical mind. Remember when you're making complex decisions, in particular, Mikels found that our gut feelings tend to be most accurate.

How do you do that? When you need to make a decision between options A and B, for example, sit with your eyes closed for a moment. How do you *feel* about each option? You might notice one makes you tense up while the other makes you feel relaxed. This will take practice. You may not notice much at first. Try it in different situations, when you're dealing with people, for example.

And finally, be aware if anything else—e.g., fear—might be getting in the way of your decision. Are you tense because one decision is scary? Or because it feels wrong? Sometimes, the scary option feels right, it just requires courage.

Make room for quiet.

We've talked about the need for silence and time away from the onslaught of imprints coming our way (Chapter 4). Our intuition is dimmed if we are constantly listening to news, opinions, and entertainment. Shut out the noise for a little while. Amplify time for listening to something other than the loud and raucous everyday.

I once heard a Buddhist monk describe meditation as listening to the grass grow. Not that you always need to be meditating, but make time for quiet, make time to hark for the messages that lie beyond the din of the world. Chances are, you'll find treasure.

Schedule idle time.

Instead of always trying to be productive, having the music on, scanning your phone for news and notifications, and engaging with someone or something, make time to allow your mind to daydream, to be in an unfocused space—the alpha wave mode we discussed that is key to receptivity and creativity. You don't have to carve out special time for this. Just choose not to take calls or listen to podcasts while you're driving. Walk your dog or go grocery shopping without your phone so you have time to just be, rather than focusing on your screen. Take hikes without your technology. Allow your mind to be in that gently unfocused state—the alpha wave mode—that is receptive to novel ideas, insights, and innovation.

A meditation practice, which you've hopefully started by this time in the book, will help you attain and value this unfocused time all the more. You have become used to spending time with yourself and hopefully enjoy it. You won't find it quite so hard anymore to put your phone away. Think of it as your sovereignty time.

Many of the same takeaways from previous chapters apply here: meditation, breathing, time spent alone and in nature, calming the nervous system. But also make sure you nurture your alpha wave time by doing the following:

- Listen to music—think of Einstein's source of inspiration and Mozart's effect on alpha waves
- Creative activities may let your mind wander and allow you to access an alpha wave state of mind
- Any activity that is not highly focused—even cleaning the dishes—can help you tune in to alpha wave mode
- Unplug from your devices, from screens, from anything that tunes you into high-focus mode. Give yourself downtime where your mind is receptive and quiet.

Create opportunities for contemplation.

Our ancestors had time for contemplation when the sun went down, around night fires, during solitary moments, or walking in nature. They had no phones, no distractions. They just spent those moments *being*. Allow yourself to spend time unplugged on hikes or nature. Observe the night sky. Read poetry. Do the things that allow you to be in a contemplative state of mind. It's hard to be in tune with yourself when your attention is always elsewhere. Allow your mind to come back home. To itself.

For additional tools and resources, visit my website at www.iamsov.com.

Intuition

They made you feel
You would die
If you did not obey
If you did not abide.

Little did they know
That because you listened
Not to them
But to your heart
You came alive.

Silence the mind
For it is only in that silence,
That stillness,
That you can hear
The music of your Heart.

CHAPTER 7

SOVEREIGN BODY

Our bodies evolved for survival, meaning physical and mental health. Yet modern life often finds us anxious, depressed, stressed, burned out, exhausted, and ailing, despite the fact most of us are not doing hard labor or living in a warzone. In large part, this has to do with the fact that we've given up sovereignty over our bodies. In so doing, we become bound.

JT[1] was a 45-year-old morbidly obese BBQ chef. At 348 pounds, he suffered from joint pain so severe he had to take 21 ibuprofens daily. He was prediabetic and had sleep apnea, high blood pressure, high cholesterol, elevated kidney and liver enzymes, and daily crippling anxiety. He was on anti-inflammatory medication, pain killers, and muscle relaxers for severe edema, but they didn't help his swollen hands, legs, and feet. He had such severe intestinal pain that he was hospitalized and prescribed more medication. He was dying.

The part that struck me most about his story was the fact that no health professional ever mentioned to JT that changing his lifestyle could help. Instead of suggesting he take responsibility for his healing, eat healthier, and lose weight, they gave him more medications. One piece of advice a doctor did give him was "stop living like a 35-year-old man and start living like a 45-year-old man" as he handed him eight more prescriptions. JT may have been exceptionally unlucky in his health professionals, but medication as a quick fix that allows you not to avoid taking responsibility is common.

JT had a choice to make here. Would he continue the trajectory he was on and abdicate sovereignty over his body, remaining bound to this downhill trajectory? Or would he take responsibility for it and save his life?

It was JT's mom who suggested he investigate what he could do to help himself. Unable to work by this time, and desperate, he did. Consequently, he adopted a 100 percent plant-based diet. In the span of three weeks his edema was gone and his blood pressure stabilized. As time went on, his numbers returned to normal, he got off all his medication, his anxiety resolved, he lost 168 pounds, and he was able to not only work again, but to thrive as a vegan chef and influencer.

JT took responsibility for his health, turned his life around, and gained sovereignty over his physical and mental health. Once bound, he is now profoundly self-empowered.

Our body is the ground of our existence, the root of all of our experiences. Our very foundation. In order to exercise sovereignty in any other domain, it is fundamental to first exercise it with our body.

You may not be morbidly obese, but you can still bind your body by not taking responsibility for it. Or you can have a sovereign relationship with it, enlivening, protecting, and nourishing it. In so doing, you gain the ability to live life to its fullest potential.

Our body is our closest friend and ally—when we have a sovereign relationship with it—or a source of great suffering and depletion when not. We'll first talk about how we bind our bodies and then how to attain sovereignty.

THE BOUND BODY

Humans have long been fascinated by the possibility of UFOs without realizing that we ourselves have become extraterrestrial. How? We live *on* the earth but are no longer *of* the earth. Our bodies evolved as part of nature, but our lifestyles are often totally out of sync with our body's natural needs, disrupting our physical and psychological well-being.

We Mistreat Our Bodies

Animals in the wild live in harmony with nature. Honoring their body is an *instinct*—following the rules of their circadian rhythms is normal: sleeping enough and at regular, predictable intervals; eating the right food for their systems; moving sufficiently; getting sunlight, and so on. No animal in the wild abuses its body or overindulges in any of the senses.

Humans, on the other hand . . .

- Are tired because we ignore our circadian rhythms and eat poorly, then overcaffeinate, artificially increasing our energy. This leads to anxiety, swiftly followed by a comedown—burnout, depressive feelings, and more fatigue than before. And then we start over. (I once witnessed someone downing anti-anxiety medication with a Red Bull. You've got to wonder: What are we up to?)
- Sit for six to eight hours/day.[2] The sedentary lifestyle also makes us more tired, lethargic, and craving the caffeine that overstimulates us and keeps us up.
- Eat junk food and fast food and mass-produced food filled with salt, fat, sugar, and chemicals that taste great but make us feel lethargic or overstimulated and harm our physical and mental health
- Deprive ourselves of fresh air and natural light and live in artificial light morning and night, further disturbing our circadian rhythm[3]
- Are so rarely in the sun that we lack vitamin D, spending most of the time indoors within four walls that are sometimes a part of concrete jungles as we stare into screens (phone, TV, computer, tablets, watches, etc.), harming our eyesight and mental health. A review paper showed that insufficient

sun exposure is linked to more than 300,000 deaths a year (from various cancers, hypertension, Alzheimer's, and more) as vitamin D supplementation does not make up for lack of sun exposure.[4]

. . . to name just a few of the very strange facts about our modern life.

And we wonder, perplexed, why do we feel so off? Not just physically, but also emotionally.

Instead of honoring our body, we take it for granted and override its needs: overindulging or overexercising, staying up too late or not sleeping enough, working too hard or lazing around. Either way, we are out of sync and often totally out of contact with our body's needs.

We usually only take care of our body after a long haul of driving it into the ground. Beat, we finally buy a green smoothie, go to the gym, or drive to a lake or beach to take a few days off in hopes of making up for things.

Here's the rub: We can't rely on self-care one-offs while neglecting our body the rest of the time. That's like a romantic partner taking you out for a glamorous date after being an ass for three months—it's nice, but it doesn't erase what happened yesterday.

Our body is the precious ally that houses us, not our enemy. Yet we treat it like we're at war with it, rather than listening to its needs and being grateful for it. We feel like we need to fight the flab, beat the bulge, and burn calories. We believe we need to battle our body, improve it, change it, heal it, complain about it. Yet considering the body a fiend that needs forceful taming binds us in misery and has us abuse the precious piece of equipment that gives us life.

We forget how extraordinary it is to have a body in the first place, except in those rare moments when we see a newborn baby and are reminded of the miracle that life is—a body complete with organs and bones created out of another body—or when we're sick and realize how important health is, or when someone we know passes away and we stand in shock at the fact that our own body has an end and how fortunate we are to still be alive.

Toxicity

Before our boys could speak to us in words, they spoke to us in eczema. On day two of our firstborn's life, his entire body was covered in the stuff. Our pediatrician himself winced as he suggested we could use a cortisone cream on our newborn. He also recommended we look into what might be causing the rash. I went on a mad investigation like only a new mom can do. Turns out it was our detergent. We were using an organic and natural detergent, but it had a "natural fragrance" that can be irritating for hypersensitive skins, especially those of newborns. When baby number two arrived, "100 percent natural and organic" American diapers gave him horrendous and painful welts. Only the finest Swedish-made compostable diapers (probably made from organic fair-trade sustainably grown non-GMO banana leaves) would do.

My children's sensitivities taught me a lot about how we can unknowingly lose sovereignty over our bodies via consumer products.

The U.S. allows the use of more than 1,000 chemicals that are illegal in many other Western countries because of health concerns. More stunning yet, there is no law requiring American companies to publicly disclose all the chemical ingredients[5] in consumer products. No surprise that a study at the University of Washington found hundreds of undisclosed chemicals and volatile organic compounds (VOCs) known to be hazardous to health, toxic, and carcinogenic[6] (as stated by the Environmental Protection Agency (EPA)) in consumer products—think teenagers' Victoria's Secret creams, our Yankee candles, and the scented Christmas trees hanging from rearview mirrors.[7]

Many of these chemicals are endocrine disruptors—they act like hormones in the body and can wreak havoc on brain function, immunity, and mental health.[8] Often, the result is that we find ourselves diagnosed with anxiety or depression that we then try to medicate away with other chemicals. And since endocrine disruptors impact our hormones, they can also lead to reproductive issues.[9] With fertility issues being so widespread (12 to 15 percent of couples are unable to conceive),[10] it makes you wonder.

In fact, some toxic consumer products are inserted directly into an area of the woman's body that produces hormones, like condoms which contain an unregulated amount of toxic chemicals.[11] Speaking of condoms, when my boyfriend-now-husband visited my parents for the first time in France, we ran out of condoms. Yeah, well, you know. Anyway, we were out in a village grocery store in Normandy when I discreetly asked my mother where such things could be purchased. Shocked, Mother promptly stomped over to poor, embarrassed, proper, small-town Midwestern boyfriend and scolded him loudly: "How could you possibly come to France without a suitcase full of condoms?!"

Of course, it being France and all, there are condom vending machines on the street, which don't work (or perhaps, it being France and all, are out of stock), despite my mother's attempts to vandalize them. Defeated, we return to local shopkeeper for advice. Shopkeeper immediately gets on phone with other local shopkeepers to try and resolve condom situation. Soon, whole village is abuzz. Finally, he surreptitiously slips Mom a small package of his own stash with a whisper: "Don't tell my wife." The condom box is yellowed with time and looks like it possibly dates from the '70s. It has a cartoon of a large smiling condom running in place. And—though doubtless past their expiration date—possibly a lot less chemicals than the ones produced today. (Though the good news is that, once you know how to look for them, you can get nontoxic condoms!)

Chemicals are even found in the urine of newborn babies[12] from the flame retardants routinely used in their pajamas, stuffed animals, and car seats. As of January 2024, Johnson & Johnson agreed to pay $700 million dollars to settle the tens of thousands of cases resulting from their iconic baby powder. It purportedly contained asbestos, causing ovarian cancer and mesothelioma.[13]

The fascinating thing is that chemicals have become such a normal part of our life that they are cherished. Most people love the smell of fresh laundry and dryer sheets whose chemicals are associated with known allergens even when labeled "baby safe" and "free and gentle."[14]

A waiter once sprayed Windex to clean the counter my baby and I were eating at. Chemical warrior I had become, I quickly pulled the baby out of the way of the spray. Confused by my reaction, the waiter protested: "But it smells *clean*!"

It smells clean. See that? Our brain associates "smell of Windex chemicals" with "smells *clean*." Chemicals = clean = good.

I'm not making this up. Psychology studies show that when you spray Windex in a room, study participants are more likely to share and play nice than make selfish choices. The hypothesis here is that the smell of Windex makes you think about cleanliness, so your actions also become more clean.[15] In sum, a spritz of Windex may come in handy once in a while when you're negotiating for a car or a raise, but over the long run, chemicals bind your physical and mental health by wreaking havoc on it.

Chemicals in Our Food

When my boys grew older, I became aware of the impact of food-based chemicals and sugar, not just on their eczema and intestines but—worse yet—on their mental health. At one birthday party, our then five-year-old had a piece of cake that morphed him into Frankenson, growling with uncontrollable rage, attacking his baby brother, and then screaming for two hours straight, managing to make even Husband, who, after 12 years in the Marine Corps can endure a fair amount, cry. Our son started apologizing. He himself couldn't understand why he was so angry. "It's not your fault," I whispered and held him tight in my arms as the food-induced stress ruthlessly coursed through his shaking little body. (I knew it was food-induced because I'd seen him react like this before.)

All nine current U.S.-approved food dyes pose toxicity risks, according to toxicology researchers.[16] While many of these are not allowed in Europe or only allowed with labeling that they "may have an adverse effect on activity and attention in children," they are widely used in the US, not just in candy and cereal but also unexpected items like ketchup.[17] Let's take, for example, the food color additive red dye No. 3, which is produced from petroleum. It has been banned from U.S. cosmetics since

1990, yet stunningly has *still been allowed* in popular U.S. foods like chewing gum and candy and icing as well as medicines and nutritional shakes.[18] After 20 consumer groups filed a report,[19] California recently banned its use.[20] It can produce behavioral changes in both animals and children[21]—a particularly alarming fact when you consider that 10 percent of U.S. children are diagnosed with attention deficit hyperactivity disorder (ADHD).[22] It is also associated with cancer in animals.[23]

I see many of my children's peers medicated for behavioral issues—5.5 million kids aged two through eight in the U.S., to be exact. (You read that right—starting at two!) The scientist in me wonders how many of them could go off their behavioral medication if their diets were chemical-free. Moreover, scientists say that because children are in the prime stage of their development, they are especially vulnerable to the effects of these chemicals.[24]

My heart breaks for the parents of children who believe there's something wrong with their child and possibly even medicate their child when it's potentially the chemicals that the kids eat that are causing the problem.

Even if you try to eat in a healthy way and don't just consume junk food and pizza for three weeks straight like my college dormmates (who ended up in the ER with scurvy), chances are you're still consuming copious amounts of chemicals unknowingly! Flavor enhancers, preservatives, colorings, emulsifiers, sweeteners, and more.

For example, ever wonder what those innocent-sounding "natural flavors" are that are in almost every packaged food? Turns out they can be made up of over 100 ingredients, including MSG and known carcinogens.[25] Regular food starts to taste boring in contrast to the excitement of "natural flavors"—which is why they are now so pervasive you can't even buy tea without them—and which is how you get bound: hooked on different foods and overeating. Even pet food is filled with them, making cats think the cornmeal they are eating is actually fish.

Parabens, preservatives known to cause cancer[26] are routinely found in medication—even for infants. A third of chocolate products test high for heavy metals[27] as does baby food[28] and pharmaceutical products.[29] The accumulation of heavy metals in the brain is associated with autism,[30] Parkinson's disease, Alzheimer's disease, Huntington's disease,[31] and more.[32]

There's so much more we could go into, like hormones in meat and dairy, pesticides, and I know this can get depressing so I'll stop here. That's not the point, because you can do your own research. My point is that, with knowledge and awareness, we can make sovereign choices.

It's critical to watch the messages coming our way—and the imprints they develop. After all, Big Agriculture spends upward of $150 million to influence our consumer choices.[33] The food industry pays influencers to promote their products on social media.[34] An energy drink marketed by a YouTube influencer to children—Prime—became really popular yet contains potentially dangerous levels of caffeine (six times the amount in Coke).[35] Caffeine products are marketed to children as young as four.[36] How many parents of toddlers and elementary school children who love soda realize their child's hyperactivity may be due to it? How many know that researchers recommend no caffeine for kids under 12 so as not to develop neurological, cardiac, and sleep problems?[37]

But aaaah! We so often just don't want to know! Life's complicated enough. Changing our lifestyle can seem impossible. Plus we have strong feelings about our food. After a healthcare professional told a colleague of mine that he might be allergic to dairy, he got so upset on the way home that he tripped, seriously injuring his leg, had to undergo surgery, and was unable to walk for three months. The idea of losing his milk literally took the legs out from under him. That's how strong our food attachments are.

We Don't Want to Take Responsibility

We would so much rather get an easy answer, a magic pill, instead of having to leave our comfort zone. Psychology research shows we tend to gravitate to the easier choices.[38] Yet one of the biggest ways we get bound is that we fall for the idea that we don't need to take responsibility if we can just find the right pill. As I'm writing this, there's a huge trend for weight-loss shots.

Why go to the trouble of getting on a healthy diet and exercise regimen if you can just get a shot?

And that's how we get bound, because reaching for the easy answer could cost us a lot—as it did for JT and the multitude of prescriptions he was handed instead of receiving recommendations to change his lifestyle. And of course, it's not entirely our fault that we think this way. Big Pharma spends $30 billion[39] a year on marketing and spends upwards of $250 million on lobbying Congress.[40] Drugs are a big and growing business after all: in 1980 nationwide spending on prescription drugs accounted for $12 billion, in 2000 $122 billion, and in 2021 $378 billion.[41]

Viola suffered from a kidney disease. After having a severe reaction to medications that sent her to the hospital and almost took her life, she looked into alternate ways to support her kidneys. She shifted to a plant-based low-protein diet and kidney-friendly foods.[42] Her cysts became smaller, and her pain disappeared. X-rays showed more improvement via her diet than ever before.

A few years ago, I met a fellow researcher at Yale Medical School who studies Viola's exact disease. I was eager to ask her what she knew about diet for the disease, having heard firsthand how much it helped Viola. Here's what she answered: "Researchers used to study diet a few decades ago, but we don't do that anymore because all our funding comes from pharmaceutical companies." Pharmaceutical companies are subsidizing medical schools,[43] directly impacting how future physicians are trained and what is researched. See that? No one stands to profit from Viola helping herself and being sovereign—only Viola stands to profit from that.

Not only does Big Pharma subsidize much of the research conducted in medical schools, it often jointly researches it[44]—a clear conflict of interest—and, worse yet, ghostwrites the results.[45] In the disturbing words of a review article on the subject, it's no wonder that "systematic bias favors products which are made by the company funding the research."[46]

I'm not saying that pills aren't often a freaking godsend. Thinking I could get away with just Tylenol after a surgeon cut my stomach open for gallbladder surgery instead of the much stronger pain meds she recommended was by far the least brilliant idea I ever had—it's up there with the time I flew into Lhasa, Tibet (12,000 feet of elevation), from Shanghai (0 elevation) without altitude sickness medication and had more than a few hard yaks in the land of yaks. My point is that relying only on pills and disregarding prevention—that isn't sovereignty.

I see a similar trend in mental health. We receive lots of information and advertisements about medical treatments for our mental health but little if any about the easy, low-cost, or free things research shows can improve our well-being without side effects or dependence. (Many of which I'm sharing throughout the book.) Many people financially benefit from you binding your body; *you* benefit from taking responsibility for it and being sovereign.

SOVEREIGN BODY

A sovereign relationship with our bodies is one that deeply respects the body. It takes awareness and that other sovereign skill: courage. But it's worth it.

So how do you become sovereign in body? Exercise and rest are obviously a given and something you've undoubtedly heard about a lot.

Eat Plant-Forward

Research is substantiating the saying attributed to Hippocrates: "Let thy food be thy medicine." In particular, it's a really good idea to be plant-forward. A plant-forward diet is a diet that doesn't restrict you from eating any foods but heavily emphasizes plants: fruits and vegetables.

Researchers at the University of Warwick tracked more than 12,000 randomly chosen individuals and discovered that people who go from a diet containing no fruit and vegetables to incorporating up to eight portions per day experienced an improvement in mood and life satisfaction "equivalent to moving from unemployment to employment."[47] The scientists, even after taking into consideration other happiness-inducing events such as income increases or new romantic relationships, discovered that happiness continued to increase incrementally for each additional daily portion of fruits and veggies, up to a maximum of eight.

Similarly, Drs. Tamlin Conner and Caroline Horwath of the University of Otago asked people to record their food consumption and mood and discovered that the more fruit and vegetables someone eats, the happier they are that day and the next.[48] Eating more fruits and vegetables is associated with a lower risk of psychological distress.[49] We know fruits and vegetables are essential for physical health, but they're also the mental health hack we've probably never heard of. This is a sovereignty tip you're not likely to hear from your psychiatrist—yet! Researchers are pushing for diet to be considered in psychiatry[50] because studies are showing that healthier diets benefit ailments like depression,[51] possibly because these diets' high-nutrient value help prevent deficiencies linked to mental health problems.

You might think, well, maybe people who are happier tend to eat more fruit so maybe these subjects were happy to begin with. To test that theory, Conner's group ran a follow-up study in which they divided people into different groups. Only one received extra fruit and vegetables to consume and only that group showed improved psychological well-being.[52]

These are not just one-off studies. A meta-analysis (a research paper that compiles many studies) of diet interventions for mental health found that "high total intake of fruits and vegetables, and some of their specific subgroups including berries, citrus, and green leafy vegetables, may promote higher levels of optimism and self-efficacy, as well as reduce the level of psychological distress [. . .] and protect against depressive symptoms."[53] Another meta-analysis looking specifically at young adults showed that a higher intake of fruit in particular appears to be preventative for depression.[54] On the flip side, unhealthy dietary patterns were associated with poorer mental health in children and adolescents.[55]

It's not just well-being that is improved but also cognitive function.[56] Several studies show that eating more fruits and vegetables could delay or prevent age-related cognitive decline. One study even showed that people consuming high amounts of fruit and vegetables end up performing better on cognitive tasks than healthy adults consuming low amounts of fruit and vegetables.[57] (If you think of the food deserts—areas with limited access to affordable and nutritious food—in many low-income communities, people are bound by the circumstances of their environment—trapped in a situation where the only food choices they have are processed with low to no access to fresh fruit and vegetables.)

No wonder high-performing athletes who continue their profession into their 40s find that avoiding unhealthy foods, chemicals, caffeine, alcohol, and excess animal products can help them continue to thrive despite their age. Tom Brady is arguably the most famous face in American football. He was the oldest NFL MVP at 40, the oldest Super Bowl MVP at 43, and the oldest quarterback selected to the Pro Bowl at 44.[58] He adheres to a strict regimen of nine hours of sleep, lots of water, and an 80 percent plant-forward diet free of dairy, sugar, gluten, refined carbohydrates, caffeine, genetically modified food like corn and soy, MSG, trans fats, overly processed foods, and processed meats.[59] Many top athletes also avoid meat, including *Sports Illustrated* Olympian of the Century Carl Lewis, top ultramarathon runner Scott Jurek, tennis legend Chris Evert, football star Ricky Williams, baseball slugger Prince Fielder, boxing champion Keith Holmes, and NBA standouts Raja Bell and Salim Stoudamire.[60]

These lifestyle choices are controversial and even triggering—think of my colleague with the broken knee. That's where courage comes in. Sometimes sovereignty means stretching your comfort zone.

If you're wondering how much fruit and vegetables you should be eating, the studies above and others recommend eight servings daily.[61]

When we find sovereignty to change our food and eat clean low-chemical, plant-forward diets, we often see that this happily leads to better farming or fishing practices that are gentle on the earth. It can feel positive and empowering to know that when you recapture sovereignty for your body by changing what you put into it, you're also becoming part of a growing movement to protect the future of our children, save biodiversity, and ensure healthy ecosystems can thrive for generations to come.[62]

Detox

Develop sovereignty over your consumer choices. This has become easier as more and more people become aware of the effects of chemicals on their health. The Environmental Working Group is a bipartisan nonprofit that offers useful information on consumer choices that are aligned with both human health and planetary health. Startup companies and even established brands are starting to develop cleaner products with fewer and less toxic ingredients. More consumers are waking up and demanding less toxic products. They're voting with their dollars and that's why you now see so many brands assuring customers that they are phthalate-free and BPA-free. You can buy toys and clothes made of organic materials like cotton, wool, and silk. Some car seat manufacturers are even using naturally flame-retardant textiles like wool, for example.

After seeing the effects of chemicals on my childrens' mental and physical health, I had to do a lifestyle overhaul. I ended up moisturizing baby two's sensitive butt with coconut oil, feeding my kids mostly plant-forward whole foods (which can be done on a budget by ordering organic food that doesn't look perfect, joining a food co-op, growing a garden, or using a shared garden), and cleaning the house with vinegar and baking soda (the former being Husband's least favorite smell in the world unless it's on a caprese salad). They are cheap, nontoxic, and effective. We're done with eczema and food-based meltdowns, but Husband leaves the house on cleaning days and happily eats out whenever he gets a chance.

It can feel like an overwhelming task when we (and our children) are used to the flavor-enhanced high-sugar treats out there—after all, some researchers have even claimed that sugar has similarly addictive properties as cocaine[63] that manifest as attention deficit disorder. But the good news is that many companies are expressly not using chemicals or refined sugars in tasty snacks and ready-made foods. There's a lot more to choose from now than there was 10 years ago.

I am not going to lie—even for my own family, it was work to change our routine. But when I am healthier and happier and my boys are healthy and feeling good, we all win. Sovereignty is making choices aligned with what is right for you.

Some people think these kinds of clean food and lifestyle choices are extreme and even offensive because it calls into question their own choices, and I get it. It's more effort to live like this in our society, and making changes is hard. So start small to make it manageable.

As with everything, no need to go overboard. It's easy to become obsessive. Take the story of my uncle who had a thing about backside hygiene. While traveling and deprived of his home bidet, he decided to wash his behind in the hotel sink. By sitting in it. Never mind that he weighed 240 pounds. Well, the sink broke away from the wall, and, as it did so, took the whole wall with it, leaving him butt naked in a sink on the floor, framed by fountains of water from the broken pipes. It's better not to take things too far (although it can make for an unforgettable vacation).

Balance

Instead, stay balanced in all things. Take our stressful lifestyles, for example. We value productivity so much, we forget the value of restoring ourselves. Question the belief that you need stress to be productive because it flies in the face of the data. You think you're getting things done better and faster, but you're actually on the superhighway to system failure. Thus the afternoon crash and, over time, the chronic fatigue and burnout. No professional athlete would dream of being in go-go-go mode all the time without periods of restoration—that would incur injury! But the rest of us do.

Here's a flashback to 10 years ago pre-kids. I had thrown my body out of whack with too many years of stress and strain, ignoring its need for proper rest and failing to take proper care of it. Husband (then fiancé), by default of being in the military, ate extreme stress for breakfast. Consequently, we were way out of balance.

Given that my biological clock was ticking and fiancé was about to deploy for an entire year, we defied his religious beliefs and started "trying" for a baby pre-wedding. When I still wasn't pregnant on our nuptials, my type-A-go-getter-won't-take-no-for-an-answer side hunted for a solution pronto. My sister-in-law had gotten pregnant thanks to acupuncture, so I found an acupuncturist who Yelp said was getting everyone in SoCal pregnant.

Picture the scene: Acupuncturist's waiting room is plastered with pictures of grateful fertile adults with the offspring the acupuncturist undoubtedly helped them produce. Needled up, I ask acupuncturist if he does dudes too. No, only the rare case of overheated testicles (sperm suffer from heatstroke too, you know). Given Husband trains in the hot California desert for weeks on end, I take zero chances and drag him to see acupuncturist.

During his session, Husband lies there stiffly, getting progressively paler—especially when acupuncturist tests Husband's testicular temperature by lifting Husband's family jewels with two bare fingers to plop a thermometer underneath. Turns out that, in addition to my unbalanced hormones, my desert-training Marine, who remains dead silent and refuses to look at me for the entire session, has the rare case of hot balls! To address this fertility fiasco and to Husband's continued horror, acupuncturist places needles in Husband's groin and—why stop there?—runs electricity through them.

A few months later, I got to send a positive pregnancy result to deployed Husband and of course add another glowing review to acupuncturist's Yelp page.

If you're anything like Husband, you associate "natural" solutions with crunchy granola yoga retreats or dance-around-the-fire-in-the-moonlight witchcraft. But that's throwing the baby away with the bathwater. Having worked as a research scientist in medical schools at Stanford and Yale for most of my career, I have a deep respect for medicine. But one thing to note is that it tends to focus on medical interventions *after* a health problem has arisen. Traditional forms of medicine (e.g., Chinese medicine) seeks to create balance in the body and prevent problems from arising in the first place while helping to manage chronic healthcare problems.

Many well-known healthcare facilities like Mayo Clinic and Duke University Medical Center now offer integrative medicine, which Mayo defines as "an approach to health care that includes practices not traditionally part of conventional medicine, such as acupuncture, massage, yoga, dietary supplements, wellness coaching, and meditation. In many situations, as evidence of their effectiveness and safety grows, these therapies are used with conventional medicine."[64]

When I had postpartum anxiety, I went to visit an integrative neurologist also trained in Ayurveda—traditional Indian medicine that has been around for thousands of years. She recommended self-massages with specific oils for my physiological makeup. From a Western perspective, we would consider giving yourself oil massages simply "hydrating the skin." How could it possibly benefit my mental health and aid my sleep? And yet it made such a difference that I still use this practice when I need to. It's easy, cheap, and can be self-administered without side effects. Most importantly, it gave me sovereignty over my postpartum mental health.

Just because there is no extensive research on it doesn't mean it's ineffective—it just means it hasn't been studied yet.

Nature

One of the best-kept secrets to having a sovereign body, is aligning it with nature. We treat nature like it's an external thing—a nice thing to go into occasionally. Maybe a hike or a few days of camping. While Indigenous traditions have long honored nature, we often tend to destroy it. But as we split from nature, we inevitably split from ourselves.

Because we forget that we are a product of nature. We were born somewhere around seven pounds and all the weight we have accumulated since then is from food and water stemming from nature. We are part and parcel of nature. Isn't it *wild*, then, that we don't work toward self-preservation?

That's probably why we benefit so much from listening to its laws: resting, exercising, and nourishing ourselves according to our circadian rhythm and physiological needs.

Exposure to nature is also a powerful way to cultivate physical, mental, and emotional sovereignty, though it is not discussed enough because nature has no marketing agents being paid to promote it like products on shelves do.

Research on more than 400,000 people showed that for every extra hour you spend outdoors during the day, you're more likely to be happier and less likely to have depression or use antidepressants. You're less tired and have less insomnia because your circadian rhythm is more balanced.[65] Another study on 16,000 urban dwellers found that visiting natural spaces (parks, lakes, etc.) three to four times a week was linked to 33 percent lower odds of being on psychiatric medication.[66] Yet Richard Louv, author of *Last Child in the Woods* (the haunting title says it all), explains that many people suffer from "nature deficit disorder."

There are too many studies on nature's health benefits to mention. Here are just a few examples:

- Natural light helps you regulate your circadian rhythm[67] and improves your emotional well-being[68]
- Seeing or hearing birds improves your mental health for hours after the encounter, even when you have drug-resistant depression.[69] Just hearing an audio recording of birdsong can alleviate anxiety, depression, and paranoia.[70]
- A "nature pill" of 20 minutes of exposure to anything that makes you feel connected to nature is sufficient to reduce levels of the stress hormone cortisol.[71] Ten minutes is the minimal dose[72] and the recommended dose per week is two hours for greater physical health and well-being.[73]
- Researchers in Finland recommend five hours in nature per month to reduce depression, alcoholism, and suicide[74]

- South Korea uses nature therapy for firefighters with post-traumatic stress[75]
- U.S. and Canadian physicians can prescribe nature therapy to help with mental and physical health[76]

Nature is even good for:

- Social health: Spending time in nature improves self-esteem in children[77] and cooperation in adults
- Brain function: Nature sounds (as opposed to urban sounds) also improves cognitive function like attention,[78] memory,[79] and creativity[80]
- Physical health: Nature protects against diseases, including depression, diabetes, obesity, ADHD, cardiovascular disease, cancer, and many more,[81] possibly via strengthening our immune system[82]

No matter how far you live from a natural environment, there is always a plant you can have on a desk and a tree you can notice down your road. There's a lunch break you can take outside, a call you can take on a walk around the block, and an evening stroll you can take when the day is done. And research shows that every single exposure to nature—even if it's a screensaver[83]—has a benefit for your mental health and well-being.

***

Are you willing to honor your self so much (as discussed in Chapter 2), that you're willing to take responsibility for your body?

Are you willing to experience your feelings (as discussed in Chapter 3) instead of physically abusing your body with addictive habits?

Are you willing to let go of imprints (as discussed in Chapter 4) that make you treat your body like an enemy instead of the loyal friend it is?

Are you willing to have a positively energizing relationship (as discussed in Chapter 5) with your body to benefit your physical and mental health?

Are you willing to go with your intuition (Chapter 6) to take care of your body in the way that it needs even if it goes against the grain or doesn't make sense to others?

If so, you will have a sovereign relationship with your body.

Your body is the only home you'll have for life. Honoring its needs makes sense. Why not resolve, once and for all, to take care of the shell in which you dwell?

Our body is the ground of our existence. It's our basis. Our root. Our very foundation. Stabilize it. Optimize it. Don't give it away. Don't betray it. It's working so hard to keep you alive.

Fall in love with this vehicle, this exquisitely fine-tuned instrument that houses you. Loyal, loving, and keeping you alive despite everything. It is your home for life. The means by which you perceive the world, interact with it, and enjoy it. It is completely devoted to you. Make it a good relationship filled with gratitude, care, and respect.

SIDE EFFECTS OF HAVING A SOVEREIGN BODY ⚠

Improved mental and physical health: By reducing toxicity in your life and increasing health-promoting lifestyle habits, you will see an improvement in both your mood and your physical health.

Less stress: As you start to respect your body's need for rest and balance, you'll find your stress will decrease significantly.

Choosiness: You'll become picky, picky, picky with food and consumer products, but you'll feel better for it. It might be a little more complicated than usual to go out to eat or to shop for things, but it's worth it. If you don't look out for you and your loved ones, who will?

Nature love: You'll develop a greater appreciation for plants, trees, parks, and natural environments.

SOVEREIGN BODY TOOL KIT

Relate to your body as your best friend, because that's what it is.

Sovereignty is learning to love your body, learning to care for it, learning to listen to it, and learning to live in harmony with its natural needs because you are so grateful to it. It gave you life! Your relationship with your body can be a deeply respectful, mutually beneficial relationship. Prioritize resting it well whenever possible, eating well whenever possible, and hydrating and exercising it well. Connect with nature whenever you can. This requires that sovereign skill: awareness. Listen for your body's needs; tune in to when you need to rest, exercise, eat better, hydrate, and spend time outside.

Get off the stress bandwagon.

There are many unavoidable stressors in life. But don't pile on more by believing you need to be in go-go-go mode all the time. Quit overcaffeinating, overcommitting, overdoing. Remember that's just the highway to burnout.

Even if you think you have no ability to make restorative choices for yourself, consider what you do during the times you are home. You may have an extremely busy schedule, but presumably you have at least an hour or 30 minutes to yourself a day. Consider what you're choosing to do during that time. Watching shows? Social media? Scrolling? Are these activities regenerating your energy and calming you down or evoking stress and exhaustion? Consider reframing your choices around this idea. *In the few minutes I have to myself, will this activity fill my tank or empty it?*

So what if, because you did something restorative, you didn't get things done. Or you got them done imperfectly. Or you only got one teeny thing done. So what? You didn't come undone. You were happy.

Check in with yourself regularly.

I have learned to use my free time as wisely as I can. I will first check in with my energy levels, if I'm depleted, I'll go for something restorative: meditation, taking a bath, napping, reading, listening to something funny or uplifting or wise, or speaking to a friend or family member. When I'm feeling energized, my cup is full, so I'll do work, reach out to someone I know who needs a little support, do something creative like write an article that might help some readers, or bake something for my family.

Low-toxicity lifestyle.

Consider making small changes to reduce your consumption of chemicals via lifestyle products and food. This can either feel overwhelming (there's so much to take on!) or empowering (I am cleaning up my life!). Taking small incremental steps will make this more manageable. Don't tackle it all at once. I've sprinkled some tips throughout this chapter, but there is so much more to learn and valuable content you can read on websites like those of the Environmental Working Group (ewg.org).

Eat plant-forward.

You know by now how much I like to experiment. I have a show-me attitude about things and encourage you to do the same. Be a skeptical scientist: Don't believe it 'til you see it. Try to include more fruits and vegetables in your diet for a few weeks and monitor your well-being in the process. Find fun ways to do so, whether via smoothies, fruit bars or fresh juices, or new recipes.

Be in nature.

Spend more time in nature, go out for a hike, or a walk in a park. If you can't do that, bring nature into your home with plants and pictures or even screen savers of nature. Knowing that 20 minutes a day in nature reduces your stress levels, make that your daily goal with a weekly goal of a total of at least 2 hours a week.

Reflect on these questions.

Do you honor and care for your body the way you would a child or pet you are taking care of? If not, what would it look like, if you did?

For additional tools and ideas, visit my website at www.iamsov.com.

The Rhythm

The first sound,
You ever heard,
Inside your mother's
Womb,
Was a rhythm,
A cadence,
A constant
Throbbing
Beat:
Her heart.

At the core of Mother Nature
Is a rhythm,
A cadence,
A constant
Throbbing
Beat:
Her Heart.

Seasons shifting,
Moon ebbing,
Tides flowing,
Wind blowing,
Plants growing.

Light and dark,
Cold and warm,
Wet and dry,
Day and night.

Billions of
Footsteps pounding,
Vessels pumping,
Insects humming,
Raindrops plummeting.

Billions of
Beings breathing their first.
Billions of
Beings breathing their last.
A constant
Everlasting Rhythmic Sway.
Creating Equilibrium.
Perfect Equilibrium.

This Rhythm In Nature
That all
Respect.
To which all Abide.
All,
That is,
Except Humans.

How have we walked so far
From Nature's womb
That we have
Fallen
Out of her Rhythm
To the point
Of no longer hearing it
At all.

In this moment,
Inside your own chest
Feel the rhythm of
Your own heart
Loving you
Every second
Into life.

Honor your body
Honor your life.
Get back into the Rhythm.
Dance.

PARTING NOTE

This book came to me as a current. A current of energy and insight. It compelled me to write this book. I felt it long before I put pen to page.

And I hope you too have felt it. A current of energy, of delight, of truth, of boldness, and of profound awareness. Perhaps it felt like a remembering. Because somewhere, deep down, you've always known that you are sovereign. You were born sovereign.

This book is an invitation. An invitation to come home to yourself. And as you honor yourself more and more, you will find you also honor others and the planet as a whole—because you realize we are all connected, not separate.

Besides, sovereignty is profoundly natural. Isn't it only natural to have a life-supportive relationship with yourself? To let emotions flow? To clear your mind? To uplift yourself and others? To listen to your gut? And to honor your body? It's common sense.

Sovereignty introduces greater ease to your life, clarity to your mind, and peace to your heart. As you live in greater alignment with yourself, you feel energized, integrated, whole, healed, and complete.

But sovereignty is more than that. Sovereignty puts you in touch with your potential. The full-blown field of possibility that is YOU.

What will you choose to do with this potential?

You have the option—if you choose—to be of great service to the world and to deeply benefit others by offering your unique gifts: your wisdom, your skill set, your knowledge, your personality, your values, your humor, and so much more.

Having looked at the research on happiness and fulfillment over the last 20 years, here is my summary in one sentence: the people who are the happiest and live the healthiest and longest lives are those whose lives are characterized by compassion for others balanced with compassion for themselves.

Millions of people can love you and that can be nice, but the greatest fulfillment you'll feel is in the act of loving. The love so many of us seek is the love that already exists inside of us—waiting to be deployed. The most profound experience of love is the one you feel in your own heart for others and for yourself.

Research shows that even small acts of kindness have ripple effects that impact three degrees of separation away from us. You offering a kind word to the person at the cash register of your local supermarket will ripple out in a cascade reaction of kindness to that woman's son's teacher. The impact one person can have is unfathomable. Your potential is immense.

And don't forget that, by being sovereign, you are modeling sovereignty for other people. You are showing them that they, too, have the option of living with freedom. Your very life becomes an act of service.

Of course, there will be days when you won't feel sovereign, when you will feel tired, and stressed, and anxious, and may even feel downright sorry for yourself or mind-blowingly angry. Totally bound and tied up in knots.

But the fact of the matter is, no matter how upset you get, there will still be a part of you that's sovereign.

Because even then, the awareness you've developed will be quietly observing the scene, waiting for you to come back to center, which you will—it might take a nap or a meal or a month, but you will. Because once you are aware—and you are now after reading this book—you will never be asleep again. You've woken up.

Sovereignty is a journey you have begun and an adventure that you will continue. If you meditate or engage in other habits that cultivate sovereignty, such as the ones I've described throughout this book, the current of sovereignty will continue to grow and enliven within you and your awareness will continue to strengthen and expand.

I encourage you to revisit and dive into the takeaways at the end of each chapter again and again.

And so I now raise my glass to YOU, my dear (full of some sort of nonalcoholic, uncaffeinated, healthy sovereignty-inducing beverage, no doubt).

To your freedom, to your happiness, to your fullest potential, to the gift that you are to this world. Remember it always. Remember your song. Sing yourself home.

May you be sovereign.

Love,
Emma

Remember Your Majesty

You are so much more powerful
Than you think,
Than you know,
Than you ever dreamed.
But confined inside a box of limited
Identities
Fears
Rules and regulations
Should and should nots
Beliefs
You have made yourself small.
And in your smallness
You have forgotten.
Plain forgotten.
Like the elephant
Who was once tied to a peg
As a baby
And still thinks
As an adult
That that wimpy peg
Is sufficient to keep him
Bound.
Laughable, really.
A multi-ton
Elephant
Bound
By
A teeny-weeny
Peg.
That's us too.
Forgotten.
Our multi-ton
Potential
And strength.
Mightiness
And
Majesty.
Do not ever
Forget
Again
The power
In your loins
In your veins
In your guts.
We need you
As you
Fierce
Warrior
Creator
Lover
You.
We need you
To sing us
Your song.
Sing
It to us.
Sing.

RESOURCES

The journey of sovereignty is rich, and there are many things you can do to support yourself in the process. There is, in fact, more than I could fit in the chapters' tool kits. So, if you want to dive deeper, I offer you some resources:

- A website where you can find additional tools to help you on your journey—videos, audio recordings, graphics, exercises, a newsletter, and more. Go to iamsov.com or scan the QR code on this page to take you there.
- Social media platforms where I aim to post only sovereignty-supportive material, and—in the spirit of sovereignty—not too much of it!

Instagram: @thehappinesstrack

Facebook: facebook.com/emma.seppala

LinkedIn: linkedin.com/in/emmaseppala

X: twitter.com/emmaseppala

ENDNOTES

Chapter 1

1. Nasreen Sheikh, n.d., https://www.nasreensheikh.org/.

2. Julie Piering, "Diogenes of Sinope," *The Philosophers' Magazine*, accessed December 28, 2003, https://archive.philosophersmag.com/diogenes-of-sinope/.

3. Richard Stoneman, *Legends of Alexander the Great* (London: I.B. Tauris, 2011), 43–47.

4. "Stepping or Step Dancing, A Story," African American Registry, accessed December 28, 2023, https://aaregistry.org/story/stepping-or-step-dancing-a-brief-story/.

5. Heather Longley, "Step Afrika's C. Brian Williams Discusses a Rebellion's Role in the History of Percussive Dance," Center for the Performing Arts at Penn State, Penn State College of Arts and Architecture, accessed December 28, 2023, https://cpa.psu.edu/features/williams-discusses-rebellion's-role-percussive-dance.

6. Alvin Powell, "Pandemic Pushes Mental Health to the Breaking Point," *Harvard Gazette*, January 27, 2021, https://news.harvard.edu/gazette/story/2021/01/pandemic-pushing-people-to-the-breaking-point-say-experts/.

7. Adam Grant, "There's a Name for the Blah You're Feeling: It's Called Languishing," *The New York Times*, April 19, 2021, https://www.nytimes.com/2021/04/19/well/mind/covid-mental-health-languishing.html.

8. "Hybrid Work Is Just Work: Are We Doing It Wrong?" Work Trend Index Special Report, September 22, 2022, accessed December 28, 2023, https://www.microsoft.com/en-us/worklab/work-trend-index/hybrid-work-is-just-work?wt.mc_id=AID_M365Worklab_Corp_HQ_Charter.; "Winter Snapshot 2022/2023," Future Forum Pulse, February 15, 2023, https://futureforum.com/research/future-forum-pulse-winter-2022-2023-snapshot/.; "Cigna Healthcare Vitality Study 2023," Cigna Global, October 2023, https://www.cignaglobal.com/blog/thought-leadership/cigna-healthcare-vitality-study-2023#How.

9. Jim Harter, "U.S. Employee Engagement Drops for First Year in a Decade," Gallup Workplace, January 7, 2022, https://www.gallup.com/workplace/388481/employee-engagement-drops-first-year-decade.aspx; Jim Harter, "U.S. Employee Engagement Needs a Rebound in 2023," Gallup Workplace, January 25, 2023, https://www.gallup.com/workplace/468233/employee-engagement-needs-rebound-2023.aspx.

10. "Anxiety Disorders - Facts & Statistics," Anxiety and Depression Association of America, accessed September 7, 2023, https://adaa.org/understanding-anxiety/facts-statistics.; "Mental Health by the Numbers," National Alliance on Mental Illness, accessed January 18, 2023, https://nami.org/mhstats.; Covid-19 Mental Disorders Collaborators, "Global Prevalence and Burden of Depressive and Anxiety Disorders in 204 Countries and Territories in 2020 Due to the Covid-19 Pandemic," *The Lancet*, October 8, 2021, accessed January, 24, 2023, https://www.thelancet.com/journals/lancet/article/PIIS0140-6736(21)02143-7/fulltext.; "Quick Facts and Statistics about Mental Health," Mental Health America, Accessed January 18, 2023, https://mhanational.org/mentalhealthfacts.; "Workplace Benefits Trends: Employee Well-Being and Mental Health," Aflac WorkForces Report 2022-2023, Aflac, https://www.aflac.com/docs/awr/pdf/2022-trends-and-topics/2022-aflac-awr-employee-well-being-and-mental-health.pdf.

Chapter 2

1. Rob Knight, "Eight in 10 Young Adults Feel They Are Not Good Enough, Poll Claims," *The Independent*, Home News section November 1, 2019, https://www.independent.co.uk/news/uk/home-news/millennials-mental-health-love-young-adults-social-media-poll-alpro-a9181296.html.

2. R.F. Baumeister et al., "Bad is Stronger Than Good," *Review of General Psychology*, 5 no.4 (December 2001): 323–370, https://doi.org/10.1037/1089-2680.5.4.323.

3. Larry Stevens, and C. Chad Woodruff, *The Neuroscience of Empathy, Compassion, and Self-Compassion* (Cambridge, MA, 2018).

4. Ricks Warren, Elke Smeets, and Kristin Neff, "Self-Criticism and Self-Compassion: Risk and Resilience: Being Compassionate to Oneself Is Associated with Emotional Resilience and Psychological Well-Being," *Current Psychiatry* 15, no. 12 (December 2016), link.gale.com/apps/doc/A474714850/AONE?u=anon~25cfd642&sid=googleScholar&xid=059a891c.; S. J. Blatt et al., "Dependency and Self-Criticism: Psychological Dimensions of Depression," *Journal of Consulting and Clinical Psychology* 50 (1982): 113–124.; Blatt, "Representational Structures in Psychopathology," in D. Cicchetti & S. Toth (Eds.), *Rochester Symposium on Developmental Psychopathology: Emotion, Cognition, and Representation* 6 (Rochester: University of Rochester Press, 1995): 1–34.

5. Amy Cantazaro and Meifen Wei, "Adult Attachment, Dependence, Self-Criticism, and Depressive Symptoms: A Test of a Mediational Model," *Journal of Personality* 78, no. 4 (2010): 1135–1162, https://doi.org/10.1111/j.1467-6494.2010.00645.; Paul Gilbert and Jeremy N.V. Miles, "Sensitivity to Social Put-Down: It's Relationship to Perceptions of Social Rank, Shame, Social Anxiety, Depression, Anger and Self-Other Blame," *Personality and Individual Differences* 29, no. 4 (2000): 757–774, https://doi.org/10.1016/S0191-8869(99)00230-5.; Norman Fazaa and Stewart Page, "Personality Style and Impulsivity as Determinants of Suicidal Subgroups," *Archives of Suicide Research* 13, no. 1 (January 2, 2009): 31–45, https://doi.org/10.1080/13811110802572122.

6. Brenna M. Williams and Cheri A. Levinson, "A Model of Self-Criticism as a Transdiagnostic Mechanism of Eating Disorder Comorbidity: A Review," *New Ideas in Psychology* 66, (August 2022): 100949, https://doi.org/10.1016/j.newideapsych.2022.100949.; Alexandra V. Rose and Katharine A. Rimes, "Self-Criticism Self-Report Measures: Systematic Review," *Psychology and Psychotherapy* 91, vol. 4 (January 18, 2018): 450–489, https://doi.org/10.1111/papt.12171.; Ruth McIntyre, Patrick Smith, and Katharine

Rimes, "The Role of Self-Criticism in Common Mental Health Difficulties in Students: A Systematic Review of Prospective Studies," *Mental Health & Prevention*, (June 1, 2018): 13–27, https://doi.org/10.1016/j.mhp.2018.02.003.; David M. Dunkley and Carlos M. Grilo, "Self-Criticism, Low Self-Esteem, Depressive Symptoms, and Over-Evaluation of Shape and Weight in Binge Eating Disorder Patients," *Behaviour Research and Therapy* 45, no. 1 (January 2007): 139–149, https://doi.org/10.1016/j.brat.2006.01.017.

7. Marc Brackett, *Permission to Feel: Unlocking the Power of Emotions to Help Our Kids, Ourselves, and Our Society Thrive* (New York: Celadon Books, 2019), 214.
8. Roy F. Baumeister and Mark R. Leary, "The Need to Belong: Desire for Inter personal Attachments as a Fundamental Human Motivation." *Psychological Bulletin* 1117, no. 3 (May 1995): 497–529. PMID: 7777651.
9. Naomi I. Eisenberger, "The Neural Bases of Social Pain: Evidence for Shared Representations with Physical Pain," *Psychosomatic Medicine* 74, no. 2 (Feb–Mar 2012): 126–135, https://doi.org/10.1097/psy.0b013e3182464dd1.
10. Baumeister, "The need to belong." *Psychological Bulletin.*
11. Julianne Holt-Lunstad, Timothy B. Smith, and J. Bradley Layton, "Social Relationships and Mortality Risk: A Meta-Analytic Review," *PLoS Medicine* 7, no. 7 (July 27, 2010), https://doi.org/10.1371/journal.pmed.1000316.
12. Sarah D. Pressman et al., "Loneliness, Social Network Size, and Immune Response to Influenza Vaccination in College Freshmen," *Health Psychology* 24, no. 3 (May 2005): 297–306, https://doi.org/10.1037/0278-6133.24.3.297.
13. Holt-Lunstad, "Social Relationships and Mortality Risk: A Meta-Analytic Review," *PLoS Medicine.*
14. Baumeister, "The need to belong." *Psychological Bulletin.*
15. Louise C. Hawkley and John T. Cacioppo, "Loneliness Matters: A Theoretical and Empirical Review of Consequences and Mechanisms," *Annals of Behavioral Medicine* 40, no. 2 (October 2010): 218–227, https://doi.org/10.1007/s12160-010-9210-8.
16. Anne Fernald, "Intonation and Communicative Intent in Mothers' Speech to Infants: Is the Melody the Message?" *Child Development* 60, (1989): 1497–1510, https://doi.org/10.2307/1130938.
17. Clara Dollar, "My So-Called (Instagram) Life," *The New York Times*, May 5, 2017, New York edition, Modern Love section, https://www.nytimes.com/2017/05/05/style/modern-love-my-so-called-instagram-life.html.
18. Erica J. Boothby et al., "The Liking Gap in Conversations: Do People Like Us More Than We Think?" *Psychological Science* 29, no. 11 (Nov 2018): 1742–1756, https://doi.org/10.1177/0956797618783714.; M. D. Lieberman and R. Rosenthal, "Why Introverts Can't Always Tell Who Likes Them: Multitasking and Nonverbal Decoding," *Journal of Personality and Social Psychology* 80, no. 2 (February 2001): 294–310, https://doi.org/10.1037/0022-3514.80.2.294.
19. Kristin Neff, *Self-Compassion: The Proven Power of Being Kind to Yourself* (New York: William Morrow, 2015).
20. "Psychologist: Asking Yourself 'What Do I Need' is an Act of Kindness," Full Circle with Anderson Cooper (video), https://www.cnn.com/videos/us/2021/08/09/psychologist-chris-germer-self-compassion-acfc-full-episode-vpx.cnn.
21. Timothy D. Wilson et al., "Just Think: The Challenges of the Disengaged Mind," *Science* 345, no. 6192 (July 4, 2014): 75–77, https://www.science.org/doi/10.1126/science.1250830.

22. Kristin D. Neff, Stephanie S. Rude, and Kristin L. Kirkpatrick, "An Examination of Self-Compassion in Relation to Positive Psychological Functioning and Personality Traits," *Journal of Research in Personality 41*, no. 4, (August 2007): 908–916, https://doi.org/10.1016/j.jrp.2006.08.002.

23. Eric Hernandez, "The Modern Native American Story," TEDxUCIrvine, TEDx Talks, YouTube, https://youtu.be/XuPxhromP3w?si=_-q5OwNP9qwqf-MJ.

24. Audre Lorde, *A Burst of Light and Other Essays* (Calabasas, CA: Ixia Press, 2017), 130.

25. Quoted in Francesca Rice, "Maya Angelou: An Extraordinarily Wise Woman," *Marie Claire*, April 4, 2014, https://www.marieclaire.co.uk/entertainment/people/maya-angelou-an-extraordinarily-wise-woman-84132.

26. Emily B. Reilly and Corri L. Stuyvenberg, "A Meta-Analysis of Loving-Kindness Meditations on Self-Compassion," *Mindfulness* 14 (September 9, 2022): 2299–2310, https://doi.org/10.1007/s12671-022-01972-x.

27. Johannes Graser and Ulrich Stangier, "Compassion and Loving-Kindness Meditation: An Overview and Prospects for the Application in Clinical Samples," *Harvard Review of Psychiatry* 26, no. 4 (July/August 2018): 201–215, https://doi.org/10.1097/hrp.0000000000000192.

Chapter 3

1. Shawn N. Katterman et al., "Mindfulness Meditation as an Intervention for Binge Eating, Emotional Eating, and Weight Loss: A Systematic Review," *Eating Behaviors* 15, no. 2 (April 2014): 197–204, https://doi.org/10.1016/j.eatbeh.2014.01.005.; Kathryn M. Godfrey, Linda C. Gallo, and Niloofar Afari, "Mindfulness-Based Interventions for Binge Eating: A Systematic Review and Meta-Analysis," *Journal of Behavioral Medicine* 38, no. 2 (April 2015): 348–362, https://doi.org/10.1007/s10865-014-9610-5.

2. Chai M. Tyng et al., "The Influences of Emotion on Learning and Memory," *Frontiers in Psychology* 24, no. 8 (August 2017): 1454, https://doi.org/10.3389/fpsyg.2017.01454.; Robert W. Levenson, "Stress and Illness: A Role for Specific Emotions," *Psychosomatic Medicine* 81, no. 8 (Oct 2019): 720–730, https://doi.org/10.1097/psy.0000000000000736.; Sarah Stewart-Brown, "Emotional Wellbeing and Its Relation to Health. Physical Disease May Well Result from Emotional Distress." *The BMJ* 317, no. 7173 (December 12, 1998): 1608–1609, https://doi.org/10.1136/bmj.317.7173.1608.; Gerben A. van Kleef and Stéphane Côté, "The Social Effects of Emotions," *Annual Review of Psychology* 73, no. 1 (January 4, 2022): 629–658, https://doi.org/10.1146/annurev-psych-020821-010855.

3. A. M. Kring and A. H. Gordon, "Sex Differences in Emotion: Expression, Experience, and Physiology," *Journal of Personality and Social Psychology* 74, no. 3 (March 1998): 686–703, https://doi.org/10.1037/0022-3514.74.3.686.

4. Rob Cross and Karen Dillon, "The Hidden Toll of Microstress" *Harvard Business Review*, Health and Wellness section, February 7, 2023, https://hbr.org/2023/02/the-hidden-toll-of-microstress.

5. Iris B. Mauss and James J. Gross, "Emotion Suppression and Cardiovascular Disease," *Emotional Expression and Health* (Oxfordshire: Routledge, 2004).; Iris B. Mauss, Silvia A. Bunge, and James J. Gross, "Automatic Emotion Regulation," *Social and Personality Psychology Compass* 1, no. 1 (September 5, 2007): 146–67, https://doi.org/10.1111/j.1751-9004.2007.00005.x.; Iris B. Mauss et al., "Emotion Control Values and Responding to an Anger Provocation in Asian American and European American Individuals," *Cognition*

and Emotion 24, no. 6 (September 1, 2010): 1026–1043, https://doi.org/10.1080/02699930903122273.

6. Philippe R. Goldin et al., "The Neural Bases of Emotion Regulation: Reappraisal and Suppression of Negative Emotion," *Biological Psychiatry* 63, no. 6 (March 15, 2008): 577–86, https://doi.org/10.1016/j.biopsych.2007.05.031.

7. Irene Messina, Alessandro Grecucci, and Roberto Viviani, "Neurobiological Models of Emotion Regulation: A Meta-Analysis of Neuroimaging Studies of Acceptance as an Emotion Regulation Strategy," *Social Cognitive and Affective Neuroscience* 16, no. 3 (January 21, 2021): 257–267, https://doi.org/10.1093/scan/nsab007.

8. Alia J. Crum et al., "The Role of Stress Mindset in Shaping Cognitive, Emotional, and Physiological Responses to Challenging and Threatening Stress," *Anxiety, Stress, & Coping* 30, no. 4 (January 25, 2017): 379–395, https://doi.org/10.1080/10615806.2016.1275585.

9. Jamil Zaki and W. Craig Williams, "Interpersonal Emotion Regulation," *Emotion* 13, no. 5 (October 2013): 803–810, https://doi.org/10.1037/a0033839.; Brett Marroquín and Susan Nolen-Hoeksema, "Emotion Regulation and Depressive Symptoms: Close Relationships as Social Context and Influence," *Journal of Personality and Social Psychology* 109, no. 5 (November 2015): 836–855, https://doi.org/10.1037/pspi0000034.

10. Emma Seppälä and Christina Bradley, "Handling Negative Emotions in a Way That's Good for Your Team," *Harvard Business Review*, June 11, 2019, https://hbr.org/2019/06/handling-negative-emotions-in-a-way-thats-good-for-your-team.

11. Brett Q. Ford and Allison S. Troy, "Reappraisal Reconsidered: A Closer Look at the Costs of an Acclaimed Emotion-Regulation Strategy," *Current Directions in Psychological Science* 28, no. 2 (February 27, 2019): 195–203, https://doi.org/10.1177/0963721419827526.

12. Amy F. T. Arnsten, "Stress Signalling Pathways That Impair Prefrontal Cortex Structure and Function," *National Reviews Neuroscience* 10, no. 6 (June 2009): 410–422, https://doi.org/10.1038/nrn2648.

13. Elizabeth Woo et al., "Chronic Stress Weakens Connectivity in the Prefrontal Cortex: Architectural and Molecular Changes," *Chronic Stress* 29, no. 5 (August 2021): 24705470211029254, https://doi.org/10.1177/24705470211029254.

14. Marc A. Russo, Danielle M. Santarelli, and Dean O'Rourke, "The Physiological Effects of Slow Breathing in the Healthy Human," *Breathe* 13, no. 4 (December 2017): 298–309, https://doi.org/10.1183/20734735.009817.

15. Russo, "The Physiological Effects of Slow Breathing in the Healthy Human," *Breathe*.

16. Pierre Philippot, Gaëtane Chapelle, and Sylvie Blairy, "Respiratory Feedback in the Generation of Emotion," *Cognition and Emotion* 16, no. 5 (2002): 605–627, https://doi.org/10.1080/02699930143000392.

17. Artin Arshamian et al., "Respiration Modulates Olfactory Memory Consolidation in Humans," *The Journal of Neuroscience* 38, no. 48 (November 28, 2018): 10286–10294, https://doi.org/10.1523/JNEUROSCI.3360-17.2018.

18. Sufyan Ashhad et al., "Breathing Rhythm and Pattern and Their Influence on Emotion," *Annual Review of Neuroscience* 8, no. 45 (July 2022): 223–247, https://doi.org/10.1146/annurev-neuro-090121-014424.

19. M. Allen, S. Varga, and D. H. Heck, "Respiratory Rhythms of the Predictive Mind," *Psychological Review 130*, no. 4 (2023): 1066–1080, https://doi.org/10.1037/rev0000391.

20. Adriano B. L. Tort, Jurij Brankačk, and Andreas Draguhn, "Respiration-Entrained Brain Rhythms Are Global but Often Overlooked," *Trends in Neurosciences* 41, no. 4 (April 2018): 186–197, https://doi.org/10.1016/j.tins.2018.01.007.

21. Pierre Philippot, "Respiratory Feedback in the Generation of Emotion," *Cognition and Emotion.*

22. Roderik J. S. Gerritsen and Guido P. H. Band, "Breath of Life: The Respiratory Vagal Stimulation Model of Contemplative Activity," *Frontiers in Human Neuroscience* 9, no. 12 (October 2018): 397, https://doi.org/10.3389/fnhum.2018.00397.

23. Yanli Lin et al., "On Variation in Mindfulness Training: A Multimodal Study of Brief Open Monitoring Meditation on Error Monitoring," *Brain Sciences* 6, no. 9 (September 2019): 226, https://doi.org/10.3390/brainsci9090226.

24. Kieran C. R. Fox et al., "Is Meditation Associated with Altered Brain Structure? A Systematic Review and Meta-Analysis of Morphometric Neuroimaging in Meditation Practitioners," *Neurosciences and Biobehavioral Reviews* 43, (June 2014): 48–73, https://doi.org/10.1016/j.neubiorev.2014.03.016.

25. Fox et al., "Is Meditation Associated with Altered Brain Structure?" *Neurosciences and Behavioral Reviews.*

26. Jian Xu et al., "Nondirective Meditation Activates Default Mode Network and Areas Associated with Memory Retrieval and Emotional Processing," *Frontiers in Human Neuroscience* 8 (February 2014): 86, https://doi.org/10.3389/fnhum.2014.00086.

27. Remi Daviet et al., "Associations between Alcohol Consumption and Gray and White Matter Volumes in the UK Biobank," *Nature Communications* 13, no. 1 (2022), https://doi.org/10.1038/s41467-022-28735-5.

28. Johannes Knabbe et al, "Single-Dose Ethanol Intoxication Causes Acute and Lasting Neuronal Changes in the Brain," *Proceedings of the National Academy of Sciences* 119, no. 25 (June 21, 2022), https://doi.org/10.1073/pnas.2122477119.; Harish R. Krishnan et al., "Unraveling the Epigenomic and Transcriptomic Interplay during Alcohol-Induced Anxiolysis," *Molecular Psychiatry* 27 (September 12, 2022): 4624–4632, https://doi.org/10.1038/s41380-022-01732-2.

29. Jared B. Torre and Matthew D. Lieberman, "Putting Feelings into Words: Affect Labeling as Implicit Emotion Regulation," *Emotion Review* 10, no. 2, (March 20, 2018): 116–124, https://doi.org/10.1177/1754073917742706.

30. James W. Pennebaker, *Writing to Heal: A Guided Journal for Recovering from Trauma and Emotional Upheaval* (Oakland, CA: New Harbinger Publications, 2004), 18–26.

31. Frederick S. Barrett and Petr Janata, "Neural Responses to Nostalgia-Evoking Music Modeled by Elements of Dynamic Musical Structure and Individual Differences in Affective Traits," *Neuropsychologia* 91 (October 2016): 234–246, https://doi.org/10.1016/j.neuropsychologia.2016.08.012.

32. Yifan Zhang et al., "How Does Exercise Improve Implicit Emotion Regulation Ability: Preliminary Evidence of Mind-Body Exercise Intervention Combined with Aerobic Jogging and Mindfulness-Based Yoga," *Frontiers in Psychology* 27, no. 10 (August 2019): 1888, https://doi.org/10.3389/fpsyg.2019.01888.; Emily E. Bernstein and Richard J. McNally, "Acute Aerobic Exercise Helps Overcome Emotion Regulation Deficits," *Cognition and Emotion* 31, no. 4 (April 2016): 834–843, https://doi.org/10.1080/02699931.2016.1168284.; Bernstein and McNally, "Acute Aerobic Exercise Hastens Emotional Recovery from a Subsequent Stressor," *Health Psychology* 36, no. 6 (June 2017): 560–567, https://doi.org/10.1037/hea0000482.

33. A. Byrne and D. G. Byrne, "The Effect of Exercise on Depression, Anxiety, and Other Mood States: A Review," *Journal of Psychosomatic Research* 37, no. 6 (September 1993): 565–574, https://doi.org/10.1016/0022-3999(93)90050-P.; Shawn M. Arent, Alan J. Walker, and Michelle A. Arent, *The Effects of Exercise on Anxiety and Depression* (Hoboken, NJ: John Wiley & Sons, 2020), https://doi.org/10.1002/9781119568124.ch42.; Alia J. Crum and Ellen J. Langer, "Mind-Set Matters: Exercise and the Placebo Effect," *Psychological Science* 18, no 2 (February 2007): 165–171, https://doi.org/10.1111/j.1467-9280.2007.01867.x.

34. Jeffrey Conrath Miller and Zlatan Krizan, "Walking Facilitates Positive Affect (Even When Expecting the Opposite)," *Emotion* 16, no. 5 (August 2016): 775–785, https://doi.org/10.1037/a0040270.; Jo Barton and Jules Pretty, "What Is the Best Dose of Nature and Green Exercise for Improving Mental Health? A Multi-Study Analysis," *Environmental Science & Technology* 44, no. 10 (March 2010): 3947–3955, https://doi.org/10.1021/es903183r.; Emily E. Scott et al., "Measuring Affect and Complex Working Memory in Natural and Urban Environments," *Frontiers in Psychology* 14 (March 6, 2023), https://doi.org/10.3389/fpsyg.2023.1039334.; Peter A. Coventry et al., "Nature-Based Outdoor Activities for Mental and Physical Health: Systematic Review and Meta-Analysis," *SSM Population Health* 16 (December 2021), https://doi.org/10.1016/j.ssmph.2021.100934.

35. James L. Oschman, Gaetan Chevalier, and Richard Brown, "The Effects of Grounding (Earthing) on Inflammation, the Immune Response, Wound Healing, and Prevention and Treatment of Chronic Inflammatory and Autoimmune Diseases," *Journal of Inflammation Research* 24, no. 8 (March 2015): 83–96, https://doi.org/10.2147/JIR.S69656.; Gaetan Chevalier et al., "The Effects of Grounding (Earthing) on Bodyworkers' Pain and Overall Quality of Life: A Randomized Controlled Trial," *Explore* (NY) 16, no. 3 (May–June 2019): 181–190, https://doi.org/10.1016/j.explore.2018.10.001.; Wendy Menigoz et al., "Integrative and Lifestyle Medicine Strategies Should Include Earthing (Grounding): Review of Research Evidence and Clinical Observations." *Explore* (NY) 16, no. 3 (May–June 2020): 152–160, https://doi.org/10.1016/j.explore.2019.10.005.

Chapter 4

1. "Justin Guilbert, From Nomad to Harmless Harvest Founder," *The Kreatures of Habit Podcast*, March 31, 2021, https://www.kohpodcast.com/justin-guilbert-from-nomad-to-harmless-harvest-founder/.

2. James Short, "How Much Media? 2013 Report on American Consumers," Institute for Communications Technology Management (CTM) at the University of Southern California's Marshall School of Business.; James E. Short, "How Much Media 2: An Analysis of Media Attention and Its Impact on Viewership," Institute for Communications Technology Management (CTM), Marshall School of Business, University of Southern California, November 2014.

3. Wilhelm Hofmann, Kathleen D. Vohs, and Roy F. Baumeister, "What People Desire, Feel Conflicted About, and Try to Resist in Everyday Life," *Psychological Science* 23, no. 6 (April 30, 2012): 582-588. https://doi.org/10.1177/0956797612437426.

4. Stephen J. Kim, "'Viewer Discretion Is Advised': A Structural Approach to the Issue of Television Violence," *University of Pennsylvania Law Review* 142,no. 4 (April 1994): 1383–1441, https://doi.org/10.2307/3312455.

5. Robert B. Lull and Brad J. Bushman, "Do Sex and Violence Sell? A Meta-Analytic Review of the Effects of Sexual and Violent Media and Ad Content

on Memory, Attitudes, and Buying Intentions," *Psychological Bulletin* 141, no. 5 (September 2015): 1022–1048, https://doi.org/10.1037/bul0000018.

6. Craig A. Anderson et al., "The Influence of Media Violence on Youth," *Psychological Science in the Public Interest* 4, no. 3 (December 2003): 81–110, https://doi.org/10.1111/j.1529-1006.2003.pspi_1433.x.; L. Rowell Huesmann and Leonard D. Eron (Eds.), *Television and the Aggressive Child: A Cross-National Comparison* (1st ed.), (Oxfordshire, UK: Routledge, 1986), https://doi.org/10.4324/9780203380130.; L. Rowell Huesmann et al., "Longitudinal Relations between Children's Exposure to TV Violence and Their Aggressive and Violent Behavior in Young Adulthood: 1977–1992." *Developmental Psychology* 39, no. 2 (March 2003): 201–221, https://doi.org /10.1037/0012-1649.39.2.201.

7. Anjana Madan, Sylvie Mrug, and Rex A. Wright, "The Effects of Media Violence on Anxiety in Late Adolescence," *Journal of Youth and Adolesence* 43, no. 1 (January 2014): 116–126, https://doi.org/10.1007/s10964-013-0017-3.

8. Nicolas Rapp and Aric Jenkins, "These 6 Companies Control Much of U.S. Media," *Fortune*, July 24, 2018, https://fortune.com/longform/media -company-ownership-consolidation/.

9. Kyle T. Bernstein et al., "Television Watching and the Risk of Incident Probable Posttraumatic Stress Disorder: A Prospective Evaluation," *Journal of Nervous and Mental Disease* 195, no. 1 (January 2007): 41-47, https://doi.org /10.1097/01.nmd.0000244784.36745.a5.

10. Stephanie Mazza et al., "Relearn Faster and Retain Longer: Along With Practice, Sleep Makes Perfect," *Psychological Science* 27, no. 10 (August 20, 2016): 1321–1330. https://doi.org/10.1177/0956797616659930.

11. Elisabeth Simoes et al., "How Negative Is Negative Information," *Frontiers in Neuroscience* 15, (September 7, 2021), https://doi.org/10.3389/fnins.2021 .742576.

12. David P. Phillips, "The Influence of Suggestion on Suicide: Substantive and Theoretical Implications of the Werther Effect," *American Sociological Review* 39, no. 3 (June 1974): 340–354, https://doi.org/10.2307/2094294.

13. Jeffrey M. Elliot, Ed., *Conversations with Maya Angelou* (Jackson, MS: University of Mississippi Press, 1989).

14. Emma M. Seppälä et al., "Breathing-based Meditation Decreases Posttraumatic Stress Disorder Symptoms in U.S. Military Veterans: A Randomized Controlled Longitudinal Study," *Journal of Traumatic Stress* 27, no. 4 (August 2014): 397–405, https://doi.org/10.1002/jts.21936.

15. Peter J Bayley et al., "Randomised Clinical Non-Inferiority Trial of Breathing-Based Meditation and Cognitive Processing Therapy for Symptoms of Post-Traumatic Stress Disorder in Military Veterans," *BMJ Open* 12, no. 8 (August 2022): e056609, https://doi.org/10.1136/bmjopen-2021-056609.; Danielle C. Mathersul et al., "Emotion Dysregulation and Heart Rate Variability Improve in US Veterans Undergoing Treatment for Posttraumatic Stress Disorder: Secondary Exploratory Analyses from a Randomised Controlled Trial," *BMC Psychiatry* 22, no. 1 (April 15, 2022), https://doi.org/10.1186/ s12888-022-03886-3.

16. Emma M. Seppälä et al., "Promoting Mental Health and Psychological Thriving in University Students: A Randomized Controlled Trial of Three Well-Being Interventions," *Frontiers in Psychiatry* 11 (July 15, 2020), https:// doi.org/10.3389/fpsyt.2020.00590.

17. Michael R. Goldstein, Rivian K. Lewin, and John J. Allen, "Improvements in Well-Being and Cardiac Metrics of Stress Following a Yogic Breathing

Workshop: Randomized Controlled Trial with Active Comparison," *Journal of American College Health* 70, no. 3 (July 15, 2020): 918–28, https://doi.org/10.1080/07448481.2020.1781867.

18. Rachel Yehuda and Amy Lehrner, "Intergenerational Transmission of Trauma Effects: Putative Role of Epigenetic Mechanisms," *World Psychiatry* 17, no. 3 (October 2018): 243–257, https://doi.org/10.1002/wps.20568.; Amy Lehrner and Rachel Yehuda, "Cultural Trauma and Epigenetic Inheritance," *Development and Psychopathology* 30, no. 5 (December 2018): 1763–1777, https://doi.org/10.1017/S0954579418001153.; Hunter Howie, Chuda M. Rijal, and Kerry J. Ressler, "A Review of Epigenetic Contributions to Post-Traumatic Stress Disorder," *Dialogues in Clinical Neuroscience* 21, no. 4 (December 2019): 417 428, https://doi.org/10.31887/DCNS.2019.21.4/kressler.

19. Maddalena Boccia, Laura Piccardi, and Paola Guariglia, "The Meditative Mind: A Comprehensive Meta-Analysis of MRI Studies," *Biomed Research International* 2015 (June 4, 2015), https://doi.org/10.1155/2015/419808.; Christina M. Luberto et al., "A Systematic Review and Meta-Analysis of the Effects of Meditation on Empathy, Compassion, and Prosocial Behaviors," *Mindfulness* 9, no. 3 (June 2018): 708–724, https://doi.org/10.1007/s12671-017-0841-8.; Caio Fabio Schlechta Portella et al., "Meditation: Evidence Map of Systematic Reviews," *Frontiers in Public Health* 2, no. 9 (December 2021), https://doi.org/10.3389/fpubh.2021.742715.; Lorenza S. Colzato et al., "Prior Meditation Practice Modulates Performance and Strategy Use in Convergent–and Divergent–Thinking Problems," *Mindfulness* 8 (October 29, 2014): 10–16, https://doi.org/10.1007/s12671-014-0352-9.

20. Willoughby B. Britton et al., "Defining and Measuring Meditation-Related Adverse Effects in Mindfulness-Based Programs," *Clinical Psychological Science* 9, no. 6 (May 18, 2021): 1185–1204, https://doi.org/10.1177/2167702621996340.; Willoughby B. Britton, "Can Mindfulness Be Too Much of a Good Thing? The Value of a Middle Way," *Current Opinion in Psychology* 28 (August 2019): 159–165, https://doi.org/10.1016/j.copsyc.2018.12.011.

21. Geyze Diniz et al., "The Effects of Gratitude Interventions: A Systematic Review and Meta-Analysis," *Einstein* (Sao Paulo) 11, no. 21 (August 2023): eRW0371, https://doi.org/10.31744/einstein_journal/2023RW0371.

22. Emma Seppälä et al., "Breathing-Based Meditation Decreases Posttraumatic Stress Disorder Symptoms in U.S. Military Veterans: A Randomized Controlled Longitudinal Study," *Journal of Trauma and Stress* 27, no. 4 (August 2014): 397–405. https://doi.org/10.1002/jts.21936.; Peter J. Bayley et al., "Randomised Clinical Non-Inferiority Trial of Breathing-Based Meditation and Cognitive Processing Therapy for Symptoms of Post-Traumatic Stress Disorder in Military Veterans," *BMJ Open* 12, no. 8 (August 25, 2022), https://doi.org/10.1136/bmjopen-2021-056609.; Emma Seppälä et al., "Promoting Mental Health and Psychological Thriving in University Students: A Randomized Controlled Trial of Three Well-Being Interventions," *Frontiers in Psychiatry* 11 (July 15, 2020): 590, https://doi.org/10.3389/fpsyt.2020.00590.

23. Often attributed to Charles Bukowski.

Chapter 5

1. "Mighty Earth's Etelle Higonnet Named to France's National Order of Merit," Mighty Earth, November 30, 2023, https://mightyearth.org/article/mighty-earths-etelle-higonnet-named-to-frances-national-order-of-merit/.

2. Kim Cameron et al., "Effects of Positive Practices on Organizational Effectiveness," *The Journal of Applied Behavioral Science* 47, no. 3 (January 26, 2011): 266–308, https://doi.org/10.1177/0021886310395514.; David S. Bright, Kim Camero, and Arran Caza, "The Amplifying and Buffering Effects of Virtuousness in Downsized Organizations," *Journal of Business Ethics* 64, (March 2006): 249–269, https://doi.org/10.1007/s10551-005-5904-4.; Kim Cameron, *Positively Energizing Leadership: Virtuous Actions and Relationships That Create High Performance* (Oakland, CA: Berrett-Koehler Publishers, 2021).

3. Gail Cornwall, "Why Mattering Is a Key Part of Mental Health," *New York Times*, September 27, 2023, https://www.nytimes.com/2023/09/27/well/mind/mental-health-mattering-self-esteem.html.

4. Sara B. Algoe, Shelly L. Gable, and Natalya C. Maisel, "It's the Little Things: Everyday Gratitude as a Booster Shot for Romantic Relationships," *Personal Relationships* 17, no. 2 (May 21, 2010): 217–233, https://doi.org/10.1111/j.1475-6811.2010.01273.x.

5. Adam M. Grant et al., "Impact and the Art of Motivation Maintenance: The Effects of Contact with Beneficiaries on Persistence Behavior," *Organizational Behavior and Human Decision Processes* 103, no. 1 (May 2007): 53–67, https://doi.org/10.1016/j.obhdp.2006.05.004.

6. Yoobin Park and Geoff MacDonald, "Consistency between Individuals' Past and Current Romantic Partners' Own Reports of Their Personalities," *Proceedings of the National Academy of Sciences 116,* no. 26 (June 10, 2019): 12793–12797, https://doi.org/10.1073/pnas.1902937116.

7. James Baldwin and Nikki Giovanni, "A Conversation," LoVetta Jenkins, YouTube, 1971, https://www.youtube.com/watch?v=y4OPYp4s0tc.

8. Emily J. Cross et al., "An Interdependence Account of Sexism and Power: Men's Hostile Sexism, Biased Perceptions of Low Power, and Relationship Aggression," *Journal of Personality and Social Psychology* 117, no. 2 (2019): 338–363, https://doi.org/10.1037/pspi0000167.

9. Marina Catallozzi et al., "Understanding Control in Adolescent and Young Adult Relationships," *Archives of Pediatrics and Adolescent Medicine* 165, no. 4 (April 2011): 313–319, https://doi.org/10.1001/archpediatrics.2011.32.

10. University of Waterloo, "Intimate Partners with Low Self-Esteem Stay in Unhappy Relationships," *ScienceDaily*, February 27, 2015. accessed July 6, 2023, www.sciencedaily.com/releases/2015/02/150227154826.htm.

11. Bianca P. Acevedo and Arthur Aron, "Does a Long-Term Relationship Kill Romantic Love?" *Review of General Psychology* 13, no. 1 (March 21, 2009): 59–65, https://doi.org/10.1037/a0014226.; American Psychological Association, "Contrary to Widely Held Beliefs, Romance Can Last in Long-Term Relationships, Say Researchers," *ScienceDaily*, March 21, 2009. Retrieved July 5, 2023. www.sciencedaily.com/releases/2009/03/090317153039.htm.

12. Robert Körner and Astrid Schüt, "Power in Romantic Relationships: How Positional and Experienced Power Are Associated with Relationship Quality," *Journal of Social and Personal Relationships* 38, no. 9 (September 2021): 2653–2677, https://doi.org/10.1177/02654075211017670.

13. Human Genomic Variation Fact Sheet, National Human Genome Research Institute, https://www.genome.gov/about-genomics/educational-resources/fact-sheets/human-genomic-variation.

14. E. O'Brien and S. Kassirer, "People Are Slow to Adapt to the Warm Glow of Giving," *Psychological Science* 30, no. 2 (2019): 193–204, https://doi.org/10.1177/0956797618814145.; Tristen K. Inagaki and Edward

Orehek, "On the Benefits of Giving Social Support: When, Why, and How Support Providers Gain by Caring for Others," *Current Directions in Psychological Science* 26, no. 2 (April 2017): 109–113, https://doi.org/10.1177/0963721416686212.; E. W. Dunn and L. B. Aknin LB, "Spending Money on Others Promotes Happiness," *Science* 319, no. 5870 (March 21, 2008): 1687–8, https://doi.org/10.1126/science.1150952.

15. Michael J. Poulin et al., "Giving to Others and the Association between Stress and Mortality," *American Journal of Public Health* 103, no. 9 (September 2013): 1649–1655, https://doi.org/10.2105/AJPH.2012.300876.
16. B. L. Fredrickson et al., "A Functional Genomic Perspective on Human Well-Being," *Proceedings of the National Academy of Sciences* 110, no. 33 (Aug 13, 2013): 13684–13689, https://doi.org/10.1073/pnas.1305419110.
17. Poulin et al., "Giving to Others and the Association between Stress and Mortality," *American Journal of Public Health.*
18. Kristin D. Neff and S. Natasha Beretvas, "The Role of Self-Compassion in Romantic Relationships," *Self and Identity* 12, no. 1 (February 2012): 78–98, https://doi.org/10.1080/15298868.2011.639548.
19. Sara B. Algoe, Shelly L. Gable, and Natalya C. Maisel. "It's the Little Things: Everyday Gratitude as a Booster Shot for Romantic Relationships," *Personal Relationships 17, no. 2* (June 2010): 217–233, https://doi.org/10.1111/j.1475-6811.2010.01273.x.
20. Alexander Karan, Robert Rosenthal, and Megan L. Robbins, "Meta-Analytic Evidence that We-Talk Predicts Relationship and Personal Functioning in Romantic Couples," *Journal of Social and Personal Relationships* 36, no. 9 (August 2018): 2624–2651, https://doi.org/10.1177/0265407518795.
21. Amy B. Brunell et al., "Dispositional Authenticity and Romantic Relationship Functioning," *Personality and Individual Differences* 48, no. 8 (June 2010): 900–905, https://doi.org/10.1016/j.paid.2017.08.014.
22. I first wrote on this topic for *Washington Post*: Emma Seppälä, "Forgiving Others Literally Lightens Your Step, and 6 Other Ways Science Shows It Helps," *Washington Post*, March 30, 2015, https://www.washingtonpost.com/news/inspired-life/wp/2015/03/30/feel-lighter-jump-higher-the-science-on-how-forgiving-others-can-help-you-too.
23. Charlotte vanOyen Witvliet et al., "Granting Forgiveness or Harboring Grudges: Implications for Emotion, Physiology, and Health," *Psychological Science* 12, no. 2 (March 2001): 117–123, https://doi.org/10.1111/1467-9280.00320.; P. A. Hannon et al., "The Soothing Effects of Forgiveness on Victims' and Perpetrators' Blood Pressure," *Personal Relationships* 19, no. 2 (2012): 279–289, https://doi.org/10.1111/j.1475-6811.2011.01356.x; J. C. Karremans et al., "Forgiveness and Its Associations with Prosocial Thinking, Feeling, and Doing Beyond the Relationship with the Offender," *Personality and Social Psychology Bulletin* 31,no 10 (2005): 1315–1326. https://doi.org/10.1177/0146167205274892.; Loren Toussaint et al.,"Effects of Lifetime Stress Exposure on Mental and Physical Health in Young Adulthood: How Stress Degrades and Forgiveness Protects Health," *Journal of Health Psychology* 21, no. 6 (June 2016): 1004–1014, https://doi.org/10.1177/1359105314544132.; Loren Toussaint et al., "Why Forgiveness May Protect Against Depression: Hopelessness as an Explanatory Mechanism," *Personality and Mental Health* 2 (March 2008): 89–103, https://doi.org/10.1002/pmh.35.; S. Noreen, R. N. Bierman, and M. D. MacLeod, "Forgiving You Is Hard, but Forgetting Seems Easy: Can Forgiveness Facilitate Forgetting?" *Psychological Science* 25, no 7 (May 2014): 1295–1302, https://doi.org/10.1177/0956797614531602.

24. X. Zheng et al., "The Unburdening Effects of Forgiveness: Effects on Slant Perception and Jumping Height," *Social Psychological and Personality Science* 6, no 4 (December 2015): 431–438, https://doi.org/10.1177/1948550614564222.

Chapter 6

1. *Online Etymology Dictionary*, https://www.etymonline.com/word/understand.
2. Kristen Jule, Lisa Leaver, and Stephen Lea, "The Effects of Captive Experience on Reintroduction Survival in Carnivores: A Review and Analysis," *Biological Conservation* 141, no 2 (February 2008): 355–363, https://doi.org/10.1016/j.biocon.2007.11.007.
3. Kevin Loria, "How Much Do We Really Know about the Human Brain?" World Economic Forum, May 28, 2015, https://www.weforum.org/agenda/2015/05/how-much-do-we-really-know-about-the-human-brain.
4. D. J. Bem, "Feeling the Future: Experimental Evidence for Anomalous Retroactivelinfluences on Cognition and Affect," *Journal of Personality and Social Psychology* 100, no. 3 (2011): 407–425, https://doi.org/10.1037/a0021524.
5. For a great summary of Bem's paper and the reactions to it, see: Daniel Engber, "Daryl BEM Proved ESP Is Real. Which Means Science Is Broken.," Slate Magazine, June 7, 2017, https://slate.com/health-and-science/2017/06/daryl-bem-proved-esp-is-real-showed-science-is-broken.html.
6. C. A. Hutcherson, E. M. Seppala, and J. J. Gross, "Loving-Kindness Meditation Increases Social Connectedness," *Emotion* 8, no. 5 (October 2008):720–724, https://doi.org/10.1037/a0013237.
7. M. Maidique, "Decoding Intuition for More Effective Decision-Making," *Harvard Business Review*, August 15, 2011. Retrieved August 12, 2020, https://hbr.org/2011/08/decoding-intuition-for-more-ef.
8. David Axe and Matthew Gault, "How U.S. Marines Are Using ESP to Weaponize Intuition," *Daily Beast*, July 2, 2017, updated October 30, 2017, https://www.thedailybeast.com/how-us-marines-are-using-esp-to-weaponize-intuition.
9. Channing Joseph, "U.S. Navy Program to Study How Troops Use Intuition," *New York Times*, March 27, 2012, https://archive.nytimes.com/atwar.blogs.nytimes.com/2012/03/27/navy-program-to-study-how-troops-use-intuition/.
10. Mark Divine, The Way Of The SEAL: "Build Your Intuition," April 25, 2018, in *The Mark Divine Show*, podcast, https://unbeatablemind.com/the-way-of-the-seal-4.
11. Army Public Affairs, "Army Reserve Staff Sgt. Martin K. Richburg," U.S. Army, February 2, 2007, https://www.army.mil/article/1669/army_reserve_staff_sgt_martin_k_richburg.
12. Maurice L. Naylon IV, *The New Ministry of Truth: Combat Advisors in Afghanistan and America's Great Betrayal* (Ashland, OR: Hellgate Press, 2019), https://www.newministryoftruth.us/p/the-book.html.
13. Marine Corps Training Command, "Introduction to Combat Hunter B1E0795 Student Handout," United State Marine Corps, https://usmcofficer.com/wp-content/uploads/2014/01/Introduction-to-Combat-Hunter.pdf.
14. P. Seli et al., "How Pervasive Is Mind Wandering, Really?" *Consciousness and Cognition* (November 2018): 74–78, https://doi.org/10.1016/j.concog.2018.10.002.

15. Nadav Amir, Naftali Tishby, and Israel Nelken, "A Simple Model of the Attentional Blink and Its Modulation by Mental Training," *PLOS Computational Biology* 18, no. 8 (August 29, 2022): e1010398, https://doi.org/10.1371/journal.pcbi.1010398.; Heleen A. Slagter et al., "Mental Training Affects Distribution of Limited Brain Resources," *PLoS Biology* 5, no. 6 (May 8, 2007): e138, https://doi.org/10.1371/journal.pbio.0050138; Antoine Lutz et al., "Mental Training Enhances Attentional Stability: Neural and Behavioral Evidence," *The Journal of Neuroscience* 29, no. 42 (October 21, 2009): 13418–27, https://doi.org/10.1523/jneurosci.1614-09.2009.; Sara van Leeuwen, Notger G. Müller, and Lucia Melloni, "Age Effects on Attentional Blink Performance in Meditation," *Consciousness and Cognition* 18, no. 3 (September 2009): 593–99, https://doi.org/10.1016/j.concog.2009.05.001.; Marieke K. van Vugt and Heleen A. Slagter, "Control over Experience? Magnitude of the Attentional Blink Depends on Meditative State," *Consciousness and Cognition* 23 (January 2014): 32–39, https://doi.org/10.1016/j.concog.2013.11.001.; Brandon T. Saxton et al., "Do Arousal and Valence Have Separable Influences on Attention across Time?," *Psychological Research* 84, no. 2 (February 28, 2018): 259–75, https://doi.org/10.1007/s00426-018-0995-6.

16. Tom Klisiewicz, "The Latest in Military Strategy: Mindfulness," *The New York Times*, April 5, 2019, https://www.nytimes.com/2019/04/05/health/military-mindfulness-training.html.; Carl D. Smith et al., "Impact of Mindfulness Training and Yoga on Injury and Pain-Related Impairment: A Group Randomized Trial in Basic Combat Training," *Frontiers in Psychology* 14 (October 6, 2023), https://doi.org/10.3389/fpsyg.2023.1214039.

17. Jonathan L. Helm, David Sbarra, and Emilio Ferrer, "Assessing Cross-Partner Associations in Physiological Responses via Coupled Oscillator Models," *Emotion* 12, no. 4 (August 2012): 748–62, https://doi.org/10.1037/a0025036.; Emilio Ferrer and Jonathan L. Helm, "Dynamical Systems Modeling of Physiological Coregulation in Dyadic Interactions," *International Journal of Psychophysiology* 88, no. 3 (June 2013): 296–308, https://doi.org/10.1016/j.ijpsycho.2012.10.013.; Pavel Goldstein, Irit Weissman-Fogel, and Simone G. Shamay-Tsoory, "The Role of Touch in Regulating Inter-Partner Physiological Coupling during Empathy for Pain," *Scientific Reports* 7, no. 1 (June 12, 2017), https://doi.org/10.1038/s41598-017-03627-7.; Lei Li et al., "Neural Synchronization Predicts Marital Satisfaction," *Proceedings of the National Academy of Sciences* 119, no. 34 (August 18, 2022): e2202515119, https://doi.org/10.1073/pnas.2202515119.

18. Sylvie Guillem, "Sylvie Guillem (Official Full Documentary)," Dance Masterclass, YouTube, https://www.youtube.com/watch?v=2vlN8DiJvpw.

19. Joseph A. Mikels et al., "Should I Go with My Gut? Investigating the Benefits of Emotion-Focused Decision Making," *Emotion* 11, no. 4 (2011): 743–753, https://doi.org/10.1037/a0023986.

20. Joseph A. Mikels et al., "Following Your Heart or Your Head: Focusing on Emotions Versus Information Differentially Influences the Decisions of Younger and Older Adults, " *Journal of Experimental Psychology: Applied* 16, no. 1 (March 2010): 87–95, https://doi.org/10.1037/a0018500.

21. G. Lufityanto, C. Donkin, and J. Pearson, "Measuring Intuition: Nonconscious Emotional Information Boosts Decision Accuracy and Confidence," *Psychological Science* 27, no. 5 (May 2016): 622–634, https://doi.org/10.1177/0956797616629403.

22. Joel Pearson, "How to Get Your Intuition Back (When It's Hacked by Life)" *New York Times*, July 17, 2018, https://www.nytimes.com/2018/07/17/well/intuition-gut-instinct-psychology-midlife-crisis.html.

23. A. Dijksterhuis and L. F. Nordgren, "A Theory of Unconscious Thought," *Perspectives on Psychological Science* 1, no. 2 (June 2006): 95–109, https://doi.org/10.1111/j.1745-6916.2006.00007.x.

24. R. P. Nalliah, "Clinical Decision Making–Choosing between Intuition, Experience, and Scientific Evidence," *British Dental Journal 221*, no. 12 (2016): 752–754, https://doi.org/10.1038/sj.bdj.2016.942.

25. Scott Cohn, "Think You Can Spot a Fraud? This $80 Million Art Scam Fooled the Experts," CNBC.com, American Green, August 17, 2018. https://www.cnbc.com/2018/08/16/think-you-can-spot-a-fraud-this-80-million-art-scam-fooled-experts.html.

26. Alice Calaprice (Ed.), *The Expanded Quotable Einstein.* (Princeton, N.J.: Princeton University Press, 2000), 287.

27. Shinichi Suzuki, *Nurtured by Love: A New Approach to Education* (New York: Exposition Press, 1969), 90.

28. W. Verrusioet et al., "The Mozart Effect: A Quantitative EEG Study," *Consciousness and Cognition* 35 (September 2015): 150–155, https://doi.org/10.1016/j.concog.2015.05.005.

29. Jonathan Smallwood and Jonathan Schooler, "The Science of Mind Wandering: Empirically Navigating the Stream of Consciousness," *Annual Review of Psychology* 66 (January 2015): 487–518, https://doi.org/10.1146/annurev-psych-010814-015331.

30. John Lynch, "The Average American Watches So Much TV It's Almost a Full-Time Job," Yahoo! Finance, June 28, 2016, https://finance.yahoo.com/news/average-american-watches-much-tv-205729319.html.

31. Peter J. Renfrow, Lewis R. Goldberg, and Ran Zilca, "Listening, Watching, and Reading: The Structure and Correlates of Entertainment Preferences," *Journal of Personality* 79, no. 2 (April 2011): 223–258, https://doi.org/10.1111/j.1467-6494.2010.00662.x.

32. Kyung Hee Kim. *The Creativity Challenge: How We Can Recapture American Innovation* (Amherst, NY: Prometheus Books, 2016).

33. R. T. Proyer, "Playfulness as a Personality Trait in Adults: Its Structure, Definition, and Measurement" (unpublished habilitation thesis, University of Zurich, 2015).

34. René T. Proyer and Lisa Wagner, "Playfulness in Adults Revisited: The Signal Theory in German Speakers," *American Journal of Play* 7, no. 2 (February 2015): 201–227, https://files.eric.ed.gov/fulltext/EJ1053424.pdf.

35. René T. Proyer, "A New Structural Model for the Study of Adult Playfulness: Assessment and Exploration of an Understudied Individual Differences Variable," *Personality and Individual Differences* 108 (2017): 113–122, https://doi.org/10.1016/j.paid.2016.12.011.; L. A. Barnett, "The Nature of Playfulness in Young Adults," *Personality and Individual Differences* 43 (September 2007): 949–958. https://doi.org/10.1016/j.paid.2007.02.018,; C. D. Magnuson and L. A. Barnett, "The Playful Advantage: How Playfulness Enhances Coping with Stress," *Leisure Sciences* 35, no. 2 (March 2013): 129–144. https://doi.org/10.1080/01490400.2013.761905.; X. L. Qian and C. Yarnal, "The Role of Playfulness in the Leisure Stress-Coping Process among Emerging Adults: An SEM Analysis," *Leisure* 35 (May 13, 2011): 191–209, https://doi.org/10.1080/14927713.2011.578398.

36. Yang Bai et al., "Awe, the Diminished Self, and Collective Engagement: Universals and Cultural Variations in the Small Self," *Journal of Personality and Social Psychology* 113, no. 2 (August 2017): 185–209, https://doi.org/10.1037/pspa0000087.

37. L. A. Barnett, "How Do Playful People Play? Gendered and Racial Leisure Perspectives, Motives and Preferences of College Students," *Leisure Sciences* 33, no. 5 (September 2011): 382–401, https://doi.org/10.1080/01490400.2011.606777.

38. Todd Kashdan and Jonathan Rottenberg, "Psychological Flexibility as a Fundamental Aspect of Health," *Clinical Psychology Review* 30, no. 7 (November 2010): 865–878, https://doi.org/10.1016/j.cpr.2010.03.001.; George A. Bonanno et al., "The Importance of Being Flexible: The Ability to Both Enhance and Suppress Emotional Expression Predicts Long-Term Adjustment," *Psychological Science* 15, no. 7 (July 2004): 482-487, https://doi.org/10.1111/j.0956-7976.2004.0070.

39. Z. L. Dabelina and M. D. Robinson, "Child's Play: Facilitating the Originality of Creative Output by a Priming Manipulation," *Psychology of Aesthetics, Creativity, and the Arts* 4, no. 1 (2010): 57–65, https://doi.org/10.1037/a0015644.

40. "Overcoming the Innovation Readiness Gap: Most Innovative Companies 2021," BCG, April 15, 2021. https://www.bcg.com/publications/2021/most-innovative-companies-overview.

41. Ruth Ann Atchley, David L. Strayer DL, and Paul Atchley, "Creativity in the Wild: Improving Creative Reasoning through Immersion in Natural Settings," *PLoS ONE* 7, no. 12 (December 2012): e51474, https://doi.org/10.1371/journal.pone.005147.

42. C. Remmers and J. Michalak, "Losing Your Gut Feelings: Intuition in Depression," *Frontiers in Psychology* 23, no. 7 (August 2016): 1291, https://doi.org/10.3389/fpsyg.2016.01291.

Chapter 7

1. Jeff T., "How I Went from Being an Obese BBQ Chef to a Healthy Vegan Chef," *Forks and Knives*, July 19, 2018, https://www.forksoverknives.com/success-stories/how-i-went-from-being-an-obese-bbq-chef-to-a-healthy-vegan-chef.

2. Emily N. Ussery et al., "Joint Prevalence of Sitting Time and Leisure-Time Physical Activity among US Adults, 2015-2016," *JAMA* 320, no. 19 (November 20, 2018):2036–2038, https://doi.org/10.1001/jama.2018.17797.

3. Jaime M. Zeitzer et al., "Sensitivity of the Human Circadian Pacemaker to Nocturnal Light Melatonin Phase Resetting and Suppression," *The Journal of Physiology* 526, no. 3 (August 2000): 695–702, https://doi.org/10.1111/j.1469-7793.2000.00695.x.

4. Lars Alfredsson et al., "Insufficient Sun Exposure Has become a Real Public Health Problem," *International Journal of Environmental Research and Public Health* 17, no. 14 (July 2020): 5014. https://doi.org/10.3390/ijerph17145014.

5. "Emergency Planning and Community Right-to-Know, Title 42: The Public Health and Welfare," essay, in United States Code: Armed Forces (as Amended through January 7, 2011) (Washington, D.C.: U.S. G.P.O., 2011), https://www.govinfo.gov/content/pkg/USCODE-2011-title42/html/USCODE-2011-title42-chap116.htm.

6. Anne Steinemann, "Fragranced Consumer Products and Undisclosed Ingredients," *Environmental Impact Assessment Review* 29, no. 1 (January 2009): 32–38, https://doi.org/10.1016/j.eiar.2008.05.002.

7. Anne Steinemann, "Fragranced Consumer Products: Exposures and Effects from Emissions," *Air Quality Atmosphere and Health* 9, no. 8 (2016): 861–866, https://doi.org/10.1007/s11869-016-0442-z.

8. "Endocrine," National Institute of Environmental Health Sciences, updated June 2, 2023, https://www.niehs.nih.gov/health/topics/agents/endocrine/index.cfm.

9. Kristen E. Knox et al., "Identifying Toxic Consumer Products: A Novel Data Set Reveals Air Emissions of Potent Carcinogens, Reproductive Toxicants, and Developmental Toxicants," *Environmental Science and Technology* 57, no. 19 (May 2, 2023): 7454–7465. https://doi.org/10.1021/acs.est.2c07247.

10. "How Common Is Infertility," Eunice Kennedy Shriver National Institute of Child Health & Development, February 8, 2018, https://www.nichd.nih.gov/health/topics/infertility/conditioninfo/common.

11. N. A. Motsoane et al., "An In Vitro Study of Biological Safety of Condoms and Their Additives," *Human and Experimental Toxicology* 22, no. 12 (December 2003): 659–664, https://doi.org/10.1191/0960327103ht410oa.

12. K. Hoffman et al., "High Exposure to Organophosphate Flame Retardants in Infants: Associations with Baby Products," *Environmental Science and Technology* 49, no. 24 (November 9, 2015): 14554-14559, https://doi.org/10.1021/acs.est.5b03577.

13. Jef Feeley, J&J to pay $700 million to settle states' Talc Investigation, Bloomberg, January 8, 2024, https://www.bloomberg.com/news/articles/2024-01-08/j-j-to-pay-700-million-to-settle-states-talc-marketing-probe.

14. H. Bai, I. Tam, and J. Yu, "Contact Allergens in Top-Selling Textile-Care Products," *Dermatitis* 31, no. 1 (ebruary 2020): 53–58. http://doi.org/10.1097/DER.0000000000000566.

15. Katie Liljenquist, Chen-Bo Zhong, and Adam D. Galinsky, "The Smell of Virtue: Clean Scents Promote Reciprocity and Charity," *Psychological Science* 21, no. 3 (February 2010): 381–383. https://doi.org/10.1177/0956797610361426.

16. S. Kobylewskia and M. F. Jacobson, "Toxicology of Food Dyes," *International Journal of Occupational and Environmental Health* 18, no. 3 (November 12, 2013): 220–246. https://doi.org/10.1179/1077352512Z.00000000034.

17. Roni Caryn Rabin, "What Foods Are Banned in Europe but Not Banned in the U.S.?," *The New York Times*, December 28, 2018, https://www.nytimes.com/2018/12/28/well/eat/food-additives-banned-europe-united-states.html.

18. Lauren Kirchner, "Why Is Red Dye No. 3 Banned in Cosmetics but Still Allowed in Food?" *Consumer Reports*, updated October 31, 2023. https://www.consumerreports.org/health/food-additives/red-dye-3-banned-in-cosmetics-but-still-allowed-in-food-a3467381365.; Stephanie Breijo, "So Long Red Dye No. 3? Why Lawmakers Want to Cancel a Chemical Found in Your Skittles and Strawberry Yoohoo," *Los Angeles Times*, March 27, 2023. https://www.latimes.com/food/story/2023-03-27/red-dye-no-3-california-bill-ban-food-chemicals.

19. Center for Science in the Public Interest, "Red 3 Petition," October 24, 2022. https://www.cspinet.org/resource/red-3-petition.

20. Kelly McCarthy, "California 1st in US to Ban 4 Chemicals in Food: What to Know," GMA.com, October 12, 2023. https://abcnews.go.com/GMA/Food/landmark-ca-bill-ban-harmful-food-chemicals-spares/story?id=103150822.

21. M. D. Miller et al., "Potential Impacts of Synthetic Food Dyes on Activity and Attention in Children: A Review of the Human and Animal Evidence," *Environmental Health* 21, no, 1 (April 29, 2022): 45, https://doi.org/10.1186/s12940-022-00849-9.

22. "Data and Statistics about ADHD," Centers for Disease Control and Prevention, updated October 16, 2023. https://www.cdc.gov/ncbddd/adhd/data.html.

23. Malcolm Gladwell, "FDA: Red Dye's Reluctant Regulator," *The Washington Post,* February 7, 1990.

24. Dana G. Smith, "Two States Have Proposed Bans on Common Food Additives Linked to Health Concerns," *New York Times*, April 13, 2023, accessed May 23, 2023.

25. David Andrews, "Synthetic Ingredients in Natural Flavors and Natural Flavors in Artificial Flavors," Environmental Working Group, https://www.ewg.org/foodscores/content/natural-vs-artificial-flavors/#.WvTAAdPwaRt.

26. S. Iacobelli et al., "Paraben Exposure through Drugs in the Neonatal Intensive Care Unit: A Regional Cohort Study," *Frontiers in Pharmacology* 14 (June 8, 2023): 1200521. https://doi.org/10.3389/fphar.2023.1200521.

27. Kevin Loria, "A Third of Chocolate Products Are High in Heavy Metals, CR's Tests Find," *Consumer Reports*, October 25, 2023. https://www.consumerreports.org/health/food-safety/a-third-of-chocolate-products-are-high-in-heavy-metals-a4844566398/.

28. Loria, "Are There Still Heavy Metals in Baby Foods?" *Consumer Reports*, July 6, 2023. https://www.consumerreports.org/babies-kids/baby-food/are-heavy-metal-levels-in-baby-foods-getting-better-a1163977621/.

29. F. Nessa, S. A. Khan, and K. Y. Abu Shawish, "Lead, Cadmium and Nickel Contents of Some Medicinal Agents," *Indian Journal of Pharmaceutical Sciences* 78, no. 1 (January-February 2016): 111–119, https://doi.org/10.4103/0250-474x.180260.

30. C. N. Amadi et al., "Association of Autism with Toxic Metals: A Systematic Review of Case-Control Studies," *Pharmacology Biochemistry and Behavior* 212 (January 2022): 173313. https://doi.org/10.1016/j.pbb.2021.173313.

31. O. M. Ijomone et al., "The Aging Brain: Impact of Heavy Metal Neurotoxicity." *Critical Review in Toxicology* 50, no. 9 (November 19, 2020): 801–814. https://doi.org/10.1080/10408444.2020.1838441.

32. M. Jaishankar et al., "Toxicity, Mechanism and Health Effects of Some Heavy Metals," *Interdisciplinary Toxicology* 7, no. 2 (June 2014): 60–72, https://doi.org/10.2478/intox-2014-0009.

33. "Sector Profile: Agribusiness," Open Secrets, https://www.opensecrets.org/federal-lobbying/sectors/summary?cycle=2021&id=A.

34. A. O'Connor, "The Food Industry Pays Influencer Dieticians to Shape Your Eating Habits," *Washington Post*, September 13, 2023, https://www.washingtonpost.com/wellness/2023/09/13/dietitian-instagram-tiktok-paid-food-industry/.

35. David Rossiaky, "FDA Asked to Investigate YouTube Star Logan Paul's Prime Energy Drink. What to Know.," *Healthline*, June 7, 2023, https://www.healthline.com/health-news/why-prime-and-other-energy-drinks-can-be-dangerous-especially-for-kids.; Ashley Abramson, "The Truth about What's Really in Prime Energy Drinks," *Consumer Reports*, July 14, 2023, https://www.consumerreports.org/health/hydration-beverages/the-truth-about-whats-really-in-prime-energy-drinks-a2960180425/.; "US Food Agency Called on to Investigate Prime Energy Drink over Caffeine Levels," *The*

Guardian, July 10, 2023, https://www.theguardian.com/us-news/2023/jul/10/prime-energy-drink-logan-paul-fda-investigation.

36. J. L. Temple, "Caffeine Use in Children: What We Know, What We Have Left to Learn, and Why We Should Worry," *Neuroscience and Biobehavioral Review* 33, no. 6 (June 2009): 793–806, https://doi.org/10.1016/j.neubiorev.2009.01.001.

37. R. Soós et al., "Effects of Caffeine and Caffeinated Beverages in Children, Adolescents and Young Adults: Short Review," *International Journal of Environmental Research and Public Health* 18, no. 23 (November 25, 2021): 12389, https://doi.org/10.3390/ijerph182312389.; G. Richards and A. Smith, "Caffeine Consumption and Self-Assessed Stress, Anxiety, and Depression in Secondary School Children," *Journal of Psychopharmacology* 29, no. 12 (October 27, 2015): 1236–1247, https://doi.org/10.1177/0269881115612404.

38. Nobuhiro Hagura, Patrick Haggard, and Jörn Diedrichsen, "Perceptual Decisions Are Biased by the Cost to Act," *eLife* 6 (February 21, 2017): e18422, https://doi.org/10.7554/elife.18422.

39. Lisa M. Schwartz and Steven Woloshin, "Medical Marketing in the United States, 1997–2016," *JAMA* 321, no. 1 (January 2019): 80–96, https://doi.org/10.1001/jama.2018.

40. Kris van Cleave, "They Have Really Endless Resources: Big Pharma Spending $263 Million to Keep Drug Prices High," CBS News, November 3, 2021. https://www.cbsnews.com/news/big-pharma-lower-prescription-drug-prices.

41. "Prescription Drugs: Spending, Use, and Prices," Congressional Budget Office, January 2022, https://www.cbo.gov/publication/57772.

42. "Eating, Diet, and Nutrition for Polycystic Kidney Disease," National Institute of Diabetes and Digestive and Kidney Disease, National Institutes of Health, updated January 2017, https://www.niddk.nih.gov/health-information/kidney-disease/polycystic-kidney-disease/eating-diet-nutrition.

43. Rijul Kshirsagar and Priscilla Vu," The Pharmaceutical Industry's Role in U.S. Medical Education," In-Training.com, April 3, 2016, https://in-training.org/drugged-greed-pharmaceutical-industrys-role-us-medical-education-10639.; Laura Hensley, "Big Pharma Pours Millions into Medical Schools – Here's How It Can Impact Education – National," *Global News*, August 12, 2019, https://globalnews.ca/news/5738386/canadian-medical-school-funding.; Howard Brody, "Pharmaceutical Industry Financial Support for Medical Education: Benefit, or Undue Influence?," *Journal of Law, Medicine & Ethics* 37, no. 3 (2009): 451–60, https://doi.org/10.1111/j.1748-720x.2009.00406.x.; Marcia Angell (speaker), "Drug Companies and Medicine: What Money Can Buy," Edmond and Lily Safra Center for Ethics, Harvard University, December 10, 2009. https://ethics.harvard.edu/event/drug-companies-and-medicine-what-money-can-buy.

44. S. S. Buchkowsky and P. J. Jewesson, "Industry Sponsorship and Authorship of Clinical Trials over 20 Years," *Annals of Pharmacotherapy* 38, no. 4 (April 2004): 579–585, https://doi.org/10.1345/aph.1D267.

45. John Abramson, "Big Pharma Is Hijacking the Information Doctors Need Most," *Time*, April 28, 2022, https://time.com/6171999/big-pharma-clinical-data-doctors/.; Dennis K Flaherty, "Ghost- and Guest-Authored Pharmaceutical Industry–Sponsored Studies: Abuse of Academic Integrity, the Peer Review System, and Public Trust," *Annals of Pharmacotherapy* 47, no. 7–8 (June 26, 2013): 1081–83, https://doi.org/10.1345/aph.1r691.; Peter C Gøtzsche et al., "Ghost Authorship in Industry-Initiated Randomised Trials," *PLoS Medicine* 4, no. 1 (January 16, 2007): e19, https://doi.org/10.1371/journal.pmed.0040019.

46. J. Lexchin et al., "Pharmaceutical Industry Sponsorship and Research Outcome and Quality: Systematic Review," *BMJ* 326, no. 7400 (May 31, 2003): 1167–1170, https://doi.org/10.1136/bmj.326.7400.1167.

47. Redzo Mujcic and Andrew J. Oswald, "Evolution of Well-Being and Happiness After Increases in Consumption of Fruit and Vegetables," *American Journal of Public Health* 106, no. 8 (August 2016): 1504–1510, https://doi.org/10.2105/AJPH.2016.303260.

48. Bonnie A. White, Caroline C. Horwath, and Tamlin S. Conner, "Many Apples a Day Keep the Blues Away—Daily Experiences of Negative and Positive Affect and Food Consumption in Young Adults," *British Journal of Health Psychology* 18, no. 4 (November 2013): 782–798, https://doi.org/10.1111/bjhp.12021.

49. B. Nguyen, D. Ding, and S. Mihrshahi, "Fruit and Vegetable Consumption and Psychological Distress: Cross-Sectional and Longitudinal Analyses Based on a Large Australian Sample," *BMJ Open* 7, no. 3 (Mar 15, 2017). https://doi.org10.1136/bmjopen-2016-014201.

50. Jerome Sarris, Ph.D. et al., "Nutritional Medicine as Mainstream in Psychiatry," *The Lancet Psychiatry* 2, no. 3 (January 2015), https://doi.org/10.1016/S2215-0366(14)00051-0.

51. J. Firth, et al., "The Effects of Dietary Improvement on Symptoms of Depression and Anxiety: A Meta-Analysis of Randomized Controlled Trials," *Psychosomatic Medicine* 81, no. 3 (April 2019): 265–280, https://doi.org/10.1097/PSY.0000000000000673.

52. T. S. Conner et al., "Let Them Eat Fruit! The Effect of Fruit and Vegetable Consumption on Psychological Well-Being in Young Adults: A Randomized Controlled Trial. " *PLoS One* 12, no. 2 (February 3, 2017), https://doi.org/10.1371/journal.pone.0171206.

53. D. Głąbska et al., "Fruit and Vegetable Intake and Mental Health in Adults: A Systematic Review," *Nutrients* 12, no. 1 (January 1, 2020):115, https://doi.org/10.3390/nu12010115.

54. PNA Dharmayani et al., "Association between Fruit and Vegetable Consumption and Depression Symptoms in Young People and Adults Aged 15–45: A Systematic Review of Cohort Studies," *International Journal of Environmental Research and Public Health* 18, no. 2 (January 18, 2021):780, https://doi.org/10.3390/ijerph18020780.

55. A. O'Neil et al., "Relationship between Diet and Mental Health in Children and Adolescents: A Systematic Revie," *American Journal of Public Health* 104, no. 10 (October 2014): e31–e42, https://doi.org/10.2105/AJPH.2014.302110.

56. Daniel J Lamport et al., "Fruits, Vegetables, 100% Juices, and Cognitive Function," *Nutrition Reviews* 72, no. 12 (December 2014): 774–89, https://doi.org/10.1111/nure.12149.; Sujatha Rajaram, Julie Jones, and Grace J Lee, "Plant-Based Dietary Patterns, Plant Foods, and Age-Related Cognitive Decline," *Advances in Nutrition* 10 (November 2019): S422–36, https://doi.org/10.1093/advances/nmz081.; Monika A. Zielińska et al., "Vegetables and Fruit, as a Source of Bioactive Substances, and Impact on Memory and Cognitive Function of Elderly," *Postępy Higieny i Medycyny Doświadczalnej* 71 (April 2017): 267–80, https://doi.org/10.5604/01.3001.0010.3812.

57. M. Cristina Polidori et al., "High Fruit and Vegetable Intake Is Positively Correlated with Antioxidant Status and Cognitive Performance in Healthy Subjects," *Journal of Alzheimer's Disease* 17, no. 4 (2009): 921–27, https://doi.org/10.3233/jad-2009-1114.

58. Chris Wesseling, "Tom Brady Named NFL's MVP for Third Time of Career," *NFL.com*. February 3, 2018. accessed January 29, 2020.; Shanna McCarriston, "Tom Brady Admits He's Sore after Week 1 Win over Cowboys: 'There's No Margin for Error When You're 45,'" *CBS Sports*. accessed September 16, 2022.

59. Tom Brady. *The TB 12 Method: How to Achieve a Lifetime of Sustained Peak* (New York: Simon & Schuster, 2020).

60. "A Vegan Diet Can Help with Impotence," PETA.org, June 24, 2010. https://www.peta.org/living/food/impotence/.

61. Redzo Mujcic and Andrew J.Oswald, "Evolution of Well-Being and Happiness after Increases in Consumption of Fruit and Vegetables," *American Journal of Public Health* 106, no. 8 (July 11, 2016): 1504–10, https://doi.org/10.2105/ajph.2016.303260.; Bonnie A. White, Caroline C. Horwath, and Tamlin S. Conner, "Many Apples a Day Keep the Blues Away—Daily Experiences of Negative and Positive Affect and Food Consumption in Young Adults," *British Journal of Health Psychology*.

62. H. Lynch, C. Johnston, and C. Wharton, "Plant-Based Diets: Considerations for Environmental Impact, Protein Quality, and Exercise Performance," *Nutrients* 10, no. 12 (December 1, 2018): 1841, https://doi.org/10.3390/nu10121841.

63. J. J. DiNicolantonio, J. H. O'Keefe, and W. L. Wilson, "Sugar Addiction: Is It Real? A Narrative Review," *British Journal of Sports Medicine* 52 (2018): 910–913, https://doi.org/10.1136/bjsports-2017-097971.

64. "Integrative Medicine and Health Overview," Mayo Clinic, June 24, 2023, https://www.mayoclinic.org/departments-centers/integrative-medicine-health/sections/overview/ovc-20464567.

65. A. C. Burns et al., "Time Spent in Outdoor Light Is Associated with Mood, Sleep, and Circadian Rhythm-Related Outcomes: A Cross-Sectional and Longitudinal Study in Over 400,000 UK Biobank Participants," *Journal of Affective Disorders* 295 (December 1, 2021): 347–352, https://doi.org/10.1016/j.jad.2021.08.056.

66. A. W. Turunen et al., "Cross-Sectional Associations of Different Types of Nature Exposure with Psychotropic, Antihypertensive and Asthma Medication," *Occupational and Environmental Medicine* 80, no. 2 (February 2023): 111–118. https://doi.org/10.1136/oemed-2022-108491.

67. R. Nagare et al., "Access to Daylight at Home Improves Circadian Alignment, Sleep, and Mental Health in Healthy Adults: A Crossover Study," *International Journal of Environmental Research and Public Health* 18, no. 19 (September 23, 2021): 9980. https://doi.org/10.3390/ijerph18199980.

68. Javiera Morales-Bravo and Pablo Navarrete-Hernandez,"Enlightening Well-being in the Home: The Impact of Natural Light Design on Perceived Happiness and Sadness in Residential Spaces," *Building and Environment* 223 (September 2022): 109317, https://doi.org/10.1016/j.buildenv.2022.109317.

69. R. Hammoud et al., "Smartphone-Based Ecological Momentary Assessment Reveals Mental Health Benefits of Birdlife. *Science Reports* 12, 17589 (October 27, 2022): 17589, https://doi.org/10.1038/s41598-022-20207-6.

70. Michelle Tester-Jones et al., "Results from an 18 Country Cross-Sectional Study Examining Experiences of Nature for People with Common Mental Health Disorders," *Scientific Reports* 10, article 19408 (November 6, 2020), https://doi.org/10.1038/s41598-020-75825-9.; E. Stobbe et al. "Birdsongs Alleviate Anxiety and Paranoia in Healthy Participants," *Science Report* 12, article 16414 (October 13, 2022), https://doi.org/10.1038/s41598-022-20841-0.

71. MaryCarol R. Hunter, Brenda W. Gillespie, and Sophie Yu-Pu Chen, "Urban Nature Experiences Reduce Stress in the Context of Daily Life Based on Salivary Biomarkers," *Frontiers in Psychology* 10 (April 2019): 722, https://doi.org/10.3389/fpsyg.2019.00722.

72. Genevive R. Meredith et al., "Minimum Time Dose in Nature to Positively Impact the Mental Health of College-Aged Students, and How to Measure It: A Scoping Review," *Frontiers in Psychology* 10 (January 2020): 2942. https://doi.org/10.3389/fpsyg.2019.02942.

73. Mathew P. White et al., "Spending at Least 120 Minutes a Week in Nature Is Associated with Good Health and Wellbeing," *Scientific Reports* 9, no. 1 (June 2019), https://doi.org/10.1038/s41598-019-44097-3.

74. Florence Williams, "Call to the Wild: This Is Your Brain on Nature," *National Geographic,* January 1, 2016, https://www.nationalgeographic.com/magazine/article/call-to-wild.

75. Florence Williams, "Call to the Wild," *National Geographic.*

76. Victoria Forster, "Canadian Physicians Can Now Prescribe Nature To Patients," *Forbes,* February 8, 2022, accessed July 14, 2022. https://www.forbes.com/sites/victoriaforster/2022/02/08/canadian-physicians-can-now-prescribe-nature-to-patients/?sh=c451c586f202.; Jillian Mock, "Why Doctors Are Prescribing Nature Walks," *Time,* April 27, 2022. https://time.com/6171174/nature-stress-benefits-doctors.; "Nature Prescribed," Park Rx America, n.d., https://parkrxamerica.org/.

77. Deborah S. McCraken et al., "Associations between Urban Greenspace and Health-Related Quality of Life in Children," *Preventative Medicine Reports* 3 (June 2016): 211–221, https://doi.org/10.1016/j.pmedr.2016.08.013.

78. S. C. Van Hedger et al., "Of Cricket Chirps and Car Horns: The Effect of Nature Sounds on Cognitive Performance," *Psychonomic Bulletin and Review* 26, no. 2 (April 2019): 522–530, https://doi.org/10.3758/s13423-018-1539-1.

79. K. E. Schertz and M. G. Berman, "Understanding Nature and Its Cognitive Benefits," *Current Directions in Psychological Science* 28, no. 5 (June 2019): 496–502, https://doi.org/10.1177/0963721419854100.

80. R. A. Atchley, D. L. Strayer, and P. Atchley, "Creativity in the Wild: Improving Creative Reasoning through Immersion in Natural Settings. *PLoS ONE* 7, no. 12 (2012): e51474, https://doi.org/10.1371/journal.pone.005147.

81. "Immune System May Be Pathway between Nature and Good Health," University of Illinois College of Agricultural, Consumer, and Environmental Sciences, September 16, 2015, https://www.sciencedaily.com/releases/2015/09/150916162120.htm.

82. Ming Kuo, "How Might Contact with Nature Promote Human Health? Promising Mechanisms and a Possible Central Pathway," *Frontiers in Psychology* 6 (August 2015). https://doi.org/10.3389/fpsyg.2015.01093.

83. Katherine R. Gamble, James H. Howard, and Darlene V. Howard, "Not Just Scenery: Viewing Nature Pictures Improves Executive Attention in Older Adults," *Experimental Aging Research* 40, no. 5 (October 2014): 513–30, https://doi.org/10.1080/0361073x.2014.956618.; Meredith A. Repke et al., "How Does Nature Exposure Make People Healthier?: Evidence for the Role of Impulsivity and Expanded Space Perception," *PLOS ONE* 13, no. 8 (August 22, 2018), https://doi.org/10.1371/journal.pone.0202246.

INDEX

A

B

C

N

O

P

T

U

V

W

Y

ACKNOWLEDGMENTS

This book was made possible by the kindness and time of many.

Mark Tauber—you are so kind, supportive, and thoughtful—thank you. I feel so lucky to work with you.

A deep bow of gratitude to my super delightful, charming, talented, meticulous, caring, gracious editor Anne Barthel—you are amazing (and hilarious!).

A big thanks also to Melody Guy for first bringing me on board.

Thanks to Reid, Patty, and the entire Hay House team for your warm welcome and for setting me up with Anne—you are my people. Thank you, Monica, for being so attentive to detail and making sure the manuscript turned out so perfectly! Lindsay and Nusrah for being so skilled and energizing and amazing. And of course dear, dear Ashley, I love you.

Thanks also to the Yale School of Management and Yale Executive Education for all the support—it's a privilege to work with you.

A heartfelt thank-you to those of you who graciously helped edit parts (or all) of the manuscript at various times, giving me fantastic feedback: Sarah I., who helped me put my early thoughts on paper when the whole fam was down with scabies (a fun and itchy story that will make it into my next book no doubt!)—you gave me such relief. My many early readers who gave great suggestions and edits on my first drafts, the rewrites, the re-rewrites, the re-re-rewrites, and the 500th drafts—Bryant, Etelle, Stephanie, Katie, Indu, Frali, Randy, Dara, Kohar, Liz, Jacqui,

Lucia, Mona, MeiMei, Daisy, Steffi, Dhruv, Mark, Nika, Jackie, Dhvani, Meredith, Haley, Kritika, Damon—thank you for your generosity and insights, your contributions helped immensely!

Thanks to all those who generously agreed to have their stories told: Starr, Johane, Etelle, Lynn, "Maya," "Stephanie," "Deana," Moria, Eric, Deonne, Mihir, Mark, Jake, Kushal—you are all so inspiring!

Thanks for taking the time to talk to me so I could write about your findings and brilliant insights: Premal, Justin, Chipp, Kristin, Joe, Bryant, Dena, Troy, Aman, Julien, and Robert.

For the continuous loving support and encouragement: Leslye, Johann, Uma, Carolan, Priya, Auntie Liz, Karishma, Shubhu, Emilia, Jameela, Faith, Ashley, Susan, Maya, Tina, LisaMarie, Marissa, Damiane, Ria, Radhika, Dr. Doty, Andrew K., Bill H., Bill and Leslie, Willow, Gersende, Miia, Emilia, Susan B., Jana, Bala, Ameya, Siva and the CT crew, and so many more I may be forgetting.

Thank you so very much to the kind and generous endorsers who took the time to read and blurb the book: Dr. Doty, Faith, Tom, Jennifer, Dan, Sharon, Alison, and April. Thanks also to the members of the Silicon Guild for all of their wisdom, support, and guidance.

Jacqui, LeeAnn, and Amber, thank you for all your astute guidance throughout the process—you are amazing, love you!

Maya and Dani for nourishing me during intense deadline weeks. Jennifer Jai Jai, Connie, Cassandra, and Maddy, Trystan, Cindy, and Joe for giving me the energy I needed to keep writing.

A deep bow to Jehanne for being my muse.

Thank you to Gurudev for all of the inspiration, wisdom, and daily breathing and meditation practices. Thank you for giving me sovereignty.

Most of all, thank you to my dearly beloved parents, family, husband, and children. You did so much to support me as I put forth this book—especially dear Andrew. You mean everything.

ABOUT THE AUTHOR

A Yale lecturer and international keynote speaker, **Emma Seppälä** teaches at the Yale School of Management and directs its Women's Leadership Program. She is also the science director of Stanford University's Center for Compassion and Altruism Research and Education. Her first book, *The Happiness Track*, has been translated into dozens of languages.

She regularly speaks and consults for Fortune 500 companies and contributes to *Harvard Business Review*, *The Washington Post*, *Psychology Today*, and *TIME*. A repeat guest on *Good Morning America*, she has spoken at TEDx Sacramento and TEDx Hayward.

A psychologist and research scientist by training, Seppälä's expertise is the science of happiness, emotional intelligence, and social connection. Her research has been published in top academic journals and featured in news outlets including *The New York Times*, NPR, and CBS News and featured in documentaries like *Free the Mind*, *The Altruism Revolution*, *What You Do Matters*, and *Bullied*. **www.emmaseppala.com** and **www.iamsov.com**

Hay House Titles of Related Interest

YOU CAN HEAL YOUR LIFE, the movie,
starring Louise Hay & Friends
(available as an online streaming video)
www.hayhouse.com/louise-movie

THE SHIFT, the movie,
starring Dr. Wayne W. Dyer
(available as an online streaming video)
www.hayhouse.com/the-shift-movie

***

LOVE YOUR ENEMIES: How to Break the Anger Habit & Be a Whole Lot Happier, by Sharon Salzberg and Robert Thurman

POWER UP YOUR BRAIN: The Neuroscience of Enlightenment, by David Perlmutter, M.D., and Alberto Villoldo, Ph.D.

THE POWER OF VITAL FORCE: Fuel Your Energy, Purpose, and Performance with Ancient Secrets of Breath and Meditation, by Rajshree Patel

THAT SUCKED. NOW WHAT?: How to Embrace the Joy in Chaos and Find Magic in the Mess, by Dr. Neeta Bhushan

All of the above are available at your local bookstore,
or may be ordered by contacting Hay House (see next page).

***

We hope you enjoyed this Hay House book. If you'd like to receive our online catalog featuring additional information on Hay House books and products, or if you'd like to find out more about the Hay Foundation, please contact:

Published in India by:
Hay House Publishers (India) Pvt Ltd
Muskaan Complex, Plot No. 3,
B-2, Vasant Kunj, New Delhi 110 070
Phone: +91 11 41761620
www.hayhouse.co.in

Published in Australia by:
Hay House Australia Publishing Pty Ltd
18/36 Ralph St., Alexandria NSW 2015
Phone: +61 (02) 9669 4299
www.hayhouse.com.au

Published in the United Kingdom by:
Hay House UK Ltd
The Sixth Floor, Watson House,
54 Baker Street, London W1U 7BU
Phone: +44 (0) 203 927 7290
www.hayhouse.co.uk

Published in the United States of America by:
Hay House LLC
P.O. Box 5100, Carlsbad, CA 92018-5100
(760) 31-7695 or (800) 654-5126
www.hayhouse.com® • www.hayfoundation.org

'The gateways to wisdom and knowledge are always open.'

Louise Hay